MYRON FISH & CO.,
MANUFACTURERS OF
Oak Belting, Lace and Picker Leather.
ALSO,
LOOM HARNESS AND REEDS.
DEALERS IN SUPPLIES FOR COTTON, WOOLEN, AND SILK MILLS.
AGENTS FOR JOSEPH NOONE'S SONS' ROLLER, SLASHER AND CLEARER CLOTHS.
Agents for Reddish's Patent Improved Oil Cans.   We have unequaled facilities for furnishing Needles and Heddle Frames, Wire Heddles and Wire Goods of all descriptions.
Special Notice to Worsted and Silk Mills.
We manufacture both worsted and cotton machine-knit Mail Harness for weaving fine worsted and silk goods.   Also a full line of supplies for Jacquard Looms.
VALLEY FALLS, R. I.

TAFT-PEIRCE MFG. CO.
T-P
4283

Heywood
BOOTS AND SHOES.

"Say, Jimmy! get on to de Sign—'Heywood Shoes Wear.' Look at de shoes, yer can bet dey'll wear.   When I'se a man, them's de kind I'se a-goin' to buy!   Mer feet won't be all de time out in de air den."   *Heywood Shoes* are admired by all who see them, and appreciated by those who wear them.

Heywood Shoe

$3.50
is the price of our new winter shoe, in black or tan.   Sold by leading dealers everywhere.   Our Catalogue D, which we will send you if YOUR shoe man does not sell the Heywood Shoe, describes all leading styles.

Honesty of material and care in making the *Heywood Shoe* account for the satisfactory way it **wears**, and its stylish appearance,—hence its popularity.

Heywood Boot & Shoe Co.,
WORCESTER, MASS.

W'S
IMPROVED
AMP
ICE CLUB SKATES
AND PATENT
VINEYARD ROLLER SKATES
QUICKLY ATTACHED, EASILY ADJUSTED.
MANUFACTURED BY
SAMUEL WINSLOW SKATE MFG. CO., U.S.A.

FIRE

Landscape of Industry

BLACKSTONE RIVER

Landscape of Industry

An Industrial History of the Blackstone Valley

Published by UNIVERSITY PRESS OF NEW ENGLAND

Hanover and London

In Cooperation with the WORCESTER HISTORICAL MUSEUM

and the JOHN H. CHAFEE BLACKSTONE RIVER VALLEY

NATIONAL HERITAGE CORRIDOR

Published by University Press of New England,

One Court Street, Lebanon, NH 03766

www.upne.com

© 2009 by Worcester Historical Museum

Printed in China

5 4 3 2 1

Library of Congress Cataloging-in-Publication Data

Landscape of industry: an industrial history

of the Blackstone Valley.

    p. cm.

"In Cooperation with the Worcester Historical Museum

and the John H. Chafee Blackstone River Valley

National Heritage Corridor."

Includes index.

ISBN 978-1-58465-777-4 (cloth: alk. paper)

1. Industrialization—Blackstone River Valley (Mass. and R.I.)
—History. 2. Industries—Blackstone River Valley (Mass.
and R.I.)—History. I. Worcester Historical Museum.
II. John H. Chafee Blackstone River Valley National Heritage
Corridor Commission.

HC107.M42B635 2009

338.09744'3—dc22   2008054068

ENDSHEET IMAGES

Center image: Collection of Judy Zaleski & Family

Border images, left to right:

National Worsted Mills.

    Courtesy of the American Antiquarian Society

Pawtucket Hair Cloth Company.

    Courtesy of Slater Mill, Pawtucket, RI

Blackstone Valley Prints. Courtesy of Slater Mill, Pawtucket, RI

E. W. Vaill Patent Folding Chairs. From the Collections

    of the Worcester Historical Museum, Worcester, MA

Myron Fish Co. Courtesy of John H. Chafee Blackstone River

    Valley NHC/National Park Service

Taft-Pierce Company Pin.

    Courtesy of the Museum of Work & Culture, Woonsocket, RI

Heywood Shoe.

    From the Collections of the Worcester Historical Museum,

    Worcester, MA

Winslow's Skates.

    From the Collections of the Worcester Historical Museum,

    Worcester, MA

Contents

Foreword

Senator Edward M. Kennedy

Over the years, I've had the privilege of working with outstanding leaders on both sides of the aisle, and I have many warm memories of our work together. In thinking about the Blackstone Valley, my good friend and colleague the late GOP Senator John Chafee comes to mind as one of those unique persons who had a great impact in the Senate, his state, and our region. One day, he came up to me on the Senate floor, took my arm, and said that one of the truly remarkable areas in our states, the Blackstone Valley, needed attention.

During my many visits to the valley, whether to Waters Farm in Sutton, Massachusetts, or by train along the river, this extraordinary historical area stands out as one of the jewels of our nation, a living landscape that speaks to our nation's past, present, and future. It's been the setting for some of the nation's great social movements and technological advances, and it helped lay the foundation for the world power the nation would become.

Today, few remnants remain of our early industrial period. Many of the old mill buildings have been demolished and replaced with modern structures, or put to entirely different uses. That's why the Blackstone River Valley National Heritage Corridor, which preserves and promotes understanding about mill community living, is so important. It offers a glimpse of America as a young nation on the way to becoming a world power, and it honors the ingenuity and hard work that led us forward.

The authors have meticulously researched this extraordinary history and assembled it into an appealing volume that captures the region's basic significance for modern readers in all walks of life.

On the broadest level, *Landscape of Industry: An Industrial History of the Blackstone Valley* is the story of the rapid industrialization of what was largely a rural area of New England whose technological advances and related changes sent ripples across the country and helped build a powerful nation. The discussion of how industrialization started seeds of change in all facets of life make it an especially fascinating and revealing summary of the nation's evolving social consciousness on challenges that still confront us today—such as religion, race, and the rights of women, employees, and property owners—all in the context of a growing nation expanding westward and developing its extraordinary natural and human resources.

Rare treasures like the Blackstone Valley grace all our states and are endlessly inspiring places that we should all work hard to preserve. I'm sure that many of those who read and learn from this fascinating history will be inspired to visit the Corridor in person, and they will be amazed to see this remarkable history come alive.

Edward M Kennedy

Landscape of Industry

Introduction A River Transformed, a Valley Remade DR. JOSEPH F. CULLON

The Blackstone River. John H. Chafee Blackstone River Valley NHC/National Park Service

The Blackstone River quickly descends 438 feet over 46 miles as it speeds its way along a course from Worcester, Massachusetts, to Providence, Rhode Island. With every inch that it drops, the river releases energy. Initially, this power carved the river's bed and gradually eroded the soil and rock along the river's banks. Earth crumbled in the torrent of water as the Blackstone cascaded toward the sea.

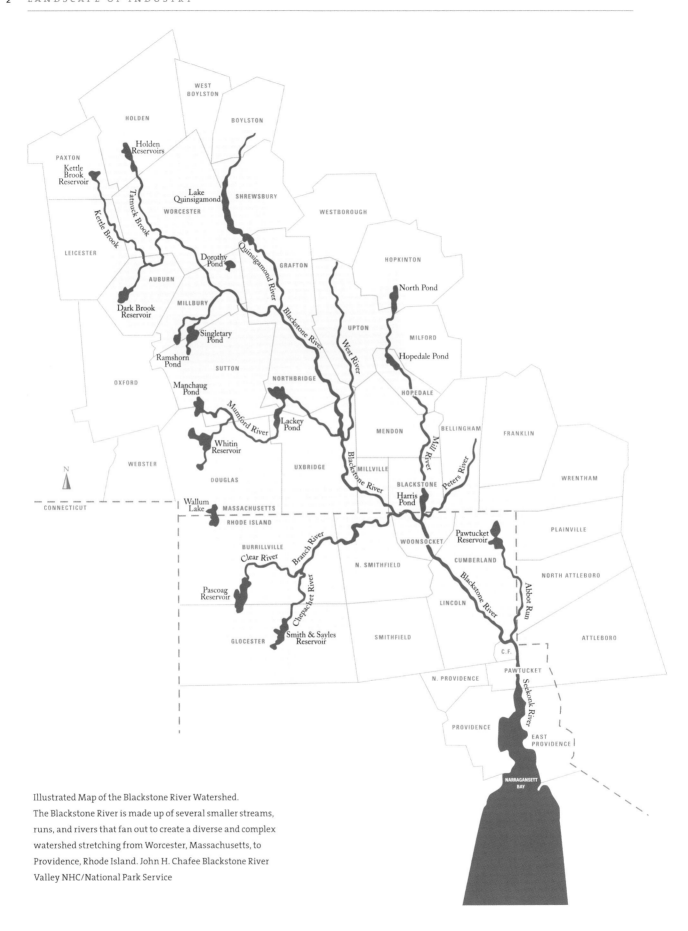

Illustrated Map of the Blackstone River Watershed.
The Blackstone River is made up of several smaller streams,
runs, and rivers that fan out to create a diverse and complex
watershed stretching from Worcester, Massachusetts, to
Providence, Rhode Island. John H. Chafee Blackstone River
Valley NHC/National Park Service

Untapped, the river's energy created a watershed drawing the runoff and engrossing the power of tributary streams, brooks, and smaller rivers. These tributaries fanned out across the landscape, gathering waters from an area of approximately five hundred square miles. Near Worcester, the Kettle, Beaver, Tatnuck, and Mill brooks joined to form the Blackstone's source; south of the city, these headwaters wedded with the water of the Quinsigamond, West, and Mumford rivers. Further south, the Clear River flowed into the Branch before the combined flow of both merged with the Blackstone River, and near Woonsocket, the Peters and Mill rivers joined forces with the rising waters. Before the river released its water to the bay, the Abbott Run spilled into the Blackstone, adding still more force to the torrent. Although the river intermittently released energy along the way, at two points—the falls at Woonsocket and Pawtucket—its release was torrential. Elsewhere, such as the rapids at Valley Falls, the roiling white waters testified to the river's considerable power.[1]

The Blackstone still largely follows the course established long ago by the geological and physical forces that carved its initial bed. While the river's moving water has continuously moved the earth and altered its banks over the centuries, the boundaries of the Blackstone's watershed have shifted imperceptibly to the untrained eye. Its quick descent, numerous tributaries, and frequent rapids are now channeled and contained by more than two centuries of human intervention.

Those Native Americans and early English settlers who encountered the unencumbered Blackstone saw it as a resource and used it accordingly.[2] Until the late eighteenth century, however, the Blackstone's power was a resource that remained only partially tapped. Indeed, it was the river's reservoir of fish protein that initially focused attention on its banks. Native Americans harvested the anadromous fish, including Atlantic salmon, shad, and alewives, that annually swam upriver to spawn. Following the habits of their Nipmuck neighbors, the region's first English settlers too relied upon the runs of anadromous fish to supplement their diet and made a ritual of the annual event. With the maturation of the valley's colonial settlements, Anglo-American residents built gristmills, iron forges, and sawmills that appropriated only a small part of the river's energy to move waterwheels before 1780. Even as the new United States was taking shape after the Revolutionary War, the vast majority of the river's potential power still spilled over its banks and down its falls without intervention. Channeling the river and tapping more fully into its power offered opportunities and challenges for those who wished to place the new nation upon a solid economic base.[3]

In the 1790s, entrepreneurs sought to harness the river's energy. Some succeeded while others failed. In the process, the energies of both enterprising men and falling water conjoined to magnify the power of each. In harnessing the river's energy, these early entrepreneurs also appropriated the labor of other men, women, and children to launch mills and manufactories. In the end, the river shaped the people just as the people reshaped the Blackstone in their quest to harness its energy.

This is the story that emerges in these pages. Over the course of more than two hundred years, the Blackstone River and the residents along its banks interacted to create what we recognize now as the Blackstone Valley: an amalgamation of natural, agricultural, industrial, and urban landscapes. This is the valley's enduring legacy as a place where the power of natural forces spurred industrial development and set in motion a series of events that ever more closely intertwined the lives of a river and the people who made their homes along its banks. The essays in this volume explore the river's history from many perspectives: industrial and domestic architecture, business and labor history, transportation and industrial history. One thread—a story of becoming, of transformation and development—runs through all these essays and stories. As milldams multiplied on the river, as canal boats plied its waters, and as new immigrants settled in its valley, the Blackstone became a region distinct in its history and its habits.

Early Industrialization

In its usual telling, the story of the valley's industrial heritage starts with a chance encounter. In 1790, a recent English immigrant, Samuel Slater, traveled from New York City to Pawtucket, Rhode Island, to meet with the established merchants and novice mill own-

Slater Mill Historic Site. Unimposing by the standards of modern industrial architecture, the manufacturing revolution of the early nineteenth century started in small structures built along the watercourses that provided their power. John H. Chafee Blackstone River Valley NHC/National Park Service

ers Moses Brown and William Almy. What ensued is the stuff of legend. When Slater arrived, Brown and Almy—who were eager to succeed at manufacturing—were already well along in a project that would harness the Blackstone's power to spin cotton thread. Area mechanics had built machines to the group's specifications and assembled them in a mill building near the falls at Pawtucket. When Slater arrived to examine the machines and inquire about a position with Brown and Almy, he was not impressed with the tinkering of Yankee mechanics. Having worked in several mills in England, Slater scorned the prototypes. However, he did find the site near the falls more than serviceable.[4]

After accepting a position with Brown and Almy, Slater drew upon his experience in English mills and retooled the machinery. Soon the river's energy moved a wheel that powered his improved spinning machines. With Slater's assistance, Brown and Almy achieved something new: the first fully mechanized spinning mill in the United States. In three years, Slater and Brown moved their operations to a newly constructed building (now restored as the Slater Mill Historic Site) to better accommodate an increasing number of machines and their own growing ambitions. Their partnership earned for Pawtucket its title as the undisputed birthplace of American manufacturing.

Historians have been spinning the story of Brown, Almy, Slater, and the Blackstone ever since they first combined their energies to spin thread in Pawtucket. The achievement of Brown, Almy, and Slater, however, was as much a beginning as a crowning achievement. Their industrial experimentation resulted not only in technological innovation but also in a social model that would replicate itself across the Blackstone Valley. Later, Slater, Brown, and many others established similar mills that closely imitated the mechanical and organizational structure of their first. As in Pawtucket, these mills married the energy of the river with the labor of families in mixed agricultural settings. With the multiplication of spinning mills in the Blackstone Valley, the village emerged as a model of social organization; the mill and its boardinghouses came to define what would become an iconic New England landscape.[5]

The rise of mill villages in the valley did not go unchallenged. Since each new mill required at least a dam to channel the river's power to a waterwheel, mill owners systematically remade the river. Each new dam slowed the Blackstone, submerged land, and blocked the runs of anadromous fish. For those who had settled along the river before mills dotted its banks, these improvements conflicted with their traditional uses of the Blackstone. Small farmers, especially, protested the construction of dams that blocked the spring runs of fish, since they had come to depend upon the fish to supplement their diet and thereby their livelihood. They petitioned their legislatures and sued mill owners; when their pleas went unanswered, they sometimes destroyed the dams that they despised. Their protests signaled one of the many ways that the rise of mills and the new relations of labor and land were not unanimously embraced. Just as mill workers would grow to question the terms of their employment in the early nineteenth century, so too did small farmers challenge the reordering of their landscape in the service of industry.[6]

As the manufacturing revolution worked its way through the valley in the first decades of the eighteenth century, the small-scale resistance of farmers failed to stem the tide of transformation and the river was remade to service the interests of industry. In the first chapter of this volume, Dr. Richard Greenwood describes the changing face of the valley as mills, boarding houses, and dams displaced farms along the water's edge. The expansion of manufacturing across the valley created a new landscape of industry. Dr. Greenwood explores how manufacturers balanced their preference for traditional, pastoral landscapes with the demands of their business, opting to create mill villages that honored the past but accommodated an industrial future. Inventorying the various building forms and styles of the Blackstone, Greenwood identifies a common architectural vernacular that shaped construction in the valley and still influences preservation efforts to this day.

Angry farmers were not the only obstacle that budding industrialists confronted. Nature also conspired against them. Before Pawtucket's success and for some time after it, the Blackstone River did not provide a serviceable corridor upon which to organize regional economic life. Rapids and falls made boat transport a perilous adventure. Although settlements dotted its course and mills grew up along its banks, these early towns did not coalesce into a network focused upon and fortified by the river. Rather, settlers and mill owners moved in many different directions upon established turnpikes, and their trade was scattered among several competing market centers. Trade patterns did not move along the river, as it was too difficult to transport goods upon it.

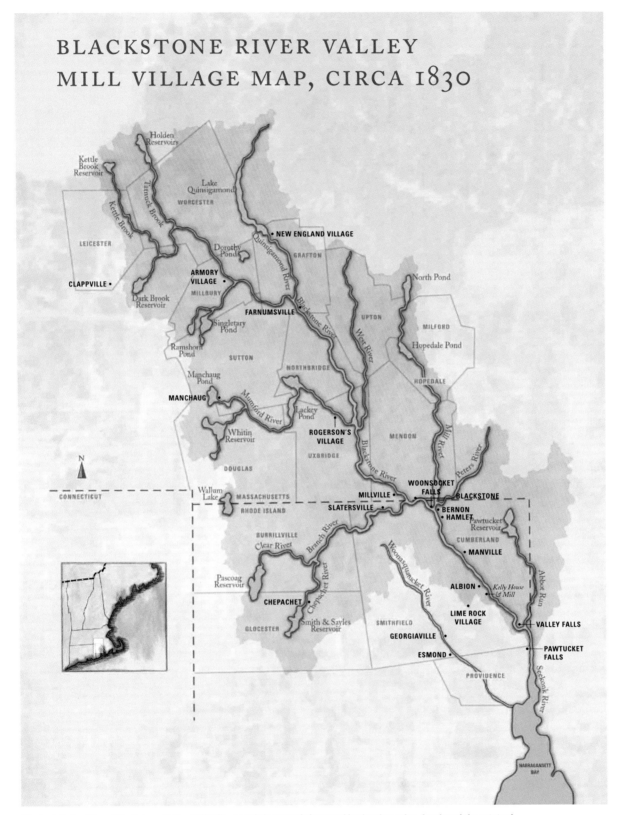

BLACKSTONE RIVER VALLEY
MILL VILLAGE MAP, CIRCA 1830

Illustrated 1830 Map of Blackstone Valley Mill Villages. While Samuel Slater and his brother, John, developed the original model for the mill village, it was quickly imitated throughout the valley as entrepreneurs opened mills along waterways based on their pioneer model. John H. Chafee Blackstone River Valley NHC/National Park Service

Although the valley's hilly topography and rock-strewn river raised transportation costs and impeded growth, the success at Pawtucket and elsewhere set in motion plans to realize the river's full potential as an engine of industry. Some called for a canal to furnish better north-south transportation as well as to squeeze every last ounce of the river's power by regulating its flow.[7]

Few people did more to reshape the Blackstone as an engine of industry than Samuel Slater and his family. As Gray Fitzsimons explores in the second chapter, members of the Slater clan consistently influenced developments in the valley as mangers, promoters, investors, and philanthropists. Samuel Slater, with his brother John, extended manufacturing by investing in new mills and building new villages. They embraced change, adapted their business practices, improved their machinery, and experimented with steam in their efforts to remake the Blackstone. Gray Fitzsimons argues that the practices of the Slater family over three generations reveal in microcosm the spirit of entrepreneurialism that moved many of the valley's manufacturers.

Only as entrepreneurs sought to improve upon the Blackstone's natural features did the river come to fulfill the expectations of the people who set up shop along its course. As its falls were channeled to power mills, its course altered to furnish transportation, and its flow regulated to sustain the delivery of energy, the Blackstone Valley emerged as a unit of social and economic organization. The raw energy of the river and the labor power of mill owners, canal diggers, managers, and mill hands reshaped one another to create a valley that was simultaneously a natural and an engineered landscape.

The Blackstone Canal

The integration of the social and economic character of the several mill towns built along the river after 1793 accelerated as several mill operators sought to improve waterborne transportation on the river. Many Blackstone mill interests championed the construction of a canal to speed the movement of raw materials and finished mill goods, and to lower the cost of freight. The construction of the canal heralded a new era for those who lived and worked in the valley, as

the canal reoriented life along a north-south axis. The canal joined Worcester and Providence in a tight economic embrace and increased the tempo of village life by integrating the river's scattered mills into an enlarged economic sphere.

Proposals for a canal flowed quickly upon the success of the first spinning mills. In 1796, John Brown (Moses's brother) first raised the idea of building a canal to improve north-south transportation through the valley. Merchants in Providence quickly endorsed Brown's proposal because such a canal would greatly enlarge their market in the hinterlands by reducing the costs of transportation. While Rhode Islanders quickly intuited the benefits of a canal, others balked at the idea of trade flowing south to Providence. Boston merchants, especially, worried that the trade of inland towns like Worcester would flow south—to Providence merchants' benefit—rather than east to their own. This opposition in Massachusetts' capital city consistently thwarted plans for a canal, and preserved the valley's status quo for a time.

Popular desire for a canal shifted during the first decades of the nineteenth century as the economic life of the region changed. The spread of mills along the Blackstone and its tributaries gradually pulled both Worcester and Providence closer together economically. Worcester merchants increasingly sought to access the markets afforded by mill villages to its south, as Providence traders looked to the manufactories to the north. Further, as the importance of the mills increased, the interests of mill owners were taken more seriously in the state houses of Massachusetts and Rhode Island. The desirability of a north-south canal corridor became increasingly obvious to interests in Worcester, Providence, and the middle villages as well as undeniable even to interests back in Boston.[8]

The spectacular success of the Erie Canal renewed interest for a similar project along the Blackstone in the 1820s. This time, both Massachusetts and Rhode Island legislators approved the project. Merchant and mill interests invested to underwrite the cost. Immigrant laborers moved the earth to tame the river so canal boats might move along it easily. Finally, in 1828, a completed canal connected Worcester to Providence and the numerous mill villages that now dotted the valley.[9]

By lowering the cost of freight and speeding the shipment of goods, canal boats changed the social and economic life of the valley. Once a natural feature of the landscape, then the site of a multitude of mills, the Blackstone River now became the primary transportation corridor connecting many villages and mill towns. From its northern origins in Worcester to its southern terminus in Providence, the river now included a network of mill villages that not only looked similar but shared a common corridor that created efficiencies and solidified a sense of shared purpose. The canal improved upon nature, making possible the efficient movement of boats up and down the river.

If the first step of industrialization along the Blackstone was to tap its energy, the second step was to temper its power. The canal conserved human energy by reducing the labor expenditures of moving goods along the river. Once again, the energy of the river was harnessed to spur the productivity of the valley's population. The technical and political challenges that canal backers faced are the subject of the third chapter, by Gray Fitzsimons. He conveys the heavy lifting required both in the legislative chambers and in the field to complete the Blackstone Canal. In the process, he reveals just how revolutionary a force the canal was in shaping the politics and economy of the region. Although the canal era in the Blackstone Valley was short lived, as Fitzsimons makes clear, its service solidified the bonds that joined the mill villages with the economic centers of Worcester, Massachusetts, and Providence, Rhode Island, and its course furnished the route for another transforming technology, the railroad.

The Railroads

Even before the canal boats had time to show signs of wear, they fell almost into obsolescence. Within a decade of the canal's completion, two railroads in the region heralded a new era. First the Boston to Providence Railroad in 1834 and then the Boston to Worcester Railroad in 1835 arrived to challenge the canal's grip upon the valley's trade. Just as the mills and canals oriented the economic life of the valley along a north-south axis, the railroads threatened to alter the region's human geography. Freed from the constraints of waterways—unlike canal boats—railroads could move in any direction or weather. Competition from the Boston-Providence and Boston-Worcester lines diminished the canal's preeminence somewhat, but the bonds that the mills and canal had forged between Worcester and Providence proved too strong for the rail lines to supplant the water corridor completely. Still, almost two decades after the completion of the canal, another rail line, the Providence & Worcester Railroad, provided a bond of iron where water was once the sole link that wedded disparate communities into a united economic entity.[10]

The canal and railroads did more than strengthen the economic ties that held the mill villages together. More efficient forms of transportation revealed the connections that bound the villages to the national economy and even to the plantation South. From the beginning, the rise of manufacturing in the valley rested upon capital accumulated in part from the West Indian and slave trades. As cotton spindles multiplied, mill owners and laborers found their fortunes ever more closely tied to the interests of slave owners in the South, who furnished the raw material spun upon the valley's machines. In the fifth chapter, Dr. Seth Rockman explores the dense web of connections that created the mutual dependence of the manufacturer and the slave driver. Even as the railroads sped the delivery of cotton to the Blackstone's mill and just as quickly took finished cloth south for use as slave clothing, their lines moved opinion hostile to the "peculiar institution." While the Blackstone's mill economy tied it the southern plantation economy, segments of the valley's population embraced anti-slavery and abolition. Dr. Rockman interrogates the meaning of these contradictions and makes clear that the stain of slavery soiled even the noblest sentiments.

The railroad connections that radiated outward from Worcester in all directions promised to transform the valley, and soon the industrial character of Worcester shifted dramatically. Shortly after the arrival of the railroad from Boston, Worcester boasted three cotton mills, eight woolen mills, two paper mills, textile machine makers, a wire company, and numerous other small shops. The arrival of railroad connections pushed Worcester's manufacturing base in new and more diverse directions. While spinning mills defined the industrial character of the middle

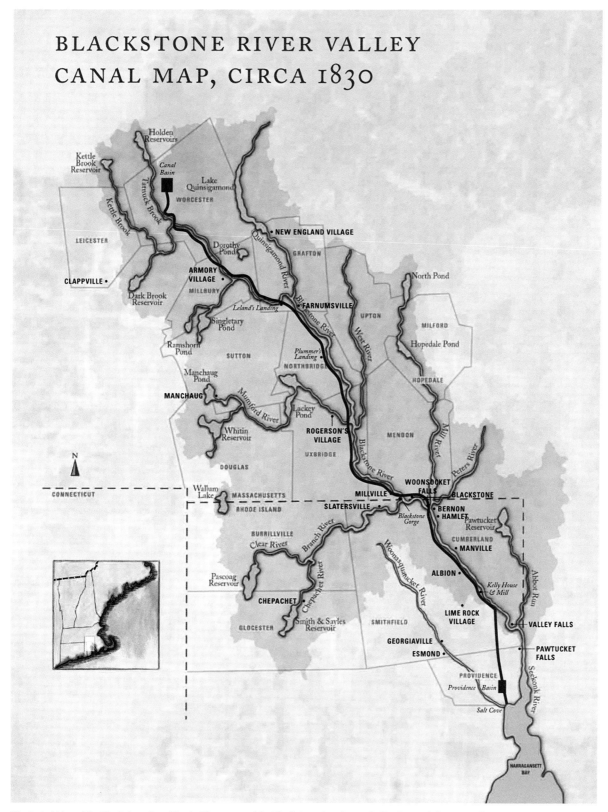

BLACKSTONE RIVER VALLEY CANAL MAP, CIRCA 1830

Illustrated Map of the Blackstone Canal Route. The course of the Blackstone Canal remade the river and the towns along its banks. In speeding travel and regulating flow, the canal facilitated the expansion of older mills, construction of new mills, and the growth of villages into towns and cities. John H. Chafee Blackstone River Valley NHC/National Park Service

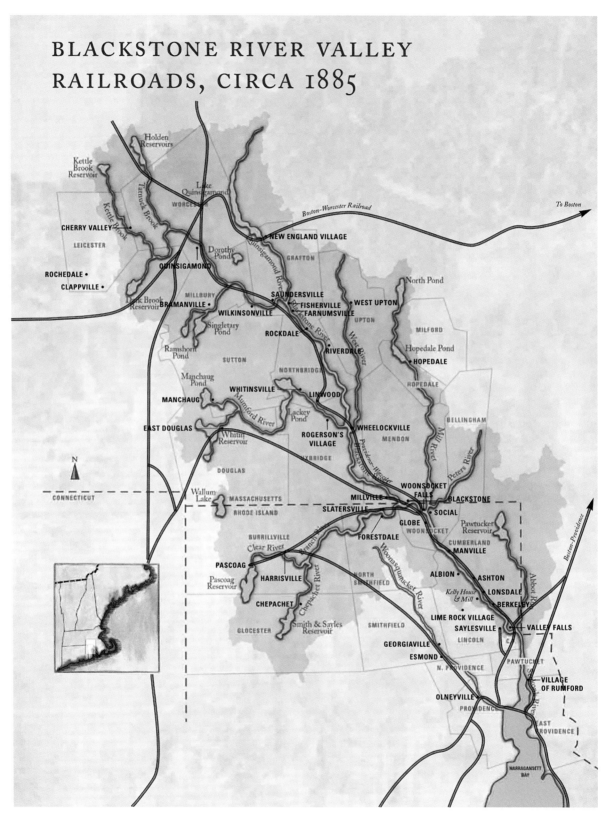

Illustrated Map of Blackstone Valley Railroads. Although the Providence and Worcester Railroad was the most important railroad serving the valley, the host of other lines moving through the Valley increased the number and diversity of manufacturing enterprises in the region. Rather than reorienting life in the valley, railroads intensified the pace of industrialization along the river. John H. Chafee Blackstone River Valley NHC/National Park Service

villages along the river, Worcester now branched out into metal trades, tool and machine manufacturing, and wire making. Within two decades of the completion of the Providence and Worcester Railroad in 1847, numerous other railroad lines threaded their way through Worcester, creating a web of tracks that sustained the city's industrialization.[11]

Diversification

As much as the railroads created new opportunities, they also solidified bonds that had first formed with the spread of Slater's mills along the lower reaches of the river. The fortunes of Worcester and Providence remained tied to the valley because the mill villages offered attractive opportunities for investment and trade. And as the villages themselves grew into large towns or small cities, their lure became even more powerful. For example, the Providence & Worcester Railroad pushed Pawtucket's industry in new directions. While once all mill activity in the town had clustered around the falls that powered Brown, Almy, and Slater's first mill, railroads and steam power allowed the development of industries along the tracks rather than the river. Like their Worcester predecessors, Pawtucket industrialists diversified their operations. Once home to spinning and textile mills, by the end of the nineteenth century Pawtucket industrial workers assembled toys, steam fire engines, tools, and water fountains. The increasingly industrialized towns of the valley relied upon road rails to serve their interests and continue to link them to the commercial centers of Providence and Worcester.[12]

Although the importance of the rivers and canals as a transportation corridor diminished, the Blackstone still gave up its energy to power the mills. Indeed, mill owners and engineers found new uses for the river. As the number of canal boats upon the river declined, the canal along with an extensive system of dams, reservoirs, feeder canals, sluices, and gates, nevertheless ensured the steady flow of water to the mills, which relied upon a steady supply to power their machinery. Although engineers could not harness all the river's energy, they did create an engineering wonder along its banks. It's not surprising that for a brief time the Blackstone River was known as the "hardest-working river" in the country.

The variety of industries that drew energy from the Blackstone in the second half of the nineteenth century defies easy summary. As new industries joined cotton mills in the valley's villages, new immigrants arrived, bringing even greater diversity to the valley. Rather than impose an arbitrary order upon the complex industrial character of the Blackstone, Rangers Chuck Arning, Ray Boswell, Peter Coffin, Kevin Klyberg, and Jack Whittaker recount the range of experience in the fourth chapter. Heavily illustrated, this chapter conveys the complexity of life in the valley and avoids easy generalizations. Rather, these authors provide glimpses into each town, village, and city in the valley and underscore that as much as they shared in common, the valley's diverse populations experienced industrialization in ways as various as the industries that made a home in the valley by 1900.

With the expansion and diversification of industry, the valley's population swelled and grew more heterogeneous. The increasingly ethnically diverse workforce experienced a mix of opportunity and oppression as steam power and railroads created a new industrial order along the Blackstone. In the sixth chapter, the emeritus director of the Rhode Island Historical Society, Dr. Albert T. Klyberg, explores workers' struggles with industrialists over wages, hours, and safety as well as their battles for local and state political rights. He reveals that the range of industries and ethnicities in the valley precluded the coalescence of a unified regional labor movement even as numerous workers took up more local fights for the wages and respect that were their due.

Just as it seemed that the river had little energy left to tap, entrepreneurs found new uses for its water. Steam engines and steam-powered mills multiplied in the valley. Heated by coal, steam from the Blackstone's waters now spun turbines to produce an array of new materials. Like railroads before it, steam power might have shifted the economic geography of the valley away from the river. But the Blackstone provided in abundance the water necessary for steam power, and the old canal now served as a conduit ensuring its steady supply.

By 1880, the Blackstone little resembled the river that Slater and Brown used to power their Pawtucket mill in 1790. With each new mill, the river gave up

The Millbury Dam, 1831. Dams such as this one at Millbury still powered the mills of the valley well into the middle of the eighteenth century. Such dams increased the energy that mills might draw from the river by guaranteeing a steady supply of water to spin waterwheels. John H. Chafee Blackstone River Valley NHC/National Park Service

a part of its energy. As the mills multiplied and the dams proliferated, the river itself changed. Yet the alterations to the river before 1820 paled in comparison with the transformation wrought by the canal. With the canal, the Blackstone River—whose wildness had once precluded easy travel by boat—became an engineered system whose power served the interests of industry. Even as the uses of the river's energy changed with the perfection of steam power, the Blackstone continued to provide the course that linked the increasingly diverse industries of the valley. For all its transforming power, the new technologies and the industries that came with them only underscored the economic bonds that nature and history had created in the wake of Slater's first success at mechanized spinning.

Timeline

1790 Samuel Slater and Moses Brown first successfully use mechanized spinning machines with power from the Blackstone River at Pawtucket.

1793 Slater and Brown move their operations to a new, larger mill building.

1806 Samuel & John Slater establish Slatersville as a mill village.

1828 The Blackstone Canal, which follows the course of the river to join Worcester and Providence, is complete.

1834 Rail service opens connecting Boston and Providence.

1835 Rail service opens connecting Boston and Worcester

1847 The Providence and Worcester Railroad opens.

1849 Providence mechanic George Corliss improves the design of steam engines to make them an efficient and affordable alternative to water power.

1870 Lonsdale Company establishes the first steam-powered factory village in the valley.

NOTES

1. Daniel P. Murray, ed., *Guidebook to Field Trips in Rhode Island and Adjacent Regions of Connecticut and Massachusetts*, (Kingston, R.I.: New England Intercollegiate Geological Conference, Ninetieth Annual Meeting, 1998); and Robert Finch, Jonathan Wallen, and Bob Finch, *The Smithsonian Guides to Natural American: Southern New England* (Washington, D.C.: Random House, 1996).

2. On the environmental history of Native American and English settlers in seventeenth-century New England, see William Cronon, *Changes in the Land: Indians, Colonists, and the Ecology of New England* (New York: Hill and Wang, 1983); and Carolyn Merchant, *Ecological Revolutions: Nature, Gender, and Science in New England* (Chapel Hill: University of North Carolina Press, 1989).

3. On the river fisheries of New England before industrialization, see Daniel Vickers, "Those Damn Shad: Would the River Fisheries of New England Have Survived in the Absence of Industrialization," *William and Mary Quarterly*, 3rd scr., 61 (2004).

4. The dealings of Salter, Brown, and Almy are the subject of a large body of scholarship; the most accessible of these studies include James Lawson Conrad, Jr., "The Evolution of Industrial Capitalism in Rhode Island: Almy, the Browns, and the Slaters" (Ph.d. dissertation, University of Connecticut, 1973); Gary B. Kulik, "The Beginnings of the Industrial Revolution in America: Pawtucket, Rhode Island, 1672–1829" (Ph.D. dissertation, Brown University, 1980); and Barbara M. Tucker, *Samuel Slater and the Origins of the American Textile Industry, 1790–1860* (Ithaca, N.Y.: Cornell University Press, 1984).

5. On the spread of the textile industry and the rise of the mill village prototype, see Jonathan Prude, *The Coming of Industrial Order: Town and Factory Life in Rural Massachusetts, 1810–1860* (New York: Cambridge University Press, 1983); Richard Candee, "New Towns of the Early New England Textile Industry," in *Perspectives in Vernacular Architecture*, vol. I, ed. Camille Wells (Columbia: University of Missouri Press for the Vernacular Architecture Forum, 1982).

6. Gary Kulik, "Dams, Fish, and Farmers: Defense of Public Rights in Eighteenth-Century Rhode Island," in *The Countryside in the Age of Capitalist Transformation: Essays in the Social History of Rural America*, ed. Steven Hahn and Jonathan Prude, 25–50 (Chapel Hill: University of Noth Carolina Press, 1985); Gary Kulik, "Pawtucket Village and the Strike of 1824: The Origins of Class Conflict in Rhode Island," *Radical History Review* 17 (Spring 1978): 21–26; and Gary Kulik, "Textile Mill Labor in the Blackstone Valley: Work and Protest in the Nineteenth Century," in *Working in the Blackstone Valley: Exploring the Heritage of Industrialization*, ed. Douglas M. Reynolds and Marjory Myers (Woonsocket, R.I.: Rhode Island Labor History Society, 1991).

7. On transportation in the Blackstone Valley before the canal, see Daniel P. Jones, "Commercial Progress versus Local Rights: Turnpike Building in Northwestern Rhode Island in the 1790s," *Rhode Island History* 48 (February 1990). The finest recent scholarship on the canal can be found in Richard E. Greenwood, "Natural Run and Artificial Falls: Waterpower and the Blackstone Canal," *Rhode Island History* 49 (May 1991).

8. On the proposed canal, see *Account of the Proposed Canal from Worcester to Providence . . . published by order*

of the Committee for Worcester County (Worcester, Mass.: William Manning, 1822). Available at the American Antiquarian Society, Worcester, Mass.

9. On the canal and its construction and use, see Israel Plummer, *History of the Blackstone Canal, read before the Worcester Society of Antiquity, 1878* (Slatersville, R.I.: Slatersville Press, 1998); and, especially, Richard E. Greenwood, "Natural Run and Artificial Falls: Waterpower and the Blackstone Canal," *Rhode Island History* 49 (May 1991).

10. William Appleton, *Massachusetts Railroads, 1842–1855* (Boston: J. H. Eastburn's Press, 1856); Stewart P. Schneider, "Railroad Development in Rhode Island during the Nineteenth Century," *Rhode Island History* 61 (2003): 36–48; and Edward Chase Kirkland, *Men, Cities and Transportation: A Study in New England History*, 2 vols. (Cambridge, Mass.: Harvard University Press, 1948).

11. The essential work on Worcester's nineteenth-century industrialization remains Charles G. Washburn, *Industrial Worcester* (Worcester, Mass.: The Davis Press, 1917). Roy Rosenzweig offers a brief treatment of this history in his *Eight Hours for What We Will: Workers and Leisure in an Industrial City, 1870–1920* (New York: Cambridge University Press, 1983).

12. John Williams Haley, *The Lower Blackstone River Valley* (Pawtucket, R.I.: Lower Blackstone River Valley District Committee of the Rhode Island and Providence Plantations Tercentenary Committee, 1936); Robert Grieve, *The Cotton Centennial 1790–1890 . . . a full account of the Pawtucket Cotton Centenary Celebration* (Providence, R.I.: J. A. & R. A. Reid, 1891); and Susan Marie Boucher, *The History of Pawtucket, 1635–1976* (Pawtucket, R.I.: Pawtucket Memorial Library, 1976).

1 A Landscape of Industry

DR. RICHARD GREENWOOD

Washburn Iron Works c. 1865–70, Worcester, Massachusetts. From the collections of Worcester Historical Museum, Worcester, MA

When Samuel Slater initiated the factory spinning of cotton thread in 1790, a short walk in any direction from his mill in the village of Pawtucket would reach an open countryside of widely spaced farms and occasional villages but no true urban settlements. In the first decades of the nineteenth century, as the revolutionary effects of Slater's success at Pawtucket became apparent, textile mills proliferated throughout the Blackstone River Valley. In the new industrial establishments springing up at intervals along the valley's rivers, owners and operatives mastered the new machine technology and, of equal importance, negotiated the new economic relationships of industrial production. As they established these rural factory villages, they developed technology, architecture, and community forms that influenced the spread of industry though the rest of the country.

New England Countryside. The present-day landscape of Mendon shows the agrarian character that exemplified the Blackstone Valley in the early nineteenth century. Several generations of farmers had cleared much of the woodland and created an open landscape of dispersed farmsteads bounded by fences and stone walls. John H. Chafee Blackstone River Valley NHC/National Park Service

Before the Factories

At the close of the eighteenth century, the Blackstone River Valley, like much of New England, was the domain of the farmer. From Providence on the coastal lowlands of Narragansett Bay to the upland plateau of Worcester, the countryside was dominated by the homestead farm, where individual families as owners or tenants produced food and other stuffs for their own use, as well as small surpluses for trade. They supplemented their work in the fields with traditional hand crafts, such as shoemaking and, significantly, spinning and weaving cloth from wool and linen. The nuclear family was the principal labor force, with all members taking part in the daily and seasonal round of work. Farmers used the surpluses they generated to trade with Providence or Worcester merchants. The merchants were eager to obtain commodities they could use in their trading ventures, while the country folk sought goods they couldn't produce on the farm, such as sugar, salt, tea, and iron. Farmers also engaged in a lively exchange of produce and services amongst themselves.

The farm families generally raised both crops and livestock, and their farms revealed distinct patterns of usage that reflected the varied qualities of the land. The land along the rivers and streams was generally more fertile than the thin sandy soils common to the valley, and farmers favored these areas for their tilled cropland and hayfields. They cleared the dryer uplands for pasturage for their cattle and sheep; and they often planted orchards on the steep and rocky hillsides.

While they steadily cleared the forest for their expanding settlements, farmers retained woodlots where they harvested trees for firewood, building materials, potash, and bark for tanning hides. The center of the valley farm was the center-chimney farmhouse of one or two stories with an adjoining kitchen garden and barnyard, generally built on higher ground with the tilled fields nearby. Grazing lands and woodlots were more far-flung and many farmers owned land parcels separate from their main farm.

This patchwork landscape of farmyards, fields, and woodland, bounded by stone walls and rail fences, was linked internally by a network of narrow farm lanes. A few wider public roads, including Great Road and Mendon Road, ran up the valley between Providence and Mendon and the other Massachusetts towns. These major roads attracted commercial and social institutions including taverns and stores, while local roads led to meetinghouses, grist and sawmills, and other industrial operations. River crossings were made at fords or wading places; there were few bridges and they were often out of repair.

Although most of the populace was spread out across the countryside, small villages or hamlets formed in a few interior locations. The largest of these in Rhode Island was Union Village (now North Smithfield), which grew up at the crossroads of the Great Road and an early road from Boston to eastern Connecticut. A tavern established by the Arnold family and the Friends Meeting House built in 1721 formed the nucleus of the village, which included two schools, a bank, and a number of residences by the early nineteenth century. What was perhaps the first industrial village, Lime Rock (now Lincoln) on the upper Moshassuck River, was fostered by the quarrying and burning of limestone ore that began in the late seventeenth century. The importance of this industry was such that it prompted the construction of the Louisquisset Turnpike in 1805–1806.

In Massachusetts, the towns originally were organized as parishes of the Congregational Church, the established or state-sponsored religion, and the meetinghouses, which housed civic as well as religious functions, typically were located in a geographically central spot for the equal convenience of the congregation. In some instances, villages gradually filled in around the meetinghouses, as at Mendon, Grafton, and Sutton. Otherwise, they remained isolated, like the Chestnut Hill Meetinghouse built for the South Parish of Mendon (Millville) in 1769.[1]

By the end of the eighteenth century, the valley towns were largely settled, with the good farmland under cultivation. As the valley's population increased, fathers had to subdivide large farms for their sons and some were forced to take up more remote and less fertile lands. The limited opportunities for farming increasingly prompted young men and women of the valley to supplement agriculture with craft work, to seek other livelihoods, or to depart for new land elsewhere.

A New Pattern of Industry

A powerful process of change in these patterns of land use and livelihood began in 1806 when Samuel Slater established Slatersville on a parcel of 122 acres along the Branch River in Smithfield (now North Smithfield) in partnership with his brother John and his original employers, William Almy and Obadiah Brown. This new Slater enterprise, modeled on the cotton factory villages they had known in Derbyshire, England, was the earliest example of this new industrial community form in the United States. Slatersville's influence was felt immediately, as the trade embargo imposed by Presidents Jefferson and Madison stimulated the first boom in the textile industry. As Moses Brown described it in 1810, "Our people have 'cotton mill fever' as it is called. Every place almost is occupied with cot-

ton mills; many villages [have been] built up within 16 miles of town [Providence]."[2] Providence merchants led the boom, but farmers, doctors, and other investors from the rural towns joined in as well.

These industrial entrepreneurs were drawn to the Blackstone Valley in search of falling water to generate the energy needed to operate the new cotton-spinning machinery. Falling water was a plentiful resource in the Blackstone River Valley. The main river or its tributaries weren't large, but they fell rapidly, their flow was sufficient, and their narrow widths made it easier for the early mill builders to construct the dams that would harness the flow.

While the river already powered numerous little country mills, the scale and character of the new factory form of industry required a different approach to water power. Unlike the saw and gristmills that served a local community and operated according to the seasonal rhythms of agrarian life, the new factory system was based on continuous year-round operation and it demanded a more constant and plentiful supply of water. The textile industry also required significant infrastructure, even in its early phases. The most obvious components were the factory and its water-power system, but with most of the available mill sites or privileges in the sparsely settled countryside, manufacturers also had to provide housing for the work force, as well as any commercial and social services. The result was, as Moses Brown noted, that the textile industry was growing through the proliferation of the mill village.

The creation of the new mill villages was a pragmatic process that began with the functional necessities of the manufacturing system and drew on the vernacular techniques of the millwright and the housewright. The basic requirement for a textile mill site was, of course, a location on a river that could be harnessed for water power. This included places where a natural waterfall could be tapped, as at Pawtucket or Woonsocket. More commonly, mills were located on stretches where the river's natural descent was more gradual and a dam was needed to concentrate the river's drop at a single point. The potential power that a mill site or, as it was also known, a mill privilege could yield depended on both this vertical drop, referred to as the "head," and the volume of water that could be

Small Dam and Mill. The Moffett Mill, built sometime between 1810 and 1818, is a rare survivor of the first generation of industrial development. Hugging the river bank alongside its dam, this little mill with its waterwheel in the basement and two floors of machinery was not much bigger than many farmhouses. Collection of Wells Pile

delivered to the waterwheel, which was known as the "flow." An accurate assessment of both factors was one of the key elements in the success of a manufacturing venture; otherwise, a mill owner might find that he had invested in more mill and machinery than his mill privilege could support.

A manufacturer could build his dam only as high as the section of river he controlled; build it any higher and the river water would back up and impede the operation of a neighboring mill upstream. He also had to be aware of seasonal fluctuations in the river's volume; flow rates dwindled significantly in the summer months, especially on the smaller rivers like the Woonasquatucket or the Mumford.

Once the location for the dam was set, the next step was determining the placement of the mill and the waterways. An upper raceway or head race carried the water from the millpond to the waterwheel

Fox Mill, Worcester, 1860. William B. Fox's woolen mill in Worcester, built during the surge of development that came with the construction of the Blackstone Canal, was typical of the early Blackstone Valley mills with its long and narrow form, its clerestory monitor lighting the attic floor, and a classical belfry housing the mill bell. From the collections of Worcester Historical Museum, Worcester, MA

set in a pit located in or immediately adjacent to the mill, and a lower raceway or tail race carried the water from the bottom of the wheelpit back into the river below the dam. The final arrangement would reflect the goals of optimizing the available waterpower, providing a convenient location for the mill, and reducing exposure to flooding.

With the mill and waterpower system established, the manufacturer laid out the workers' housing, usually in one or more rows close to the mill. He generally added a store as well, where the mill workers bought their provisions and the mill superintendent would conduct business with outworkers such as handweavers. This was the extent of many early villages: a mill and a small cluster of identical houses at the riverside. Some never grew any bigger; most often because they were located on streams with only limited waterpower. However, hopeful entrepreneurs could look to Slatersville as an example to emulate. With a main mill 154 feet long, more than twenty multi-unit houses, a tavern, a meetinghouse, and a company farm, it had a fully developed village character. One of the only groups of investors with the confidence or the capital to equal Slatersville at this time was the Blackstone Cotton Manufacturing Company, established on the Massachusetts side of the state line in 1809 by a partnership of Providence merchants that included Nicholas Brown (Moses Brown's nephew) and Thomas Poynton Ives.

In their architectural character, the early mill villages were a complex blend of tradition and innovation. Built by local carpenters and masons using common materials and forms, the buildings had an outward appearance that was familiar to the valley natives, but in both subtle and obvious ways they embodied new patterns of social and economic relationships between the employer/landlord and the workers/tenants.[3]

The factories, which were built of wood and, in some cases, stone, were rectangular timber-framed buildings, not unlike the traditional New England meetinghouse but generally larger, taller, and plainer. A common mill size was two to three stories high, and thirty feet wide by sixty feet long, though they could be taller or longer. The interior was kept as open as possible for the better arrangement of the machinery and the better distribution of daylight from the many windows. The basement typically was occupied by the mill wheel and its raceways. A system of revolving gears and shafting transmitted the motion of the waterwheel to the floors above, where one or two overhead lines of iron shafting with attached drums, or later, pulleys, ran the length of the building. Leather belts then conveyed the rotary motion from the pulleys to the individual carding and spinning machines arranged in rows underneath the shafting. Production depended on the efficiency of this mechanical power transmission system and the high narrow form of the valley mills provided the best distribution of work space for its operation. The narrow width also ensured that the interior would receive an adequate amount of daylight, an important consideration when candles or oil lamps were the only means of artificial illumination.[4]

One architectural innovation in the early factory was found on the roof. Manufacturers wanted to make full use of the top floor underneath the sloping gable roof, and to improve lighting, mill builders introduced new forms of rooftop windows. One form, known as the trapdoor monitor, consisted of a narrow strip of windows under a shed roof rising slightly above the main roof slope on either side. The other, the clerestory monitor or double roof, was a taller structure lined with windows under its own gable roof that rose above the main roof (such as the Fox Mill in the photo on the previous page). These monitors became distinctive aspects of the valley mills and sometimes were adapted for use in houses and other buildings.

Another common feature on top of the factory roof was a belfry housing the bell used to signal the daily routine from the morning's rising to the evening curfew. The rooftop bell, which was customarily a feature of the meetinghouse or the school, became the voice of authority for the new institution of the factory. The belfries were simple structures at first, but they eventually became architecturally elaborate.

The mill housing also mingled tradition and innovation. The typical forms were clapboarded houses with central chimneys, one and one-half and two and one-half stories high. On the exterior, the individual mill house might be mistaken for a farmhouse, but when they were viewed as a group, the rows of identical, plainly finished buildings were clearly not traditional housing.

Their novel character was more evident on the inside. Except for the smallest cottages, the houses were divided into identical apartments on either side, with two units in the one and one-half story cottages and four in the two and one-half story buildings. These apartments or tenements were designed for housekeeping for individual families, a natural response to the common practice of hiring entire families to work in the valley mills. A typical early unit had a combined kitchen and parlor in front with cooking fireplace and beehive oven, two bedrooms in the rear, and additional sleeping space in the garret. While they were not large, especially for a family with many children, they were within the normal size range for those of modest or middling means. Indeed, the opportunity to live in solidly built and well-maintained mill housing was often an important incentive that helped an employer attract and retain workers.

Slatersville Mill House. This simple Federal-style cottage, built in Slatersville c. 1810, was typical of early mill housing. While it resembles a farmhouse, it was built to house two separate mill families. The Rhode Island Collection at Providence Public Library

In addition to the multiple-unit tenement houses, villages often would contain a boardinghouse with a common dining room and parlor on the first floor and dormitory rooms above, occupied by single men and managed by a housekeeper. While it never became a dominant form as it did in Lowell and the similar factory towns of northern New England, the boardinghouse persisted in the Blackstone River Valley. In some cases, they housed single women, especially after the introduction of the power loom in 1817 created new jobs for young women in the mills.

An important influence on the character of the early villages was the broader concern over the effects of industrialization on American society, the debate on manufactures, as it has been termed. In the first decades of the American republic, many feared that manufacturing would create a debased working class, under the control of their employers and lacking the independence and virtue of the yeoman farmer. Even a strong advocate for the new industrial technology like Zachariah Allen acknowledged the problems caused by uncontrolled industrialization. Allen, owner of a woolen mill on the Woonasquatucket River, toured Great Britain in 1825 and saw firsthand the slums and debased social conditions that accompanied dense urban manufacturing in Manchester. He also observed how educational opportunities and other social programs helped create a model community at the textile village of New Lanark.

The sharp contrasts he found between the rural village of New Lanark and the steam-powered city of Manchester reinforced Allen's commitment to the path that he and his fellow Blackstone River Valley manufacturers were taking. Their reliance on water power, rather than coal-fired steam, compelled them to locate in the countryside in "little villages or hamlets, which often appear to spring up as if by magic in the bosom of some forest, around the waterfall which serves to turn the mill wheel." This necessity was actually a virtue, Allen argued, for when the factory workers were "distributed in small communities around waterfalls, their industry is not likely to be the means of rendering them licentious; and of impairing the purity of moral principles, without which neither nations nor individuals can become truly great or happy." He also expected the work force to be made up of "the sons and daughters of respectable farmers, who live in the neighborhood of the works" and would only work "for a time."[5] To ensure that the young women in particular could work alongside men outside the home without endangering their morals, the employer would assume a paternalistic role and maintain decorum inside the factory and throughout the village. In Allen's view, the factory village provided the means to achieve an American industrial revolution without sacrificing the civic principals of the new Republic.

Not every mill owner had the same level of social concern as Allen did, but most wanted their operations to blend in with the surrounding agrarian culture to allay the fears of the larger society and the workers they needed to attract. They also saw paternalism as a way to manage the behavior of their workers and help inculcate the habits of punctuality, sobriety, and diligence that the new factory work required. Consequently, many manufacturers took measures to create the controlled social environment that Allen envisioned.

In contrast to these model establishments, there were others where the manufacturers allowed harsh and exploitative treatment of the work force and where the living conditions were meager. Abusive behavior was widespread in part because of the vulnerability of the many children in the work force, who commonly were compelled to enter the factory by their family's poverty. Whipping, beating, and other forms of corporal punishment often went uncontested. In a notorious case in Woonsocket, an eight-year-old fatherless girl died after being hung upside down outside a factory window by an annoyed overseer. The overseer fled town hurriedly, fearing retribution from the angry community. Most manufacturers came to realize that allowing such conditions to prevail made it hard to secure a reliable work force. Self-interest along with public opinion served to correct the worst abuses, but children remained an important component of the valley work force through the nineteenth century, with only limited provisions to ensure their education.[6]

A Valley Full of Factories

Slatersville was an early demonstration of how well-capitalized manufacturing could foster a concentration of people, buildings, and institutions that was unusually dense for the rural valley. Before the valley's textile manufacturers could emulate the Slaters' success, they had to weather their first recession, which began in 1815 when English textiles flooded the American market after the end of the War of 1812. As the industry regained its vigor in the 1820s, new mill villages were built and existing ones expanded where conditions allowed. The construction of the Blackstone Canal further stimulated commercial development and its hydraulic engineering improvements improved the regularity of the Blackstone River's flow and created new industrial sites at several locations.

On the lower Blackstone, Pawtucket continued its growth from village to urban center, as manufacturers replaced or expanded mills to make more efficient use of the upper and lower dams. Just upstream, new dams across the river at Valley Falls and Central Falls harnessed enough waterpower to operate multiple mills at both locations. While they began as separate villages, these new communities eventually would expand to form an extended urban district with Pawtucket.

At Woonsocket Falls, entrepreneurs responded to the coming of the canal with major improvements in the harnessing and distribution of the considerable amount of waterpower generated by the Blackstone's 34 feet of fall. The creation of the Lyman-Arnold trench enabled the erection of a row of new mills along Main Street that used 18 feet of the fall, as well as several new mills located on a lower raceway that used the same water to capture the remaining 16 feet of fall. On the opposite bank, the Globe Mill and the Bernon Mills similarly divided their shares of the river's flow. As a result of these improvements, three distinct industrial districts now existed at Woonsocket Falls: Woonsocket Village, the large concentration of mills on the east side of the Falls; and the Globe and Bernon mill villages on the opposite side of the Falls. To the east were the Social Mills on the Mill River and the Jenckes Mills on the Peters River. Just downstream was a sixth village, Hamlet, created by Edward Carrington and Stephen Smith to capitalize on the opportunities created by the Blackstone Canal. As on the lower Blackstone, this cluster of six individual communities represented the beginnings of a major urban center.

On the upper Blackstone, Massachusetts manufacturers began to exploit the available water power with the same determination as their Rhode Island neighbors. In Millbury, Asa Waters, who had enjoyed considerable success manufacturing firearms, enlarged his Armory Village with several textile mills. On the Mumford River in Uxbridge, Robert Rogerson, a Boston merchant, reworked an existing mill site, building the Crown Mill in 1823 and adding the Eagle Mill to it in 1827. Joining these mills in the 1820s were new developments at Riverdale (now Northbridge), Wilkinsonville (now Sutton), Fisherville (now

VALUABLE
WATER POWER
FOR SALE,

Situated at the outlet of Manchaug Pond in South Sutton, Worcester County, and near Manchaug Village, so called.

The Power is one of the best in the region, sufficient to operate 3000 Cotton Spindles with preparations; having at all times the control of the water from said Pond for the above named amount, and is one of the most desirable privileges on account of its permanen[t]

The Dam is in good rep[air] [w]ith land amply sufficient to erect a building suitable for using the power for manufacturing.

For further particulars, inquire at the OXFORD BANK, Oxford, Mass.   Oxford, March 21, 1853.

C. B. Webb's Cylinder Press, Ægis Office, 206, Main street, Worcester.

Water Power for Sale. By the mid-nineteenth century, industrialists had secured virtually every opportunity to capture the power of the Blackstone River and its tributaries with dams of timber, earth, and stone. As the scale of industry grew, the mills on the smaller streams often declined, though their ponds became more important as storage reservoirs for larger mills downstream. Courtesy of American Antiquarian Society

Grafton), Farnumsville (now Grafton), and Waterford (now Blackstone) on the Blackstone River; New England Village (now Grafton) on the Quinsigamond River; Wheelocksville (now Uxbridge) on the West River; and Whitinsville (now Northbridge), Manchaug (now Sutton) and East Douglas (now Douglas) on the Mumford River.

A number of the new mills in Rhode Island and Massachusetts had their origins in the hydraulic improvements created by the Blackstone Canal, including those in New England Village, Fisherville, Waterford, and Hamlet. The last and largest of them was Lonsdale (now Lincoln), launched by the Providence merchants Brown & Ives and Edward Carrington in 1831. The extensive use of the valley's waters for both manufacturing and the canal prompted the creation of numerous ponds on the rivers and major streams where the manufacturers could store rainfall from the wet months to supplement the low flows of the dry months. Although floods and droughts continued to occur, to a great extent the natural rivers had become an interconnected industrial system, harnessed by dams and canals all along their course and running under the control of the mill engineers. This would become most apparent during periods of low water, when the river's flow might stop completely, as manufacturers filled up their depleted mill ponds.

In 1829, a national depression ensued, ruining some valley manufacturers, including the Wilkinsons of Pawtucket, and causing a general downturn in the textile industry for several years. Despite the setback (which would recur with future depressions), the previous decade of sustained growth had prompted the development of nearly every available mill site on the Blackstone and its tributaries. With the return of economic strength in the 1830s, the remaining mill sites were occupied, including those on the Clear and Chepachet rivers at the western edge of the Blackstone watershed. Many of these mills, including Bridgeton, Pascoag, and Harrisville (Burrillville), would specialize in woolen production. In Douglas, the Douglas Axe Company (1834) would become the largest of the edge-tool factories in the valley.

With these new centers of economic and commercial activity springing up along the river, the importance of the older hilltop villages such as Union Village and Mendon began to dwindle. This new demographic pattern was reinforced by the Providence & Worcester Railroad, which closely followed the canal's route.

Agriculture remained an important aspect of the countryside even as manufacturing replaced it in economic importance. Although the farming population dropped, those who continued entered a new period of prosperity. While the farmers let less-fertile lands go fallow, they kept much of the valley in productive use, supplying fruits, vegetables, meat, and dairy products to the residents of the mill villages and the fast-growing urban centers of Providence and Worcester. The industrial manipulation of the river was not entirely beneficial for the valley farmers. The mill dams that impeded the river's flow also blocked the passage of salmon, shad, and herring that had swum upstream to spawn every spring. The rural populace

had relied on the fish runs as an important source of food in the lean months, but their protests against the dams were to no avail. The ponds created by the dams also inundated some of the valley's most fertile farmland. While manufacturers were required to compensate property owners for any land they flooded, they were legally entitled to build their dams despite the objections of farmers who didn't want to lose their meadows.

Water-powered manufacturing in the Blackstone Valley reached an apogee by mid-century. Despite the financial Panic of 1837, expansion and prosperity marked the 1830s and 1840s. Manufacturers built additional mills to boost their production and housing to accommodate the increased work force and more villages acquired churches, schools, and stores. By 1850, more than forty individual mill villages lined the Blackstone and its tributaries and about half that many on the Woonasquatucket and Moshassuck rivers. Between Pawtucket and Slatersville alone, sixty mills employed four thousand men, women, and children.

Mature communities were replacing the embryonic settlements of the early years in many villages. Slatersville, which began as the largest village and had continued to grow, was now equaled in size by Lonsdale, with 1,200 residents, and surpassed by Valley Falls (1,500) and Central Falls (1,307). In Woonsocket, exclusive of Bernon and Hamlet, there were nearly 900 workers in eighteen mills and an overall population of 4,000. Only Pawtucket, which had over 5,500 residents, was larger.

This growth in industry was marked not just by the number of manufacturers, but, more importantly, by the scale of their operations. One company's establishment might now include several mills and a work force ten times the size of the twenty or thirty men, women, and children that would staff an early mill. The small hamlets that Zachariah Allen described in the 1820s were now expanding into proper villages. Allen and his fellow mill owners responded to this growth with increasingly sophisticated treatment of the physical and social setting of the mill village. This paternalistic approach was generally successful, but even a conscientious employer like Zachariah Allen, who coupled physical amenities with favorable wages and working conditions to secure a diligent and con-

tented work force, was not able to avoid labor prob-lems completely.[7]

One of the principal changes was to move beyond the simple layout of the early hamlets and develop more formal village plans, frequently ornamented with shade trees. In Woonsocket, Bernon Village was laid out in a regular grid of intersecting streets facing the mills; in the words of a nineteenth-century writer, "Broad avenues were laid out, trees planted beside them, and tenement houses were erected with a view to order, beauty and convenience."[8] Nearby in Ham-

Grafton Center, Massachusetts. The village of Grafton Center clustered around the hilltop common was one of the few pre-industrial community centers to thrive during the industrial era. Flanked by the Unitarian Church (1863) on the right, the Warren Block was a center of activity on the Common. Destroyed by fire in 1862, it was subsequently rebuilt with brick and remains a focus for Grafton Common. John H. Chafee Blackstone River Valley NHC/National Park Service

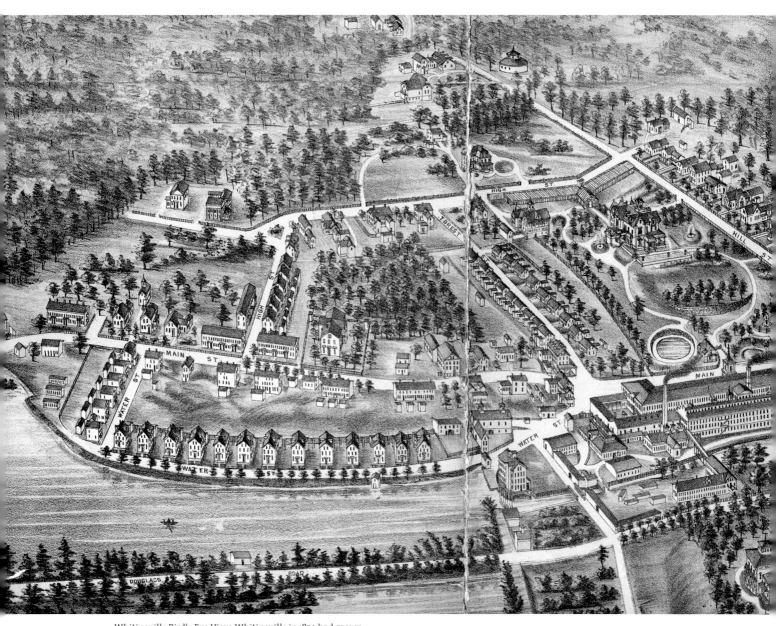

Whitinsville Bird's-Eye View. Whitinsville in 1879 had grown
into a sizeable village following a pattern that was close-knit, but
distinctly defined by social hierarchy. With the construction of the
large cotton mill and still-larger machine works in the 1840s, the
village spread across the north side of the river. To the west of the
mills, the company added successive streets of housing, including
large multiple-unit tenement houses, row houses, and duplex
cottages. More-stylish management housing and institutional
buildings occupied the east side of the village, and in the center,
the opulent mansion and grounds of John C. Whitin asserted
the family's dominant position as sole proprietor of the whole
enterprise. From the collections of Worcester Historical Museum,
Worcester, MA

let, the workers' houses faced an oval green lined with
trees. At one end of the oval was the factory and at
the other was the superintendent's house. Rogerson's
Crown and Eagle Village had a symmetrical plan arranged around the mills and their raceways; a popular view of the village epitomized the Blackstone Valley manufacturers' vision of an ordered landscape in
which the factory took its place alongside the farm in
American society.

The factories and the houses also displayed a more
sophisticated architectural quality than the simple
Federal trim of the early buildings. The large new

Crown and Eagle Landscape. Robert Rogerson's Crown and Eagle Mills, shown in this 1830 view by James Kidder, exemplified the best efforts of valley manufacturers to use architecture and landscape design to make their mill villages attractive as well as productive. John H. Chafee Blackstone River Valley NHC/National Park Service

mills were mostly of brick or stone and trimmed in current popular styles including the Greek Revival, Gothic Revival, and Italianate. A central focus for this decoration was the external stair tower that had become a common feature on textile mills in the 1820s. The towers, which were placed at one end or at the center of the long side of a mill, typically were crowned with a cupola or a belfry with an ornamental roof. The tower was one of the key elements in mill owners' efforts to reduce the significant danger of fire in the factory. Moving the stairs outside the building isolated the vertical stairwell that could allow fire to spread between floors. The tower also might contain a cistern to supply water for fighting fires. Other fire-preventive measures that began to proliferate in the 1830s were changes to the framing of the mill structure, with heavy plank-and-beam floors replacing the traditional joisted floors that contained hollow spaces that allowed fire to spread.

The decoration on the mill housing rarely exceeded a decorative cornice and front doorway trim. The overseers, the factory's middle management, generally had similarly styled residences, but with more spacious apartments. The common exception to this architectural restraint was the mill superintendent's house, which often exhibited a higher degree of architectural styling, like the Gothic Revival superintendent's residence at Allendale. These houses, often the only single-family residence in a village, usually sat in a prominent location where they overlooked the rest of the housing (as at Hamlet).

This special treatment for the superintendent's house exemplified a chief characteristic of life in the mill village—the presence of a firm hierarchical order in which authority was administered through a chain of command from the superintendent through the overseers in each of the departments to the operatives. Different jobs entailed differing levels of skill, from the highly skilled mechanics through mule spinners and weavers down to lowly bobbin boys and sweepers. As the owner's agent (or, less commonly, as the owner himself), the superintendent had the power to hire and fire employees and determine the conditions of work. The imposition of authority was not entirely one-sided; if jobs elsewhere were plentiful or a worker possessed valuable skills, he or she might simply depart for greener pastures. However, when times were bad or a worker had debts or other obligations, leaving was not easy.

Textile factory work did not require as much physical strength or exposure to the elements as many aspects of farming and other rural employments, but it was very demanding in its own way, with its long hours of repetitive unvarying actions, working at the machine's pace and exposed to the hazards of the ubiquitous moving shafts, belts, and gears. As the century progressed, the number of machines a worker tended and the speed at which they operated generally increased. Achieving a uniform product required close attention and consistent operation of the machinery. Mill managers were quick to fine or fire those who lacked the necessary dexterity, diligence, or sobriety.

The work schedule was an onerous one (though the same was true of the farmer's daily work load by to-

Charles P. Whitin Mansion. Charles P. Whitin's handsome Italianate villa and carriage house were set in a park-like setting on the south bank of the river, overlooking the mills that were the source of the family's prosperity but well-removed from the houses of the mills' many workers. Courtesy of Spaulding Aldrich

Whitinsville Mill Housing today. The Whitin Company ultimately built more than a dozen different types of worker housing; the size and quality of a worker's residence depended on his position in the work force. John H. Chafee Blackstone River Valley NHC/National Park Service

Workers in a Spinning Room. The hierarchy of the factory work force is apparent in this view of the Wuskanut Mill's spinning room, with the overseer's high collar and tie contrasting with the oily overalls of the machine tenders. The overhead shafting, pulleys, and belts driving the machines can be seen in the background. Courtesy of Judy Zaleski & Family

day's standards). The work week was six days long and the daily timetable varied somewhat from mill to mill and with the seasons. The work day typically began at sunrise and continued until sunset in the spring and summer, which meant workdays twelve to fifteen hours long, with a half-hour break for breakfast at 7:30 and an hour dinner break at noon. In the shorter days from fall through spring, candles or lamps (later replaced by gaslights) provided illumination so work could continue past sunset for an eleven- or twelve-hour day. Time was regulated by the factory bell, which rang to wake the workers up before dawn, signaled the beginning and end of the work sessions and, in some

The Dinner Hour, J. & P. Coats Thread Mills, Central Falls, R. I.

J. & P. Coats Dinner Hour. This early twentieth-century view of thread-mill workers breaking for the midday meal clearly depicts the presence of girls and boys in the valley mills even at this late date. While some of the children have come to the factory to bring lunch pails for relatives or neighbors, others are leaving their work place to dine at home. Courtesy the Rhode Island Historical Society

villages, rang curfew at night.[9] The operatives' efforts to reduce the hours of work met with only limited success. By the 1850s, manufacturers generally adhered to a sixty-nine-hour work week. The goal of the ten-hour day was finally achieved in Massachusetts for children in 1842 and for all workers in 1874; Rhode Island finally adopted the ten-hour day in 1885.[10]

The only official holidays were Christmas and the Fourth of July. Election Day might provide another holiday, especially if the mill owner wanted to encourage his work force to rally in favor of the candidate of his choice (even if many of them lacked the qualifications to vote). One of the unofficial holiday events observed by the mill workers was a springtime "blowing out" celebration that marked the end of "lighting up" (the wintertime practice of continuing to work by candle or lamplight after the sun had set).

The work regimen left the workers with little free time outside the factory, but for those who were used to the isolation of the countryside, the larger villages provided an active social environment. Religion was one of the principal social institutions, as it was elsewhere in New England, and attending services and church-sponsored gatherings was a mainstay in community life. Mill owners generally encouraged organized religion, often providing land and financial support for a church and minister, out of both their own religious convictions and a desire to promote temperance and other moral behavior that would encourage good work habits. In addition to the services in churches or schools in or near the village, workers also attended evangelical revival meetings held outdoors, under tents or, on occasion, in the factory.

Education was another aspect of village life, initially promoted by Slater and other paternalistic owners in the form of Sunday schools where children were taught the rudimentary skills of reading, writing, and arithmetic. The early schools rarely had their own buildings, but individual schoolhouses were a common village feature by mid-century as schooling for children under twelve was mandated by law. In some villages, the owners established reading rooms as well, often in conjunction with the school, and sponsored evening lectures on geography, natural history, literature, and other "improving" topics. The schools and the churches typically had an architectural quality that distinguished them as important institutions. A vernacular classicism, either Federal or Greek Revival, was most common, but the Gothic, Italianate, and Romanesque were used as well, especially in churches.

Inevitably, keeping house occupied much free time and in the growing season many households main-

Fisherville Baseball Game. The mill workers made the most of their limited free time with sports and other recreational activities. Baseball, shown here at Fisherville, was one of the most popular pastimes, from informal sandlot games, to the company-sponsored Blackstone Valley League of the 1920s. Courtesy of Steven Rodominick & Family

GEORGIAVILLE.

Georgiaville Village Painting. This folk painting of Georgiaville shows the common valley pattern, with the factories and mill housing clustered in the river valley, surrounded by open farmland and woodland on the hillsides above. This view from c. 1860 shows the village's large, new, classically styled mill and boardinghouses in the foreground, and the steep gable roof of the Gothic chapel on the far right. American Textile History Museum, Lowell, Massachusetts

tained kitchen gardens and animals such as chickens. Nonetheless, informal recreation and socializing occurred as well. Young adult workers often spent time on Sunday afternoon "promenading" in their finest clothes with their friends, while all enjoyed country pastimes that changed with the seasons, such as skating or berry-picking. The tavern was one social institution that received little support from mill owners, many of whom took active steps to regulate or even prevent the sale of alcoholic beverages in their villages. In more urban centers like Pawtucket, taverns and dram shops were common and even in the rural villages, an energetic walker usually could find the desired entertainment without difficulty.

The Tavern. The tavern was a significant aspect of the mill workers' social life, though mill owners typically barred them from their villages in their efforts to promote a temperate and diligent work force. Courtesy of Steven Rodominick & Family

Gathering places such as taverns and fraternal halls outside the company-owned village were also important for workers who wanted to voice their discontent over working conditions freely, or, if especially aggrieved, organize opposition to company policy. Worker grievances included pay cuts, longer hours, increased work load, or other conditions imposed by manufacturers who sought to increase production or bolster profits by cutting labor costs. Such opposition on occasion produced turn-outs or strikes, events that were particularly disruptive in the close quarters of a factory village.[11]

Steam Power and Industrial Expansion

In the second half of the nineteenth century, two new factors had a major effect on the established pattern of water-powered industrial development in the Blackstone Valley. One was steam power, which offered new opportunities for industry to expand, free from the limitations of water power. The other was immigration, which provided an increase in population that would sustain this new expansion and also transform the makeup of valley society.

The stationary steam engine had been a key element in the English Industrial Revolution from its beginning, but in the first decades of American industrialization its role was minor where water power was plentiful. Americans recognized steam power's potential however, and by 1827, Samuel Slater had established a steam-powered textile mill on the Providence waterfront. Providence mechanics were at the forefront of those working on improvements in the design and manufacture of the steam engine and one of those mechanics, George Corliss, achieved a major breakthrough with his automatic cutoff valve, which he patented in 1849. This valve and other improvements, such as the flyball governor, made the steam engine more efficient, less costly to run, and better able to respond smoothly to the shifting power demands in a factory. The steam engine also had the great advantage that it was completely mobile; one could build a steam mill anywhere as long as there was water for the boilers and wood or coal to turn it into steam. With the steam engine freeing them from some of the geographical constraints of water power, manufacturers in the second half of the nineteenth century increasingly chose to locate in the cities, where they were closer to the major transportation lines and the urban labor pool. The effect on Providence and Worcester, was dramatic as their relatively modest water-powered industry was soon joined by dozens of steam-powered shops and factories. Pawtucket also developed a significant steam-manufacturing district in the Church Hill neighborhood.

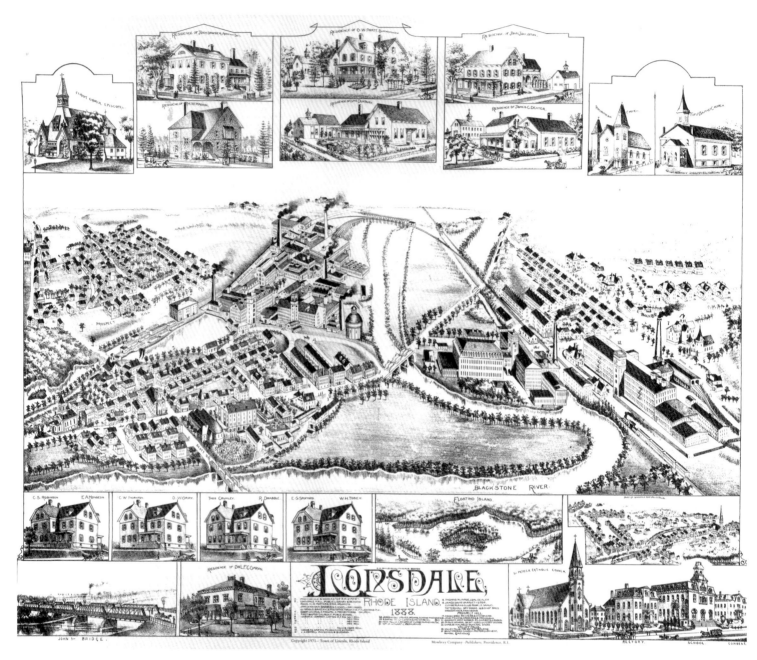

Lonsdale Bird's-Eye Map. This 1888 bird's-eye view shows how the Lonsdale
Company used steam power to double the size of their enterprise. On
the right is the company's New Village, built around the massive steam-
powered Ann & Hope Mill of 1886; on the opposite side of the Blackstone
River is the original water-powered factory village established in 1831.
Courtesy the Rhode Island Historical Society

Steam came to play an important role in the rural villages as well, not replacing water power but augmenting it. Here, mill owners first turned to steam power to deal with the recurring problem of summer drought. When there was too little water in the river and reservoirs to keep the mills running all day, a standby steam engine would provide the needed power. Without this option, the mills would have to run fewer hours or shut down, which meant that production would suffer. In addition, the operatives, who were paid only for the hours they worked, would see their earnings drop, prompting some to move on and others to run up debts at the company store. Thus the steam engine proved to be a valuable aid to the water-powered factories of the valley, allowing them to remain competitive at a time when the textile industry was expanding elsewhere.

Valley manufacturers came to rely on steam for more than just reserve power when they sought to boost their production beyond the capacity of the water power available to them. The most ambitious ventures into steam power were made by the Lonsdale Corporation. In 1870, they built the first new village in the valley in years at Berkeley (now Cumberland) with a mill that was operated entirely by steam power. The village with its rows of duplex cottages was in the same mode as the company's earlier villages at Lonsdale and Ashton, except the mill wasn't located on the river bank but alongside the railroad that brought the coal that fueled its large steam engine.

In 1886, the company employed steam again for a major expansion at Lonsdale New Village, across the Blackstone River from the original village of Lonsdale. This new enterprise had begun with one water-powered mill built in 1860 and enlarged in 1871, but this mill was dwarfed in size and capacity by the new steam mill of 1886, which was four stories high and 498 feet long. The owners proudly named it the Ann & Hope Mill, employing the name that the firm's founders first had used on their premier merchant ship in 1796. Thirty-eight multifamily houses were added to the New Village to accommodate the new mill's work force. Following the company's practice since the 1850s, the new buildings were built of brick and the majority of them fell into one of three types: one and one-half-story duplex cottages, two-story four-

family houses, and long two-story rows of attached tenements. Workers' status would determine what type of housing they would occupy, with the cottage duplex generally being the most desirable. The plain style of the new houses was little changed from the mill houses of the preceding decades, except for the overseers' houses, which were large double houses trimmed with brownstone and featuring porches and other decorative features of the Queen Anne style.

The Lonsdale Company's continued reliance on the rural village model at Berkeley and the New Village demonstrated the owners' confidence in the corporate village as an effective form of manufacturing and labor management even as urban manufacturing was accelerating rapidly. Even as these prospering operations grew to unprecedented size, the countryside still remained a short walk from the center of most villages, with private farms and fruit orchards and company-owned farms, like the large dairy farms operated by the Lonsdale and Whitin Companies, maintaining the rural character.

Throughout the valley, tall smoking chimneys became part of the landscape, as steam power supplemented existing operations or made new industry possible, both in large mills like the Ann & Hope and smaller shops. This growth depended on the cheap and efficient transportation of coal, a job best done by the railroad. Manufacturers not served by the Providence & Worcester Railroad or branch lines from the Boston & Albany Railroad invested in new rail lines and spurs, notably the Providence & Springfield Railroad, which ran through the mill villages on the Woonasquatucket and Clear rivers. Locations bypassed by the railroad, such as Chepachet, were at a disadvantage and manufacturing there remained static or went into a decline.

Immigration and the Growing Work Force

From the beginning, the industrialization of the Blackstone River Valley had depended on a redistribution of population, drawing workers from inside and outside the valley and concentrating them in the factory villages. At first, the people who came to work in the mills were mostly native-born New Englanders. The early factory workers also included a small but significant contingent of English immigrants,

Castle Hill Company Farm. The company farm was a feature of many Blackstone Valley mill villages. The farms provided foodstuffs for the village residents, fodder for the company's draft animals, and, especially in the early years, employment for fathers whose children worked in the mill. Dairy herds, like this one on the Whitins' Castle Hill Farm, supplied milk for the village schools into the twentieth century. Courtesy of Spaulding Aldrich

Fisherville Mill. After fire claimed the original Fisherville Mill in 1881, the company built a new mill powered by both water and steam. After a succession of additions, the mill as shown here in 1912 was one of the largest in the Blackstone Valley, with more than five hundred employees and operating over a thousand looms. From the Collection of Laurel Moriarty

Fisherville Mills. 1912

and English men and women, many of them experienced textile workers, continued to come to the valley through the nineteenth century. The construction of the Blackstone Canal attracted Irish canal workers, some of whom remained in the valley, but beginning in the 1830s and accelerating in the 1840s with the Potato Famine, Irish immigrants arrived at a rate that dwarfed the earlier migrations. By 1850, one of the valley's leading towns, Smithfield, Rhode Island, had twice the population it had in 1830 and one-third of its residents were foreign immigrants, mostly Irish and English. The French Canadians were the next to come, initially drawn by the labor shortage created by the Civil War. Between 1865 and 1875, they arrived at a rate that surpassed the Irish. Many other nationalities followed, though in smaller numbers than the Irish or French Canadians, including Swedes and, in the late nineteenth and early twentieth centuries, Italians, Poles, Ukrainians, Armenians, Greeks, Syrians, and Portuguese. This influx brought a new ethnic diversity to the valley's manufacturing centers. The Irish and the French Canadians (and most of the immigrants who followed) were mainly country folk with few skills who left their homes out of necessity rather than choice. Mostly poor, illiterate, and Roman Catholic, they represented an alien culture to the Yankee communities they entered. Differences in language and culture led the newcomers to hold themselves apart from both the native-born and the other immigrant groups.[12]

In the factories, the Yankees increasingly were concentrated in the ranks of management and skilled mechanics, overseeing a work force largely made up of immigrants and their children. Some manufacturers favored certain groups over others. Lonsdale Company villages had a strong British character, while the French-Canadian presence was great just up the river in the Manville and Woonsocket mills. The Washburn and Moen Company actively recruited Swedish workers for their Quinsigamond wire works, while Irish workers were the mainstay of the Allen Print Works in Providence. As new immigrant groups continued to arrive, they typically entered the work force at the bottom tier and only gradually worked their way up the ranks.

Religion was the most important focus for the immigrant communities. The first Roman Catholic congregations in the valley were founded in Pawtucket (1829), Worcester (1834), and Woonsocket (1844). The initial wave of Irish immigration stimulated a number of new parishes in the 1850s and many more followed in the 1870s with the arrival of the French Canadians. The latter group was the first to establish so-called national parishes, where they were ministered to in their native tongue. Italians and Poles were among those who also sought their own congregations, rather than English-speaking ones. Thus, large communities might have several Catholic churches, as well as various Protestant churches. These new churches were often prominent additions to the landscape, with an elaborate character that affirmed the congregation's faith and their cultural pride as well. In many villages, the church with its spire provided an architectural counterpoint to the mill and its tower, as demonstrated by the Gothic Revival St. Joseph's Church, situated halfway between the villages of Ashton and Berkeley in Cumberland.

When he retired in 1872, Zachariah Allen was one of the last manufacturers who remained from the formative years of the Blackstone River Valley's industrialization. He had begun in the experimental stage of the factory system with a single mill and a work force of twenty-four men, women, and children; in the era of expansion that began in the 1830s, he enlarged his first operation and acquired a second one, increased the combined work force to more than four hundred, and instituted an extensive system of reservoirs covering hundreds of acres. In contrast to his 1822 mill, his factories now used steam engines as well as waterwheels and he employed large numbers of foreign born, rather than sons and daughters of Yankee farmers. Nonetheless, both enterprises continued to embody the rural village character that he had promulgated fifty years earlier.

The valley's factory villages were no longer the vanguard of American industry that they had been when Allen began, but they remained a significant center of manufacturing and innovation. As the valley entered its last period of growth in the final decades of the nineteenth century, manufacturers continued

St. Anne's Band. The musical band was a common institution in mill village life. Sometimes sponsored by the mill owners or associated with a church, like this band from one of Woonsocket's French-Canadian parishes, these amateur musical groups played an important role in the social and recreational life of their communities. Courtesy of the Museum of Work & Culture Collection

their adherence to the factory village first exemplified by Slatersville in 1806. Some manufacturers turned to the new professional practices of landscape architecture and community planning to manage village growth. At model villages like Hopedale, Whitinsville, and elsewhere, mill owners provided new housing with indoor plumbing, recreational facilities, parks, and other community improvements for the benefit of the entire workforce.[13] This renewed focus on paternalistic measures, referred to as welfare capitalism, was a response to growing labor unrest nationally and among the workers in the New England textile industry. As part of their efforts, the mill owners promoted organized sports to foster better relations between company and workers, adding bowling alleys, baseball diamonds, and soccer fields to the village landscape.[14]

Although the twentieth century witnessed first the contraction of industry and then a long period of de-

View of St. Joseph's above Ashton Village. The spire of St. Joseph's Church on the hillside above Ashton was a visible symbol for the mill's Catholic workers of a significant aspect of their lives that was separate and apart from their daily routine in the company owned village. The Rhode Island Collection of Providence Public Library

industrialization, the fundamental patterns of the valley's remarkable transformation remain apparent in its villages. The landscape retains its distinctive character as the place where American industry passed through its pioneering stage and emerged as a major force on the world stage.

NOTES

1. Claire Dempsey, "The Blackstone River Valley," in *The Early Architecture and Landscapes of the Narragansett Basin*, volume II, *Blackstone River Valley and Providence*, ed. Claire Dempsey, Richard E. Greenwood, and William McKenzie Woodward, (Newport, R.I.: Vernacular Architecture Forum, 2001), 13.

2. Moses Brown to T. Rogerson, November 11, 1810, Almy & Brown MSS, RIHS.

3. Richard Candee, "New Towns of the Early New England Textile Industry," in *Perspectives in Vernacular Architecture*, ed., Camille Wells (Annapolis, Md.: Vernacular Architecture Forum, 1982), 31–50; William Pierson, Jr., *American Buildings and Their Architects*, vol. 2, *Technology and the Picturesque, The Corporate and the Early Gothic Styles* (New York: Anchor Books, 1980), 32–33.

4. For a discussion of the mechanical systems within the factories and their evolution, see Robert B. Gordon and Pat-

Canoeing and Camping on Johnny's Island, Whitinsville. The millponds and their wooded shores were well-suited to rural amusements, whether canoeing on a Sunday afternoon or, for those with more leisure time, camping like this group on the pond at Whitinsville. Courtesy of Spaulding Aldrich

rick M. Malone, *The Texture of Industry: An Archaeological View of the Industrialization of North America* (New York: Oxford University Press, 1994), 297–346.

5. Zachariah Allen, *The Practical Tourist*, vol. I (Providence, R.I.: A. S. Beckwith, 1832), 153–155.

6. See the *Second Annual Report of Industrial Statistics* (Providence, 1889), 130 ff, for the Woonsocket atrocity. Details of child labor also can be found in Brother Joseph Brennan, *Social Conditions in Industrial Rhode Island: 1820–1860* (Washington, D.C.: Catholic University of America Press, 1940), 40–46.

7. Richard E. Greenwood, "Zachariah Allen and the Architecture of Industrial Paternalism," *Rhode Island History*, 46, no. 4 (November 1988).

8. Erastus Richardson, *History of Woonsocket* (Woonsocket: S.S. Foss, 1876), 156.

9. Brother Joseph Brennan, *Social Conditions in Industrial Rhode Island: 1820–1860* (Washington, D.C.: Catholic University of America Press, 1940), 47–48.

10. Norman Ware, *The Industrial Worker, 1840–1860*, pp. 128–132.

11. See Gary Kulik, "Pawtucket Village and the Strike of 1824: The Origins of Class Conflict in Rhode Island," *Radical History Review* 17 (Spring 1978): 5–37; Paul Buhle, Scott Molloy, and Gail Sansbury, eds., *A History of Rhode Island Working People* (Providence, R.I.: Regine Printing Co., 1983).

12. For a discussion of the immigrant experience in the valley's mill villages, see Louise Lamphere, *From Working Daughters to Working Mothers: Immigrant Women in a New England Industrial Community* (Ithaca: Cornell University Press, 1987).

13. On model villages and Hopedale in particular, see John S. Garner, *The Model Company Town: Urban Design through Private Enterprise in Nineteenth-Century New England* (Amherst: University of Massachusetts Press, 1984). For Whitinsville, see Thomas R. Navin, *The Whitin Machine Works Since 1831* (New York: Russell & Russell, 1969).

14. The role of baseball in these efforts is discussed in Doug Reynolds, "Hardball Paternalism, Hardball Politics: Blackstone Valley Baseball, 1925–1955," *Labor's Heritage* 3, no. 2 (April 1991): 24–41.

"A Country So Full of Factories . . ."

RANGER CHUCK ARNING

The social, economic, and political land mass that Great Britain had known, prior to the war, as "the colonies," was changing at a rapid pace. The United States were becoming places filled with men and boys tinkering in their barns and sheds, devising new and better ways to make things. Anything and everything; such things could run the gamut from tacks to lathes to carding machines. One young lad in Kingston, Massachusetts, Ichabod Washburn, wrote in his later years that "during the winter [1813–1814], I was engaged with a Mr. Sugden, an Englishman, in running a power loom. It was so crude and primitive, that all the cog wheels were made of wood, and probably was the first power loom ever made in this country . . . At this time, I had become much interested in the operation of machinery, and felt a strong inclination to learn the machinist trade."[1]

At fifteen, Washburn was a veteran mill worker. Intensely inquisitive, he was fascinated by machinery and how each piece fit together: big pieces, small pieces, all coming together to create something new, and particularly this new engineered landscape of falling water powering the entire system. It was this complexity of machinery that intrigued Washburn, and it turns out that he was far from being alone. Men were building new tools to make new machines for new processes. Washburn was there at the ground floor, surveying this new and changing landscape, eager to try his skills in this new manufacturing environment. He wrote, "A good opportunity offering in one of the shops of the Slater's, in Pawtucket. I had a great desire to avail myself of it. But my guardian being consulted, with others, discouraged the under-taking, on the grounds of the probability, that by the time my apprenticeship should expire, the country would be so full of factories, that there would be no more machinery to be built."[2]

This conversation between a young man looking forward to a future that was radically different from anything that his guardian uncle possibly could conceive was a new one. But it was a conversation that was being held throughout the new republic, for others were seeing a future far different than anything anyone had ever imagined.[3]

What was so compelling about these young men of new ideas, new processes, and new ways of working? How did Slater and his trained operatives change the industrial landscape of America? What made some successful and others fail? These are all important questions, because the new republic's entrepreneurial environment, vastly different from anything before, was on the move. Communication systems; transportation systems; financial systems; all interacting in an environment that allowed Slater, and men like him, this new American Business class, to change the course of how business was conducted and history itself. And it was taking place at a frightening speed.

NOTES

1. Ichabod Washburn, *Autobiography and Memorials of Ichabod Washburn Showing How a Great Business was Developed and Large Wealth Acquired for the Use of Benevolence,* introduction by Rev. Henry T. Cheever (Boston: D. Lothrup & Company, 1878), 24.

2. Ibid.

3. Joyce Appleby, *Inheriting the Revolution: The First Generation of Americans* (Cambridge, Mass.: The Belknap Press of Harvard University Press, 2000), 4–8.

2 The Slaters of Rhode Island and the Rise and Fall of American Textiles GRAY FITZSIMONS

Slater Bank One Dollar Note with an image of the falls at Pawtucket with Slater Mill in the distant background.
Courtesy the Rhode Island Historical Society

Many New England families have played prominent roles in the rise and fall of American textile manufacturing. Few, however, possessed the longevity of Samuel Slater, his brother John, and their descendants, or matched the influence the Slaters wielded in shaping the nation's factory system. In fact, English-born Samuel Slater (1768–1835) has long been acclaimed as the industry's founder and even the "father of American manufacturers." The success of his waterpowered cotton-spinning mill, built in late eighteenth-century Pawtucket, Rhode Island, has led some to declare the Blackstone Valley as the "birthplace of America's Industrial Revolution." Scholars have highlighted Slater's impressive mechanical skills, as well as his important managerial and leadership role in the rise of the nation's factory system. Far less attention, however, has been paid to the later generations of Slaters who carried on the textile enterprises initiated by Samuel Slater and his Rhode Island partners Almy and Brown.

Over the years, the Slaters responded to changing textile technology, market, and labor conditions in a variety of ways: from modernizing their factories and corporate organizations, to fiercely resisting unionization, and finally to shifting their operations to the South. As a result, their companies remained consistently profitable. These returns, along with other successful investments, added to the family's considerable wealth. Several Slaters engaged in philanthropy and one gained a national reputation for aiding the freedmen of the South. By examining their careers, one may discern the broader patterns of the region's textile industry, encompassing its rise and decline in nineteenth- and twentieth-century New England.

The Slaters in Pawtucket

The roots of the Slater textile dynasty, first planted in Pawtucket, Rhode Island, in 1790, may be traced to Derbyshire in the rugged East Midlands of England. Encompassing the Derwent Valley, this region emerged in the 1770s as the center of mechanized cotton yarn production. It was here that Richard Arkwright, backed by capitalist and hosiery maker Jedidiah Strutt, developed the first successful waterpowered spinning frame. Employing families and child workers to tend Arkwright's mechanized frames, Strutt built a number of mills in the Derwent Valley, one of which was in the village of Belper, near Samuel Slater's birthplace. Slater's father, William, a tenant farmer of modest means, lived with his wife, Elizabeth Fox Slater, in a small cottage. There, they raised three daughters and five sons.[1] The second-youngest of the sons, Samuel, went to work in Jedidiah Strutt's Milford cotton mill, near the Slater farmstead, when he was around the age of thirteen. Slater was soon ap-

prenticed to Strutt. His father's death in 1782 required that Samuel sign his own indenture papers, and he began his formal apprenticeship under Strutt in January 1783.[2]

The several years that Slater spent at Strutt's mill shaped him profoundly. He gained invaluable mechanical skills while working with the most advanced textile technology of that era, the Arkwright water frame. But perhaps even more important was his exposure to the factory management and paternalistic practices of Jedidiah Strutt. As a proprietor, Strutt sought to limit competition by keeping his machinery and manufacturing knowledge proprietary, trusting only family and close associates to run his manufacturing interests. For his work force, Strutt employed families and children, including some bound labor, though the majority of his workers were wage-earners. While Strutt operated a factory for hosiery production, he contracted out some of his manufacturing, leasing his patented stocking frames to local artisans who produced hosiery goods in their homes or small workshops.[3] The preparatory machines and spinning frames that produced Strutt's yarn operated continuously and therefore required an unprecedented level of worker discipline and routine. This stringent control over his workers, as well as the regimented nature of heavily mechanized production, gave rise to suspicion and hostility toward the factory.

For Strutt, however, the factory system offered not only the opportunity of adding to his personal wealth, but also the means of uplifting the economic and moral well-being of his villagers. To this end, he paid relatively high wages, sponsored village-wide fêtes for which he provided copious amounts of food and drink, built cottages for his workers, and established chapels with Sunday schools to educate his workers in skills such as reading and arithmetic, as well as teaching them the Protestant faith. In return, he demanded loyalty, thrift, temperance, and hard work. Strutt and his overseers suffered few miscreants: Erring child workers were verbally or physically punished, while adult transgressors often were fired from the factory and cast out of the cottage.[4]

Throughout his apprenticeship, Samuel Slater absorbed the myriad lessons of his factory master, who rewarded Slater for his diligence and abilities by mak-

Portrait of Samuel Slater. The renowned Samuel Slater gained considerable experience in the textile industry in his native Derbyshire, England, prior to his immigration to the United States. Courtesy of Slater Mill, Pawtucket, RI

ing the young apprentice a factory overseer. By the time he obtained his majority, he supervised mechanical repairs. Yet, striving for even greater opportunity, Slater learned of a reward offered by Philadelphia manufacturers for a mechanic capable of introducing English spinning technology into the city's textile workshops. Undaunted by the British government's restrictions on the export of machines and the overseas migration of skilled mechanics, he decided to leave England and see what he could make of himself in America. Slater kept his plans a secret, not only to avoid apprehension as an illegal emigrant, but also fearing that his departure would upset his family. He embarked upon his voyage across the Atlantic with only a few possessions,

including the indenture papers that would attest to his skills. Slater sailed from London in September 1789 and arrived in New York nearly seven weeks later. He would never return to his native land.[5]

Soon after his arrival in New York, Slater obtained employment in a recently established jenny-spinning workshop on Veysey Street. This enterprise was crude by his standards, and offered little encouragement for improvement. By chance, he learned from a Rhode Island ship captain that Providence merchant Moses Brown, in partnership with William Almy, was constructing a mechanized spinning mill at a waterpower site in Pawtucket. Whatever notion Slater may have had of going to Philadelphia receded, and instead he began a correspondence with Brown. Having offered his services to the Quaker merchant and been offered a job, Slater sailed north to Rhode Island in January 1790. The young Englishman met Brown in Providence and then journeyed with him to the village of Pawtucket, where he found a small but thriving industrial hamlet of several hundred people. Nestled along the river were a number of mills that produced flour and snuff, along with a clothier workshop and three fulling mills. The village also contained two forges, a nail works, various artisans' workshops, at least two taverns, and some twenty or thirty houses.[6]

When taken to examine the clothier workshop and its spinning frames, Slater was unimpressed. Moses Brown noted that Slater "declined doing anything with them and proposed making a New One, Using such parts as the Old would answer."[7] Despite his initial disdain, Slater immediately set to work refashioning the existing water frames and preparatory machinery. Skilled Pawtucket metal- and woodworking artisans aided him, and by March 1790, the mill produced its first waterpowered, machine-spun cotton yarn. Offered a partnership with William Almy and Smith Brown, Slater accepted and continued overseeing the expansion of the Pawtucket mill.[8] By the end of the year, Slater, utilizing his experience with Strutt in England—along with local artisan Sylvanus Brown and ironmaster Oziel Wilkinson—built additional Arkwright machinery, including a new frame, and put them into operation. Most of the yarn spun at Pawtucket during the early years was sent by Almy and Brown to their workshops in Providence, where hand-loom weavers produced a variety of finished cotton cloth goods.[9]

Slater's reputation as a serious-minded, hard-working, and able manager quickly grew. Standing just over six feet in height and weighing more than 200 pounds, Slater was an imposing figure. His partnership in Almy and Brown enhanced his financial status in Pawtucket, and he cemented his ties to the village in late 1791 when the English émigré married Hannah Wilkinson, the seventeen-year-old daughter of Quaker ironmaster Oziel Wilkinson. The couple set up a household in an unassuming, two-story brick dwelling a short distance from the mill. Here, Hannah would give birth to eight children.[10]

Slater's marriage to Hannah Wilkinson did not lessen his intense devotion to his duties at the mill. In fact, over the next two years, he became ever more involved, as he and his partners agreed to build an entirely new waterpowered mill outfitted with Arkwright frames. Later called the "Old Mill," this two and one-half story, wood-frame factory, measuring just 26 by 40 feet—small compared to English mills—opened in 1793.[11] Being able to produce more cotton yarn at the new factory mill shored up the fledgling firm's financial strength. As the partnership was becoming known for its yarn production, a glut of cheap, imported British cloth flooded American markets and caused numerous weaving shops in Providence and elsewhere to close. By 1796, the Quaker merchants abandoned cloth production altogether, concentrating—to great advantage—in the manufacture and sale of cotton yarn.[12]

In the early years of the mill's operation, Slater hired child workers from poor as well as artisan families, and boy apprentices. For some male workers, the skills they learned at Slater's mill enabled them to become inventive mechanics, overseers, or even factory owners. Many others toiled in hardship, in unbearably oppressive conditions, with little opportunity for advancement. The mill's apprentices, in particular, objected to factory work, and Slater soon halted their employment, finding the boys costly and undependable. Instead, he turned increasingly to child labor. Typically, Slater negotiated the terms of employment with the household head after the child had entered the mill. Most of the child workers were between the ages of seven and fifteen, and their pay, amounting to three or four shillings per week (about $0.40 to $0.70), was about one-fifth that paid to adult workers. Their wages were paid to the parent who, in turn, often was employed in the village. Some such parents worked for Slater directly.[13]

Dank and dimly lit in winter, hot and humid in summer, the clamorous factory was a dirty and occasionally dangerous workplace. During peak operations —usually in the spring, summer, and early fall—Slater operated the mill six days a week, fourteen and even up to sixteen hours a day. Yet the regularity of hours, production, and oversight that characterized the factory later in the nineteenth century were not in place

Slater Mill Historic Site. The 1793 wooden Slater Mill looks far better today then when it was in full production. As the process of industrialization moved forward, the Pawtucket Falls waterfront was jammed with mills, intricate raceways, and a variety of machine shops all focused on bringing the new republic into an industrial age. The preservation efforts of the Slater Mill Association in forming the Slater Mill Historic Site allows visitors to experience the original spinning mill that had been in operation for over 160 years before becoming a museum. John H. Chafee Blackstone River Valley NHC/National Park Service

at Slater's mill in the early years. Where they existed, work rules were often informal, and work stoppages, due either to mechanical problems or lack of raw materials, were common. Within Slater's lifetime, however, these conditions changed, as workers' tasks became more specialized and repetitive, the work day was more regulated, and managerial control in the workplace was more exacting. As a result, the distance separating the mill manager and the mill hand became less easily bridged.[14]

The work force in Slater's mills included not only children and adults from poor rural families, but also a number of young males from the middle classes. Typically, these boys entered the factory with the aim of gaining the skills to become machinists, managers, and even mill owners. For example, James Tiffany, a rural merchant in South Brimfield, Massachusetts, became acquainted with Slater and, desiring that his two sons, Lyman and Bela, learn the textile business, placed them in the Pawtucket mill. Bela Tiffany advanced to the position of overseer and in the early 1810s joined Slater as a partner in a mill in Massachusetts, while still in his twenties.[15] Others, such as Elisha Waters, having learned cotton manufacturing at the Pawtucket mills, erected their own factories and competed with Almy and Brown.[16]

In its early years, Slater's mills drew upon Pawtucket and its environs for their factory labor force. Over time, however, they found it increasingly difficult to recruit local residents and instead began hiring a growing number of landless poor families from outlying rural areas and from seaports in Rhode Island and Massachusetts. With few other choices, many of these ambivalent employees viewed factory life as unhealthy and financially unrewarding, while others echoed Jeffersonian concerns over the freedom-destroying dependency that factory wage labor appeared to engender. Periodically, tensions surfaced between Samuel Slater and the heads of household who had contracted with him to employ their children. Disputes over wage rates and timeliness of payments, as well as challenges to the factory master's authority, arose not only at Slater's mill, but at other mills in the region.[17] Despite the ethnic (white and largely of English origin) and religious (primarily Protestant) homogeneity of the factory communities, and despite shared social values that emphasized deference and patriarchal authority, widening fault lines between workers and managers—especially connected to social and economic class differences—emerged during Slater's lifetime.[18]

At various times in the 1790s, Samuel Slater found himself at odds with his merchant partners. Exasperated with the inadequate delivery of raw materials and a lack of money and provisions for his workers, Slater repeatedly pleaded with and chastised Almy and Brown, occasionally threatening to curtail production or shut down the mill. On the other hand, Almy and Brown experienced a range of difficulties in running the financial and business side of their textile enterprise. The nation's poor transportation network, its inadequate banking facilities, and a lack of uniformity in currency continually hindered the ability of the Providence merchants to obtain a steady flow of raw cotton, market their cotton goods, and collect from their creditors. That Slater was focused solely

on running the Pawtucket mill and held only a limited partnership in the textile firm impaired his understanding of the larger business operations. Nevertheless, all of these factors contributed to the growing friction within the partnership.[19]

Determined to expand his role in the growing textile industry, Slater sought to establish his own company. Along with the Wilkinsons of Pawtucket, he established S. Slater and Company in 1799 and built a spinning mill on the east side of the Blackstone River in Rehoboth, Massachusetts. Within two years, the so-called "White Mill" in Rehoboth began producing cotton yarn. Legal action to prohibit Slater from gaining water-power privileges on the Blackstone slowed the company's progress and exacerbated the rift between Slater, Almy, and Brown, but the partners eventually overcame their differences and coordinated the interests of their respective companies. Such interests included the joint purchasing of raw cotton and the uniform pricing of their finished yarns. Slater also continued to manage the mills on both sides of the Blackstone River and each of these enterprises profited handsomely. For Slater, this period in the early 1800s marked his emergence not only as an accomplished factory master, but as a successful businessman. Moreover, because of the moral initiatives he had championed at Pawtucket, including the creation of one of the nation's first Sunday schools, Slater gained a reputation as a reformer and community leader.[20]

Another important event in Samuel Slater's life occurred in 1803, when he was joined in Pawtucket by his brother John. Also born in Belper, John Slater (1776–1843), like Samuel, was apprenticed in the Derbyshire mills and eventually became a millwright. By the time he was a young man, he had gained considerable knowledge of waterpower mechanics and drive trains for powering textile machinery. Shortly after arriving in Pawtucket, he joined his brother in Almy, Brown and Slater, and by 1806, he became a partner in the firm's new mill and village development in North Smithfield, Rhode Island. The following year, John Slater occupied his residence in the new village, which somewhat boldly was dubbed Slatersville, while Samuel carried on as manager of the "Old Mill" in Pawtucket and the "White Mill" in Rehoboth. In 1811, the elder Slater sought even greater opportu-

Portrait of John Slater. By the time John Slater joined Samuel in Rhode Island in 1805, the elder brother had become a partner with Providence merchants Almy and Brown and had established a reputation as a leading figure in the nation's mechanized textile industry. In 1806–07, while working under the aegis of Almy, Brown & Slater, John Slater established a mill and village in North Smithfield, Rhode Island, on the Branch River. Called Slatersville, this village quickly emerged as one of the largest producers of cotton yarn in the United States. Courtesy of Slater Mill, Pawtucket, RI

nity in New England's hinterlands, joining forces with Bela Tiffany to build a waterpowered spinning mill in Oxford, South Gore, Massachusetts. With capital obtained from Almy and Brown, the Slater and Tiffany mill opened in May 1812. At about the same time, Slater sold his shares of the "White Mill" to his in-laws. Reaching the zenith of his industrial and commercial powers, Slater would build additional mills in Dudley and Oxford, construct a steam-powered mill in Providence, maintain a large interest in the Amoskeag Mill in New Hampshire, and, with his brother, purchase cotton factories in eastern Connecticut. In addition, Slater invested in turnpikes that connected his mills in Connecticut, Rhode Island, and Massachusetts to the market centers of Worcester, Providence, and Norwich, Connecticut.[21]

Throughout the mid- and late 1820s, competition among New England's textile manufacturers intensified as prices for yarn and cloth fell. While Slater's various mills weathered this economic storm, a large number of firms became bankrupt. Slater held notes for several of these distressed companies, leaving him financially vulnerable. Then, in 1829, a financial panic hit, and banks as well as investors called in their debts. At the age of 61, Slater faced the most severe financial crisis of his adult life. To pay off his debts, Slater sold his interests in the Amoskeag Mill, the Jewett City Cotton Manufacturing Company in Connecticut, and the Slatersville, Rhode Island, mills. In addition, Slater sold his share of the Pawtucket mill to Almy and Brown, thus dissolving their partnership and severing his ties to the factory that had made his name legendary.

Slater retained principal shares in the Providence

Slater Mill and the Blackstone River. From 1829 until 1895, a number of textile companies operated Slater Mill to produce cotton yarn and cloth. For nearly 30 years thereafter, the factory housed various manufacturing concerns. In 1955 the historic property was formerly dedicated as a textile museum with some of the funds provided by Nelson Slater III, who sought to honor the memory of his great-great grandfather. John H. Chafee Blackstone River Valley NHC/National Park Service

Steam Cotton Company and the mills at Central Falls, Rhode Island, while in Massachusetts he continued to control the Slater Mills at Oxford and Dudley, as well as the factory in nearby Wilkinsonville.[22] By 1832, consolidation of his interests helped him reverse his financial losses. That year, he and his brother acquired the holdings of Almy and Brown in the Slatersville mills, reorganizing this concern as the S. & J. Slater Company. Slater also successfully petitioned the Massachusetts legislature to form the township of Webster from parts of Oxford and Dudley, a move that politically unified his three mill villages. Slater's sons assumed larger roles in running the Webster and Providence mills, while his brother John ran the Slatersville Company. Suffering from severe rheumatism and digestive ailments during the last years of his life, Samuel Slater became seriously ill in the spring of 1835 and died in late April at his home in the East Village of Webster. He left to his family an estate estimated at between $1 and $2 million. Beyond this, he left an even greater legacy as the man who established the first successful waterpowered cotton factory in the United States.

The Slaters of Slatersville, Rhode Island

In 1801, the Providence area contained four cotton-spinning mills, three of which were owned or controlled by Almy, Brown, and Slater. Over the next eight years, this industry, while still in its infancy, expanded dramatically as nearly two dozen additional cotton factories were built in the region. A cotton fever had gripped investors. Yet in the face of this rapid growth, Slater and his Providence merchant partners continued to stay ahead of manufacturers. By 1810, they operated about one-fifth of all spindles in the United States.[23] The most important development that helped them retain their leadership in cotton yarn production was a mill they built in the northern reaches of Smithfield, Rhode Island, along a tributary of the Blackstone River, in the village of Slatersville.

The key figure in establishing the Slatersville mills was Samuel Slater's brother, John. Not long after his arrival from England, John Slater was dispatched to northern Rhode Island to investigate potential factory sites. Most importantly, Slater sought out a water-power property on a stream that not only provided the requisite volume of flow and drop in height to power a large mill, but also was not encumbered by individuals who held title to water rights in the watershed above the factory site. After a few months, Slater reported favorably on a large parcel of land on the Mohegan (later named the Branch) River, where the stream dropped some 40 feet over the course of one mile. In the summer of 1805, Almy and Brown had John Slater begin acquiring land and water privileges along this stretch of the river, as well as a gristmill and sawmill. By March of the following year, the company had purchased 200 acres, and John Slater initiated improvements to an existing dam and undertook the construction of a power canal, machine shop, and cotton factory.[24] Slater also built a group of wood-frame tenements for factory managers and workers. In 1807, the cotton factory began operations.[25]

The timing of the mill's initial years of yarn production could not have been more favorable. The Embargo Act of 1807 halted international trade and gave rise to a large demand for American-produced textiles. Almy, Brown, and Slater readily sold yarn produced at Slatersville mill, and within a short time John Slater—who had relocated with his family to the village—supervised an expansion of additional waterpowered spinning frames. By 1813, the mill, which used about 20 feet of head ("head" refers to the drop of water over a waterwheel), contained 5,170 spindles, the largest in the United States. Much of the cotton yarn produced at Slatersville was shipped by wagon to Providence over the nearby Douglas-Providence Turnpike, a distance of 15 miles, which by stage was a four-hour journey.[26]

In the early 1810s, the population of Slatersville numbered around 300. Many lived in crowded, company-built, two-story houses, situated on a gently sloping hillside above the mill. The tenements measured 28 by 36 feet, with four families living in each of the dwellings. The majority of these families—among them John Slater's—included eight to twelve females and males, with nearly two-thirds of them being children under the age of seventeen.[27] Nearly all of the villagers were of Yankee stock and some heads of household, including Mowry, Robinson, and Comstock, had family ties to the surrounding countryside dating from the eighteenth century. Although later in the nineteenth century the village's housing arrangements reflected its social and economic hierarchy—managers and professionals lived in a cluster around the common, while workers lived closer to the factory and on streets nearer to the river—in the early years company managers, skilled mechanics, and overseers lived alongside the mill workers. Rents ranged from $1 to nearly $1.70 per week.[28] A stone-constructed company store furnished food and dry goods to the villagers, and a Congregational Church, built in 1838 and towering above the common, served as a religious and social center for many in the community.

Early Mill Housing on the Church Common. With the opening of the mill in 1807, Slatersville became the first planned industrial community in the United States. The Congregational Church (1838) on the common was a focal point for the community with housing lining the north side of the common with a clear view of the mill. This set of mill houses tended to be for supervisors. John H. Chafee Blackstone River Valley NHC/ National Park Service

Congregational Church and John Slater House. The present location of the John Slater home was not the original site. After John's death, his daughter moved her mother's house down the street to its present site near the church so she could claim the preferred central location for her own home. John H. Chafee Blackstone River Valley NHC/National Park Service

In addition to the textile mill, John Slater operated a farm, raising livestock and grains, a sawmill, and a gristmill. The production of timber and agricultural goods not only provided the factory village with building materials and food, but also gave work to male heads of households, whose sons and daughters toiled in the spinning mill. This combination of industry and agriculture enabled the village to gain a measure of self sufficiency, though most of the village's operations remained extensively under the control of the company.

The War of 1812 proved highly disruptive to the nation's economy and exacerbated banking, credit, and currency problems. For a brief time, Almy, Brown, and the Slaters found it difficult to sell their textile goods or collect from their buyers. As a result, John Slater became a more aggressive marketer of goods produced at Slatersville. In 1815, he traveled to Philadelphia to sell the company's textile products. At the same time, the Slatersville mill continued to reap sizable profits, with sales amounting to $575,000 between 1811 and 1815. The success of this enterprise under John Slater's leadership prompted the Providence partners to enlarge their factory. In 1821, the company built the Western Mill, several hundred feet upstream from the original factory. After a fire destroyed the oldest section of the mill in 1826, a new four-story factory, with an impressive central bell-tower, was constructed of fire-resistant stone.[29]

The other important development at the Slatersville mill was the introduction of the waterpowered loom. In 1815, John and Samuel Slater brought in mechanic William Gilmore, who was working on a variation of the British-patented Horrocks' loom, which would prove equal to the power loom developed around the same time at Waltham by Francis Cabot Lowell and Paul Moody. For several months at North Smithfield, Gilmore labored to build his durable iron-framed loom, which featured a crank-and-lever mechanism for improved weft insertion that yielded tighter weaves, as well as faster picks per minute using larger bobbins with finer threads. Gilmore continued his work at the nearby Lyman and Coventry mills where weaving with his new loom commenced in early 1818. Soon after, the Slaters installed Gilmore looms in their Slatersville factory and, in May of the same year, they

shipped the first of the woven shirtings to Philadelphia. The Slaters thus established a fully integrated mill at North Smithfield, albeit on a smaller scale than the massive Waltham factory.[30]

From the inception of textile manufacturing at Slatersville, as elsewhere in New England, managers and workers faced cycles of booms and busts. Growing regional competition, pressure from British imported goods, price fluctuations in raw cotton, technological changes, and varying managerial capabilities of the region's textile firms all contributed to the volatility of the textile market. The hardest hit during the industry's periodic slumps were the mill workers, and Slatersville's wage earners were no exception. Frequently paid in scrip, Slater's employees had their boarding charges and provisions purchased from the company store subtracted from their wages. During John Slater's years at Smithfield, he responded to downturns just as others did: He cut production costs by reducing wages, curtailing hours, or, where necessary, laying off workers entirely.

An English immigrant who worked as a mason in Slatersville village in the late 1820s observed the problems that such strategies presented to workers. "Wages in cotton factories," the Englishman proclaimed, "are getting lower every year and . . . a great part must be taken in goods and provisions at high prices and it is rare to see a silver dollar, as there is nothing but paper in circulation, the notes of which are not often worth the paper on which promises to pay are recorded."[31] When a severe slump in cotton prices struck manufacturers in 1842, Slater and other mill owners slashed wages by as much as 20 percent. One editor of a Democratic newspaper decried this action, charging, "An arbitrary old Englishman by the name of John Slater, owner of the village and factories in Slatersville, becoming incensed at his help leaving . . . declared that he would never pay them for what they had done, unless they came back to work for him."[32]

Despite fluctuations in the cotton-goods market and the periodic resistance of workers to wage cuts and harsh factory conditions, John Slater and his family prospered at Slatersville. Slater's wife, Ruth Bucklin, had eleven children, only four of whom survived into adulthood. The oldest son, John Fox Slater (1815–1884), assisted his father in the Jewett City and

Slatersville Mill No. 1. The architecturally impressive, waterpowered No. 1 Mill, constructed in 1826 with granite bearing walls and a heavy timber interior frame, originally contained carding machines, spinning frames, warping machines and power looms, all of which constituted a nearly fully integrated cotton textile factory. John H. Chafee Blackstone River Valley NHC/National Park Service

Hopeville mills in Connecticut.[33] William Smith Slater (1817–1882) lived at Slatersville and Providence and became involved in the family's banking and manufacturing interests in Rhode Island.[34]

John Slater died at Slatersville in 1843 and soon after his two sons formed a partnership, the J. & W. Slater Company. Shortly before his death, John Slater had leased the Slatersville mill for ten years to his agent Amos D. Lockwood; without this mill to run, William Smith Slater devoted his attention to banking and serving on corporate boards of Rhode Island manufacturers, in which the family held large shares

of stock. At the same time, John Fox Slater was amassing a considerable fortune in Norwich, Connecticut. In 1849, the brothers acquired the Slatersville interests of Samuel Slater's heirs and, when the lease of the Lockwood expired in 1853, William Smith Slater assumed the management of this enterprise.

Under the aegis of the J. & W. Slater Company, the aging factory buildings were extensively repaired and the old machinery was discarded in favor of new carding machines, spinning frames, and looms. A decade later, the Slater firm acquired the cotton mill of the Forestdale Manufacturing Company, about a mile

Slatersville Commercial Block. The massive commercial blocks as seen in this picture, constructed of stone and brick in 1850 and granite block added in 1870, illustrate the power and influence even the architecture had over the mill village. Courtesy of the North Smithfield Historical Society

downstream from the Slatersville factory. In addition, William S. Slater incorporated the Slater Cotton Company in 1869, acquiring a factory property in Pawtucket, and installing 20,000 spindles and 450 looms. This company employed about 350 workers and specialized in shirtings.[35] Slater had a trusted superintendent, Winsor Scott Mowry, of Providence, manage this firm, while keeping its operation separate from the Slatersville mill.

The work force at Slatersville changed markedly between 1830 and 1860, most notably in the employment of more adults and fewer children, and in the increasing ethnic mix of mill workers. This included large numbers of Irish and French Canadians—by 1872, the village's Catholic population was large enough to support a parish church—along with a range of Scottish, English, and native-born New Englanders. The supervisory positions, from superintendent to over-

seer, were filled by men from New England families, though some had immigrated from the British Isles. Similarly, native-born New Englanders and British Isle émigrés dominated the highly skilled positions of mule spinner, dresser tender, and dyer. The spinners, carders, and weavers were the most ethnically diverse and included the majority of women who worked in the Slatersville mills. Unlike the factories at Lowell, Massachusetts, in which large numbers of single women toiled, most of the women Slater hired were either the wives or daughters of heads of households in the village's company houses, or widows boarding with them.[36]

When the brothers dissolved the J. & W. Slater Company in 1872, William Smith Slater retained control of the Slatersville property and presided over its mills. He left the daily management of the factory to a superintendent, a practice his brother followed in Connecticut.[37] Slater also served as president of the Providence & Worcester Railroad and the Rhode Island Locomotive Works, while maintaining houses in Providence and Slatersville. He assumed the role of gentleman farmer, as he continued to run the large farm, gristmill, and sawmill that his father had operated since 1806. About 1842, Slater married Harriet

Morris Whipple, the daughter of a prominent Providence attorney, and had four children who lived into adulthood. His one son, John Whipple Slater (1852–1924), was groomed when he was a young man to take over his father's enterprises. This occurred in 1882, when William Smith Slater died suddenly of a stroke.[38]

Presiding over the company's affairs at Slatersville and Providence for nearly eighteen years, John Whipple Slater lacked the forceful personality of his father and was, by all appearances, an absentee mill owner. His tenure was marred by his own marital problems, a much-publicized lawsuit initiated by a selling agent, and severe labor unrest in the village.[39] Typically, for several weeks each spring and summer, he resided at Slatersville, where he took on the trappings of a country squire, surrounded by servants, butlers, and a chauffeur.[40] Relying heavily on his superintendent, Slater nominally oversaw the operation of the mill.[41] In his business affairs, he increasingly called upon his more capable cousin William Albert Slater, the son of John Fox Slater, who controlled his family's mills at Jewett City, Connecticut. Facing a crumbling marriage and financial pressures, John W. Slater ceded control of Slatersville to the newly organized

W. A. Slater Corporation. This new concern invested in a new weaving shed, adjacent to the 1826 mill. Despite the volatility of the textile industry in the 1890s, the Slatersville concern remained profitable. Like other New England textile manufacturers, however, the Slater Corporation faced increasing competition from southern mills. This competition, compounded by overproduction, made cotton goods a notoriously unstable commodity, as prices continually climbed and dropped. Management at Slatersville responded to these threats to profitability like other Northern producers: The company slashed wages, laid off workers, and sped up machines.

Despite the willingness of managers to restore wages and hours when cotton prices recovered, relations between Slatersville managers and many of the workers deteriorated. A revitalized trade union movement, supported by many New England textile workers, surged during the mid–1890s as union membership rose within the mule spinning, weaving, and carding crafts. At Slatersville and several other cities in the region, political and labor militancy grew. Managers, in turn, often fired and blacklisted the most ardent trade unionists. For a brief time in the spring of 1898, Slatersville captured the nation's attention when superintendent William P. Holt fired several weavers for belonging to the Socialist Labor Party. This action, following on the heels of a New England–wide strike in which nearly 5,000 textile workers in the Blackstone Valley participated, was met with a series of rallies and fundraisers.[42] Noted socialist and suffragist Ella Reeve Bloor traveled from her Philadelphia home to give an impassioned speech on behalf of the strikers at a boisterous demonstration in Slatersville. The strike ended with the majority of the 600 workers employed at the Slatersville mill returning to work and accepting the company's offer to rescind the 10 percent wage cut from the previous year.[43]

In 1900, not long after the strike at Slatersville, the Slater family sold the village and mill property to Boston financier James R. Hooper. Hooper renamed the enterprise the Slatersville Finishing Company, and immediately scaled down the mill's operation. He demolished most of the Western Mill and ran only the bleachery and dye house. This restructuring resulted in a loss of some 250 jobs and brought to a

close nearly 80 years of integrated textile operations at Slatersville.

In 1915, Hooper sold the village to industrialist Henry P. Kendall, who continued to run the mill as a bleachery and dye plant and employed some 350 persons. Kendall hired Canadian-born Arthur Beane, a Harvard graduate, to superintend the Slatersville operation. Beane subsequently presided over numerous improvements to the factory and the village. Deeply interested in the region's history, Kendall sought to reshape the physical character of Slatersville.[44] He hired the Pawtucket-based architectural firm of William R. Walker & Son to design a neo-Colonial town hall, which was completed in 1921. This firm also likely carried out a number of Kendall-inspired alterations to the manager's houses near the village green. This resulted in the addition of numerous highly ornamented woodworking elements to doors, windows, and main facades. Kendall also erected a series of neo-Colonial, wood-frame houses for managers and white-collar workers north of the green. He hired renowned landscape architect and planner Arthur A. Shurcliff to design the tree-lined streets and other plantings for this new housing development.[45]

Kendall maintained operations at Slatersville through the 1920s—one of the most difficult decades for New England's textile industry—and into the Depression years of the 1930s. During World War II, government contracts revived Northern textile manufacturing and the Kendall Company's Slatersville finishing plant won a prestigious "E-Award" for its superior wartime production. Beginning in the early 1950s, competition from southern states and overseas producers intensified, leading to numerous mill closings in New England. In 1955, Kendall Company managers decided that it was no longer feasible to maintain the Slatersville plant, moving its operations to Bethune, South Carolina, in the fall of 1956.[46] The Kendall firm, having sold its real estate and Slater-built homes to various individuals, ended Slatersville's era as a company town.

Conclusion

When William A. Slater sold the Slatersville property in 1900, the Slater family severed its century-long connection to the Blackstone Valley's textile industry.

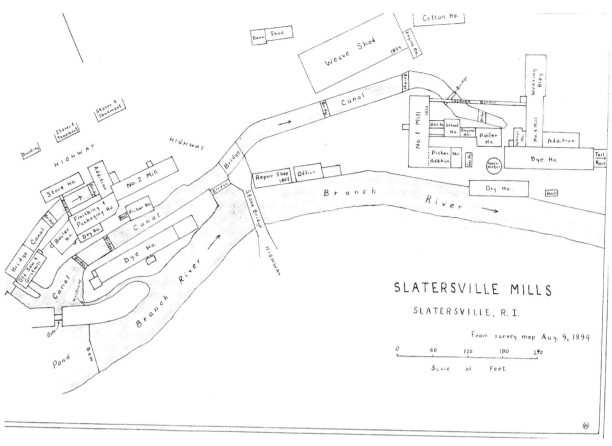

SLATERSVILLE MILLS

SLATERSVILLE, R.I.

From survey map Aug. 9, 1894

Scale of Feet

Slatersville 1904

1894 Map of Slatersville. Drawn by Rhode Island historian Walter Nebiker, this map is based on an 1894 survey of the Slatersville mills, which were owned at the time by W. A. Slater Corporation. The weave shed at the upper right had been completed the year the original survey map was executed. William A. Slater sold the property in 1900, but today, much of the mill complex remains and has been renovated into stylish apartments. Courtesy of the North Smithfield Historical Society

Slatersville Mill and Stone Bridge. This 1896 view down Railroad Street in Slatersville with the mill on the left has not changed much in over a hundred years. A portion of the original machine and repair shop that abuts the road is gone, but the weave shed to the far left still remains and has been well preserved. Courtesy the Rhode Island Historical Society

Slatersville Mill and Branch River today. John H. Chafee Blackstone River Valley NHC/National Park Service

Two decades later, the heirs of William A. Slater (who died in 1919) sold off the Connecticut mills. Nonetheless, a branch of the family headed by H. Nelson Slater, III, the great-grandson of Samuel Slater, remained active in textile manufacturing into the 1930s, with mills in Webster, Massachusetts, and Greenville, South Carolina.[47] He closed the Webster mill in 1936, unwilling to accept the unionization of his work force, but continued to operate the mill and village of Slater-Marietta in Greenville, which produced rayon goods. As a tribute to his great-grandfather, Slater had a stone removed from the Pawtucket mill and placed into the foundation of the Slater-Marietta factory. H. Nelson Slater's involvement in textiles ended in 1946 when he sold the South Carolina plant to another venerable New England manufacturer, the J. P. Stevens Company.[48] By the time of Slater's death in 1968, the South was firmly established as the leading textile-manufacturing region in the United States. Today, however, with the rise of global competition, even the most technically advanced southern operations, such as the still-functioning Slater-Marietta plant, face an uncertain future. Perhaps, like Slatersville, Slater-Marietta soon will become a relic of the nation's textile-manufacturing past.

NOTES

1. Griff Everett, Stephanie H. Hitchcock, Jane Middleton, and Rosemary H. Timms, *Samuel Slater: Hero or Traitor?* (Milford, England: Maypole Promotions, 2005), 50. This recent work on Slater features detailed research into the family's genealogy and land records in Derbyshire. Among the new information uncovered are facts about the social and economic background of William Alcock Slater, Samuel's father, who was revealed to be a landless tenant farmer and not part of the middling gentry as had been claimed since George White's biography of Samuel Slater, published in 1836. In addition, this newer study found that William Slater never owned "Holly House," which White had recorded as the birthplace of the Slater children.

2. Although a scholarly biography of Samuel Slater is badly needed, several dissertations on the American Industrial Revolution and the New England textile industry include substantial biographical material on Slater. The best of these are James Lawson Conrad, Jr., "The Evolution of Industrial Capitalism in Rhode Island, 1790–1830: Almy,

the Browns, and the Slaters" (Ph.D. dissertation, University of Connecticut, 1973); and Gary B. Kulik, "The Beginnings of the Industrial Revolution in America: Pawtucket, Rhode Island, 1672–1829" (Ph.D. dissertation, Brown University, 1980). An outstanding analysis of the writings on Slater is found in James L. Conrad, Jr., "'Drive That Branch': Samuel Slater, the Power Loom, and the Writing of America's Textile History," *Technology and Culture* 36 (January 1995): 1–28. For this essay, I have relied heavily on Conrad and Kulik, and on Jonathan Prude, *The Coming of Industrial Order: Town and Factory Life in Rural Massachusetts, 1810–1860* (New York: Cambridge University Press, 1983), which includes a fine study of Slater's life in conjunction with his mills in Webster, Massachusetts. For a lively, highly celebrative, and occasionally inaccurate biography of Slater, see Edward H. Cameron, *Samuel Slater: Father of American Manufactures* (Freeport, Maine: The Bond Wheelwright Company, 1960).

3. Similarly, Strutt appears to have contracted with hand-loom weavers in the late eighteenth century when he manufactured calico cloth. Thus Strutt's factory production occurred alongside artisanal craft production in the region's small workshops and homes. Some years later in the United States, Samuel Slater and many other textile manufacturers continued this practice of putting out the production of various goods, including the weaving of cloth. For more on Strutt, his early enterprises, and his putting out textile production, see R. S. Fitton and Alfred P. Wadsworth, *The Strutts and the Arkwrights, 1758–1830: A Study of the Early Factory System* (Manchester, England: Manchester University Press, 1958), 55–56, 295.

4. Prude, *Coming of Industrial Order*, 35–39.

5. That Slater disguised himself as a farmer's son to avoid the immigration restrictions placed on mechanics is probably a fanciful tale. However, he did conceal his indenture papers. See Kulik, "Beginnings of the Industrial Revolution," 161.

6. Conrad, "Evolution of Industrial Capitalism," 87.

7. Moses Brown, quoted in Kulik, "Beginnings of the Industrial Revolution," 141.

8. The partnership of between Slater and Almy and Brown initially centered only on the operation of the Pawtucket Mill. Slater was given a one-half share in the profits and was held liable for one-half of expenses. See Kulik, "Beginnings of the Industrial Revolution," 142, 148.

9. Ibid., 144–45.

10. Cameron, *Samuel Slater*, 66.

11. Prude, *Coming of Industrial Order*, 41.

12. Conrad, "Evolution of Industrial Capitalism," 120–25.

13. Barbara M. Tucker, *Samuel Slater and the Origins of the American Textile Industry, 1790-1860*, (Ithaca, N.Y.: Cornell University Press, 1984), 74–86.

14. Conrad, "Evolution of Industrial Capitalism," 318–20.

15. JWS, "Our Textile Industries," *American Wool and Cotton Reporter*, June 7, 1900, p. 652.

16. George S. White, *Memoir of Samuel Slater: The Father of American Manufacturers* (Philadelphia: n.p., 1836), 106–107. Mills operated by the Slaters continued to attract talented mechanics, both native-born and immigrant. Among the latter group was Robert Johnston, a spinner born in Dalston, England, in 1807. After starting as a bobbin boy in a Northumberland cotton mill, Johnston worked his way up to mule spinner and then departed England in 1830, settling in Rhode Island, where he worked in one of the Slater mills. In 1834, Johnston moved to Valitie Village, New York, taking charge of the cotton mill that produced the first muslin delaine manufactured in the United States. Johnston was then appointed agent of the large Harmony Mills, which he directed from 1850 until his death in 1890. See his obituary in the *New York Times*, September 13, 1890.

17. Workers' responses to these disputes ranged from a refusal to perform tasks in the mill, to adult workers quitting or fathers removing their children from the factory, to large-scale strikes. This latter action was rare in the antebellum period, but one strike occurred in Pawtucket in 1824. It is not clear, however, if workers at Slater's mill were active participants in the Pawtucket village strike of 1824. See Gary Kulik, "Pawtucket Village and the Strike of 1824: The Origins of Class Conflict in Rhode Island," *Radical History Review* 17 (Spring 1978): 5–37; and Tucker, *Samuel Slater*, 184–85, 253–54.

18. Among the scholars of textiles and early industrialism, Gary Kulik and Jonathan Prude stress the dynamics of class conflict in the mills of Slater and the Providence merchants. Barbara M. Tucker, on the other hand, highlights the shared cultural and religious values tied to patriarchy, family, and authority, which she claims permitted Slater's reliance on child and family labor to expand with little conflict until the 1830s, when larger-scale factory production, extreme market competition, and an increasingly permanent adult factory labor force eclipsed the Slater system. James Conrad's work on Almy, Brown, and Slater, though earlier than these other scholars, steers a middle course between the class-conflict and socio-cultural consensus "models" of early industrial capitalism. See Kulik, "Evolution of Industrial Capitalism," especially 194–222; Prude, *Coming of Industrial Order*, chapters 5 and 8, 260–63; Tucker, *Samuel Slater*, 21–28, Chapter 6, and 214–38 and 250–59. For a synopsis of Conrad's analysis, see his "Conclusion" in "Evolution of Industrial Capitalism."

19. Conrad, "Evolution of Industrial Capitalism," 114–21.

20. Ibid., 148–52. The Sunday School in Pawtucket operated sporadically and with limited funds provided by Almy and Brown. Students from Brown University instructed the factory children in reading, writing, and, very likely, in moral conduct. Slater's promotion of Sunday schools undoubtedly was influenced by his experience with similar Derbyshire institutions established by Jedidiah Strutt. See Tucker, *Samuel Slater*, 75–76.

21. Prude, *Coming of Industrial Order*, 49–52, 79.

22. Slater also maintained a financial interest in a factory at Fitchburg, Massachusetts.

23. Conrad, "Evolution of Industrial Capitalism," 195.

24. Walter Nebiker, *The History of North Smithfield* (Somersworth, N.H.: New England History Press, 1976), 60–61. Nebiker's history of North Smithfield, published as part of the nation's bicentennial celebration, includes well-documented and extensive material on Slatersville.

25. Cameron, *Samuel Slater*, 105–106.

26. An improved road that connected Slatersville to the Douglas-Providence Turnpike was initiated in 1821. See *Providence Patriot*, June 20, 1821. Stage schedules appeared periodically in the region's newspapers. For example, see *Rhode Island American*, July 15, 1828.

27. Conrad, "Evolution of Industrial Capitalism," 282–83; Federal Manuscript Census, Smithfield, Rhode Island, 1810.

28. Conrad, "Evolution of Industrial Capitalism," 281.

29. Ibid., 221–26. No injuries were recorded in the mill fire, which destroyed 5,000 spindles and resulted in a loss estimated at $80,000. A number of New England newspapers carried reports of the blaze. See, for example, the *New Hampshire Patriot*, February 6, 1826; Gary Kulik and Julia C. Bonham, *Rhode Island: An Inventory of Historic Engi-*

neering and Industrial Sites, (Washington, D.C.: U.S. Department of the Interior, 1978), 134–36.

30. Conrad convincingly rebuts the long-standing notion that Samuel Slater was not interested in developing the power loom. See Conrad's highly praised article "'Drive That Branch': Samuel Slater, the Power Loom, and the Writing of America's Textile History," *Technology and Culture* 36 (January 1995): especially 16–19.

31. This letter from an English stonemason, dated October 20, 1828, from Slatersville, originally was printed in a London newspaper and reprinted in two New England papers. See *Rhode Island American and Providence Gazette*, February 17, 1829. The English mason noted that "in fair weather girls from twelve to fourteen years-old average two dollars per week at the water looms." Children and boys, he stated, earn between fifty cents and two dollars each week. He concluded, "Wages are extremely low here and boarding very high."

32. "Present Affairs in Rhode Island," *Pittsfield Sun*, July 14, 1842. This was reprinted from an article appearing in the *Bay State Democrat*.

33. In addition to their mills in Rhode Island and Massachusetts, Samuel and John Slater undertook operations in the Quinebaug River Valley of eastern Connecticut. In 1823, the brothers purchased the factory and waterpower privileges of the Jewett City Cotton Manufacturing Company, a struggling cotton-yarn producer in Griswold, Connecticut. Within a year, the Slater brothers were producing as much as 3,500 yards of cotton cloth each week, most of which was woven on the power looms. In 1831, after John Slater purchased his brother's interests in the Jewett City Cotton Manufacturing Company, he had his son, who was but sixteen years old, assist him in managing the mills near Norwich, Connecticut. John Fox Slater took charge of the Hopeville Mill and settled in Jewett City. At the age of twenty-one, he assumed the management of both mills. In 1842, Slater moved to Norwich, spending the remainder of his life directing the Connecticut mills and engaging in several other enterprises. J. D. Van Slyck, *New England Manufacturers and Manufacturies*, vol. II (Boston: Van Slyck & Company, 1879), 560; JWS, "Our Textile Industries," *American Wool and Cotton Reporter*, May 31, 1900, 641–42.

34. Listed in the Providence city directory of 1844 as a manufacturer, William Smith Slater resided on George Street, not far from his cousin Horatio Nelson Slater, who lived on Benefit Street. For many years, both sides of the Slater family shared offices on South Water Street.

35. *History of the State of Rhode Island* (Philadelphia: Hong, Wade & Co., 1878).

36. This information is based on a sampling of about 200 villagers at Slatersville in each federal census of 1850 and 1860.

37. For many years, William Smith Slater's agent at Slatersville was George W. Holt.

38. Van Slyck, *New England Manufacturers*, vol. II, 561; JWS, "Our Textile Industries," 641–42.

39. In 1880, Slater married Elizabeth Hope Gammell, who was the granddaughter of Robert Ives, of the Providence merchant firm Borwn & Ives, and who hailed from one of Rhode Island's wealthiest families. The marriage proved disastrous. After just a few months, the couple separated, with John W. Slater charging his wife with refusal "to perform her marital duties," while she in turn claimed he had committed "numerous infidelities" and that she could not live with him. The couple attempted to reconcile before finally deciding to live apart. They divorced sometime in the 1890s. These contretemps within the Slater and Gammell families made national headlines. For example, see "A Social Sensation," *The Atchison [Kansas] Globe*, July 8, 1882.

40. Among family members, John Whipple Slater did not initiate the hiring of a coterie of servants. In fact, William Smith Slater had a large staff of domestic help as early as the 1840s. The death of his wife in 1855, at the young age 33, resulted in his children being raised largely by governesses and servants. For a listing of the various domestics in the Slater households, see the federal census for Slatersville, Rhode Island, 1850, 1860, and 1870.

41. For many years, the mill superintendent was William P. Holt, who was born in Rhode Island in 1863 and had worked his way up the ranks, beginning as an operative during his boyhood in Woonsocket. Even for his farm at Slatersville, John W. Slater had a manager. In the late 1880s, this was Zachariah J. Williams, born in Ohio in 1849. Williams cared for 1,200 acres of farm land, 40 milk cows, and several teams of work cattle. Slater paid Williams about $1,000 a year for his services. For a description of the Slatersville farm, village, and mill, see "Notes of Travel," *Newark [Ohio] Daily Advocate*, October 19, 1889.

42. "5,000 on Strike," *North Adams [Massachusetts]*

Transcript, April 7, 1899; "Slatersville Mills Closed," *Portsmouth [New Hampshire] Herald*, April 10, 1899; "Discharging Socialists," *Sandusky [Ohio] Star*, May 24, 1899.

43. The wage cut of 10 percent occurred in January 1898. "Situation in Rhode Island," *Portsmouth [New Hampshire] Herald*, January 12, 1898. Of the 600 workers at the Slatersville mills, about 150 were weavers. See "5,000 on Strike," *North Adams [Massachusetts] Transcript*, April 7, 1899.

44. Nebiker, *The History of North Smithfield*, 149–50.

45. The best source for the work of Shurcliff in Slatersville is found in the Arthur A. and Sidney N. Shurcliff papers, 1900 through c. 1981, Special Collections, Frances Loeb Library, Graduate School of Design, Harvard University. Also see "Autobiography of Arthur A. Shurcliff, Written Winter of 1943–1944 with additions Summer of 1946, Summer of 1947," available in the Arthur Asahel Shurcliff papers, 1855–1967, Massachusetts Historical Society.

46. "Rhode Island Mill Moves to Bethune," *Statesville [North Carolina] Record Landmark*, July 21, 1955.

47. "Slater: A Proud Textile Community in South Carolina and the Most Famous Name in American Textile History," brochure, n.d., published by JPS Converter & Industrial Corporation.

48. "Slater: A Proud Textile Community in South Carolina and the Most Famous Name in American Textile History," booklet published by JPS Textile Group, Inc., November 1994. The successor firm to J.P. Stevens, the JPS Textile Group was recently reorganized and now operates the Slater-Marietta, South Carolina, plant as the JPS Composite Materials Corporation.

By the Canal!

RANGER CHUCK ARNING

Surrounded by bags of grain and St. Ube's Salt, a selectman from the village of Worcester, Massachusetts, a Colonel Merrick, stood on the deck of the canal boat, *Lady Carrington*, and looked out at a celebratory mass of people along the banks of the newly dug Blackstone Canal. In the company of several of the Blackstone Canal Commissioners, Colonel Merrick began his address.

> On the completion of the great enterprise which we have here assembled to witness in the passage of the first Boat along the whole route of its peaceful waters . . . The spirit of patriotism is animated in beholding the development of the resources which have opened a new channel for industry and competition, which in their results may add alike to the wealth and the comfort of the people; and to us, who are at the head of these now navigable waters, the day should be one of unqualified gratification.[1]

Colonel Merrick pointedly made the enthusiastic crowd aware of the significant impact the coming of the canal already had made upon the small but growing village of Worcester. Citing the annual census of the minors of the Centre School District, Merrick emphasized the five-fold increase in the youth of the village enrolled in school within the space of just five years. But the Colonel did not stop there. "Look at the spot where we stand. These lands which, as it were but yesterday, were well nigh waste and desolate are now held as the most valuable of property. Ask the owners for the prices for which they will part with them, and you will find that feet are now deemed as valuable as acres once were."[2]

This new form of technology, this transportation revolution, this Blackstone Canal, had so impacted the countryside up and down its route that one could not stand still for fear of being cast aside in the construction wake of a new mill, warehouse, or some other new enterprise. Merrick and the energized crowd understood the significance of the moment.

> Far hence be the day, when widespread luxury shall embrace the hardy muscles of the vigorous race of men who dwell on the confines of these inland waters—who have subdued the rough hills and given beauty to the vallies of this heart of the Commonwealth. We rejoice this day: not that we are rich; not that we are at ease; but in the conviction that this more expanded field of enterprise will be diligently harvested by the energetic exertions of our population.[3]

The imagined opportunities presented by the new canal technology were very real and well understood by those in the crowd. Upon the ending of the speech and the exiting of the dignitaries from the *Lady Carrington*, the stevedores and teamsters took over. A local merchant, a Nathan Heard, had purchased the entire contents of this first canal boat to arrive in the Port of Worcester. The bags of grain and salt were headed for his store to be offered "for sale on the most reasonable terms." Heard, a man of vision and marketing skill, captured the moment when his ads appeared in all three of the Worcester newspapers proclaiming in big bold letters "BY THE CANAL" indicating freshly arrived goods.[4] From Indian trails to turnpikes and now the canal to be followed in short order by the railroads, these upgrades in transportation would be well utilized by men of vision who would use them and the opportunities they presented to reshape the Blackstone Valley and change America.

NOTES

1. *Worcester (MA) The National Aegis*, "Address to the Citizens of Worcester upon the arrival of the Lady Carrington by way of the Blackstone Canal on October 7, 1828 by Selectman, Colonel Merrick," October 15, 1828.

2. Ibid.

3. Ibid.

4. *The National Aegis*, "By the Canal" Advertisement, October 8, 1828.

3 Moving the Goods Roads, Canals, and the Coming of the Railroads

GRAY FITZSIMONS

North-western view in Millbury.

Canal Boat passing through Millbury. Courtesy of Worcester Historical Museum, Worcester, MA

Like other regions of early nineteenth-century New England, the hinterlands of the Blackstone Valley, with an abundance of farms and hamlets, remained largely isolated from larger market towns and seaports. Vast distances of rugged terrain and poor roads, often little more than muddy or craggy narrow trails, limited trade and contact between inland settlers and the increasingly capitalist-oriented urban centers such as Boston and Providence. As a result, most rural families followed the social and economic practices of their colonial ancestors and continued to engage in subsistence farming. Some sold or bartered surplus crops, dairy goods, and livestock to small merchants or other families within their surrounding area. And most rural families produced such goods as textiles and clothing in their households for their own use or for trade within the local economy. Similarly, artisans often bartered their goods or labor and directed much of their production toward local markets, even in the face of a growing cash economy and a nascent factory system.[1]

This is not to suggest that farmers and artisans traded exclusively within their communities or stood aloof from cash transactions. Indeed, during the first two decades of the nineteenth century, Massachusetts farmers typically traveled fifty miles or more over country lanes and highways to sell surplus goods to merchants in larger markets.[2] In fact, ties as well as tensions between the rapidly growing commercial centers—which were dominated by merchant capitalists, bankers, and members of the legal profession—and rural communities of farmers and artisans intensified throughout the early 1800s. Gradually, the cash economy, specialization of production for larger markets, and the growth of wage labor were changing the lives of inland dwellers in the Blackstone Valley and elsewhere. As historian George Rogers Taylor pointed out nearly a half century ago, the improvement to roads, the construction of canals, and finally the establishment of railroads accelerated these fundamental social and economic changes throughout the nation.[3] Nowhere is this revolutionary process more dramatically evident than in the Blackstone Valley.

Before the first English settlers arrived in the Blackstone Valley, countless generations of Nipmucs, Narragansetts, and Wampanoags traveled along the Blackstone River and established trails from the Worcester hills to the shores of Narragansett Bay. Although Native Americans canoed over stretches of the Blackstone River, they found it necessary to portage around numerous boulder-strewn shallows and falls, especially during dry summer seasons. With the arrival of colonists in the seventeenth century, commercial exchange intensified between Europeans and Indians, prompting greater travel over waterways and centuries-old trails. Much of this trade was tied to Europe's insatiable demand for pelts and fur, but as land-hungry colonists extended their settlements into the interior, they began exporting lumber, stone, and agricultural goods back to England, as well.[4] In the mid–1670s, colonial expansion in the Blackstone Valley and elsewhere was halted briefly as hostilities between Native Americans and English settlers culminated in King Phillip's War. Sporadic fighting continued for

some years, but the defeat of the region's major tribes in 1676 was followed by even larger numbers of colonial settlements, including several in the Blackstone Valley.

As English settlers penetrated more deeply into the valley's interior, they began building roads that followed the routes of Indian trails. One of the earliest of these, established shortly before King Phillip's War, was the Mendon Road, which extended from Rehoboth to the English settlement at Mendon, Massachusetts. The Mendon Road was built over a trail a few miles east and north of the Blackstone River. Another frontier route, the Great Road, opened in 1683 and ran from Providence to Smithfield, following a ridge trail along the west side of the Moshassuck River, several miles from the Blackstone, and eventually reaching Mendon. As colonial settlements multiplied, many more roads were carved from Indian paths.[5] At the same time, the Native American population, ravaged by disease and war, continued its dramatic decline.[6] By the early eighteenth century, farms, pasturelands, fences, and dirt lanes had replaced the vast forests as the dominant feature of the valley's landscape.

Into the late eighteenth century, primitive dirt roads served as main thoroughfares for pedestrian, horse, and wagon traffic. Travel remained torturously slow and often uncomfortable. One observer, who recalled a trip between Providence and Pomfret, Connecticut, in 1776 noted, "I went to Pomfret, thirty-six miles in a chaise; the road was so stony and rough that I could not ride out of a slow walk, but very little of the way; I was near two days in going, such was the general state of roads at that time."[7] In addition to poor roads, a lack of regular stagecoach service further hindered communication and commerce within the Blackstone Valley. While regularly scheduled stagecoach lines between Providence and Boston began in 1767, Providence-to-Worcester stage service was not inaugurated until 1821.[8]

In Rhode Island and Massachusetts, legislatures authorized towns to levy taxes to foster the construction of roads. Town surveyors laid out routes, and many landowners paid their tax assessments by performing labor on local road-building projects. These attempts, however, did little to improve the region's highways. Travelers continued to encounter rutted or

Blackstone River. The river systems, like the swift but shallow Blackstone River, were home to the Nipmuc Nation and provided them with many of their basic needs. John H. Chafee Blackstone River Valley NHC/ National Park Service

Road to Worcester Common. As depicted in this early nineteenth-century woodcut of a couple strolling toward the Worcester Common, this road, although muddy and rutted, appears to be in better condition than many similar lanes that ran through the region's towns and extended into the countryside. John H. Chafee Blackstone River Valley NHC/ National Park Service

Blackstone Gorge. The Blackstone Gorge presented one of the formidable barriers to navigation on the Blackstone River. Engineers Benjamin Wright and Holmes Hutchinson opted for a canal route that ran on the river's north side and skirted the treacherous rapids of the rocky chasm. John H. Chafee Blackstone River Valley NHC/ National Park Service

rough roads rife with jagged rocks and tree stumps. During rainy seasons, they often found them flooded and impassable. Fords remained the primary means for crossing the numerous streams and rivers. And where they existed, bridges, the vast majority of which were constructed of wood, were frequently in disrepair or washed out altogether.[9] At the same time, transport on waterways in the Blackstone Valley remained limited to logs and small rafts primarily along short stretches of the river. Moreover, the roiling water at Pawtucket and Woonsocket falls, and the depth of the Blackstone Gorge, made substantial riverboat navigation impossible.

The earliest successful attempts to improve overland transportation in the Blackstone Valley began in the decade following the mid-1790s, when the legislatures in Rhode Island General and Massachusetts chartered a number of turnpike companies. Modeled after the English turnpike companies, most of these firms assumed the corporate form of organization, selling company shares to finance turnpike construction. Although the charters contained provisions that permitted state regulation of tolls, limited the number of shares that could be sold, and stipulated the right of free passage to certain users—those traveling to or from public worship, for example—turnpike companies were vested with powers of eminent domain and received tax exemptions for highway land that they held. Revenue from tolls charged to turnpike users not only was directed to company shareholders as return on their investment, but also funded road maintenance and paid toll collectors.[10]

Spearheaded by wealthy Providence merchants and entrepreneurs in the Valley's small but growing manufacturing villages, the Rhode Island turnpikes that extended into Massachusetts and Connecticut were among the earliest in the nation. The Douglas Turnpike, built by a company chartered in 1804, traversed the hilly terrain northwest from Providence, paralleling the Blackstone River about four miles to its west and terminating in Douglas, Massachusetts. Begun about the same time, the Louisquisset Pike ran from Providence to the lime works at Lime Rock, a distance of seven miles and a significant early transportation connection to the growing port of Providence. It was later extended northward toward Uxbridge. The most financially successful of the valley's toll roads was the Providence and Pawtucket Turnpike, completed around 1808. Only a few miles in length, this gravel-surfaced road proved to be one of the best built in Rhode Island. During its first three decades, the turnpike generated $56,000 in revenue, with maintenance costs amounting to just $7,000. It received considerable traffic between Providence and Pawtucket, due in part to its connection, in Pawtucket, to the Massachusetts Turnpike to Boston.[11]

In New England, the turnpike era lasted about twenty-five years. Between 1805 and 1830, more than two hundred turnpike companies were chartered and, through 1840, nearly $6.5 million was invested in these firms. Most of the region's turnpike enterprises, however, were like those in the Blackstone Valley and were capitalized at around $100,000 or less. Few boasted the financial success of the Providence and Pawtucket. Only about a half dozen in all of New England yielded even a small return on shareholders' investments, largely because most turnpikes could generate only limited toll revenues. In many cases, teamsters avoided tolls by traveling on "shunpikes," which were roads that connected to private thoroughfares but were built to circumvent toll houses. Others hauled their goods

at night after toll collectors retired from their duties. In the end, turnpikes improved the condition of local travel, especially for short-haul farmers transporting their products to nearby markets or for persons being conveyed on stagecoaches or carriages, but teamsters hauling large, heavy loads long-distance didn't benefit as much from the turnpike movement—and often found the tolls too burdensome on their already slim profit margins. And in many cases, because they didn't turn a profit, turnpikes fell into disrepair years before they would have had to compete with canals and railroads.

Despite the vast improvements to overland transportation in the Blackstone Valley, producers of iron goods, stone, lime, and lumber, as well as manufacturers in the region's growing textile industry, found that overland transportation remained costly and inefficient. In 1822, several leading Providence businessmen began promoting the construction of a canal, which merchant John Brown had proposed nearly three decades earlier. Influenced by the English system of privately financed and operated canals, Brown chartered a canal company in the 1790s with the aim of building an inland waterway from Providence's tidewater wharfs, through the Blackstone Valley, to Worcester, Massachusetts, and beyond. His efforts were resisted by Boston merchants, who blocked the passage of a Massachusetts canal charter as they sought to direct hinterland trade to their city.

By the early 1820s, Boston-based opposition to a canal project in the valley had lessened. More importantly, a group of Worcester businessmen, politicians, and lawyers joined with commercial interests in Rhode Island to support of the construction of a waterway. Encouraged by the success of the Erie Canal, a 220-mile section of which was completed and operating profitably in 1822, committees formed in Providence and Worcester to promote the project. Their first task was to produce a topographic survey of the proposed canal route and prepare a plan for its execution.

With money raised by subscription, committee members contracted with Benjamin Wright, chief engineer of the Erie Canal, to conduct the survey and report his findings. Wright in turn hired Holmes

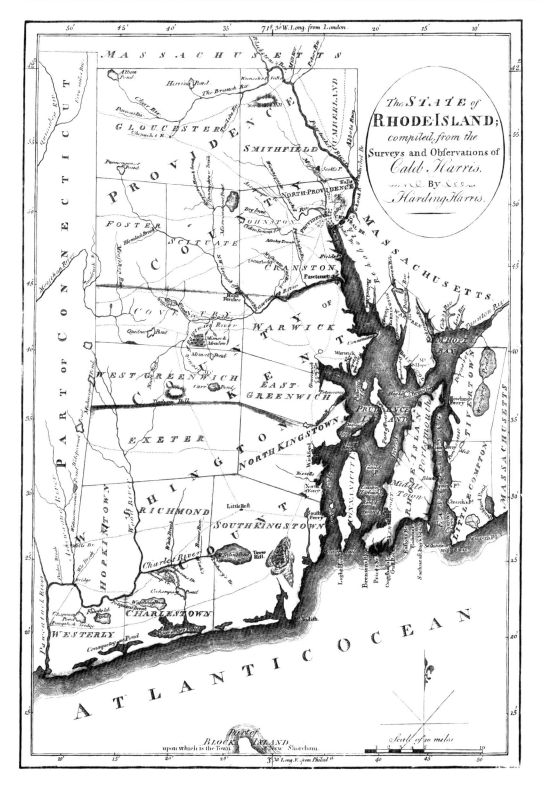

1795 Caleb Harris Map. Drawn by Caleb Harris, this map of Rhode Island from 1795 shows the major roads. Note that two of the roads extending north from Providence and into Massachusetts were constructed parallel to the Moshassuck and Pawtucket (Blackstone) rivers. Part of the road along the south and west side of the Blackstone River became the Louisquisset Pike, chartered in 1805, and extends along a portion of today's State Route 146A. Courtesy the Rhode Island Historical Society

Hutchinson, one of his assistants on the Erie Canal project, to perform the survey work. In the summer of 1822, the 28-year-old Hutchinson began the work.[12] Although it was a relatively short river, just 45 miles in length from its origin in the eastern uplands of Worcester County to its end, the Blackstone's rapid descent—nearly 440 feet over its course—would require a large number of lift locks, which were among the most costly of canal structures. In just a few months, Hutchinson completed the survey from Worcester to Providence, and a report that he prepared with Wright fully endorsed the project. They proposed building a canal 45 miles in length, containing 62 lift locks and costing nearly $325,000, provided the lift locks were constructed of wood. Further, Wright and Hutchinson recommended the use of several ponds over the course of the canal to ensure an adequate supply of water throughout the year. They stated that much of the soil was "generally easy to excavate" and that "very little solid rock [needed] to be removed."[13] The engineers also pointed out that culverts and aqueducts were required in only a few locations. Finally, Hutchinson included in the report proposals for building two branch canals, one near Millbury, Massachusetts, and the other in Smithfield, Rhode Island.

Committee members immediately endorsed the report. Leaders in Worcester—most notably Levi Lincoln, Jr., a legislator elected Speaker of the House in 1822, and John Davis, a prominent attorney who, like Lincoln, would be elected governor of Massachusetts—hailed the project, proclaiming it would benefit farmers and manufacturers alike. The valley's agricultural community, the committee boasted, "distinguished for its zeal and industry, [and] possessing a large tract of fertile soil," would reap great rewards. With reliable and less expensive canal transport, "at least twenty-four times cheaper" than roads, they remarked, the land would be "capable of yielding much beyond its present products" and would hold "a far greater population." The Worcester committee also declared that the canal would foster the use of "a great water, yet unoccupied" for "the purposes of manufacturing."[14] In January 1823, committee members enthusiastically delivered their petition for a canal company charter to the Massachusetts General Court. Undoubtedly aided by the political strength of Lincoln and Davis,

the state quickly approved a charter. It authorized the formation of the Blackstone Canal Company for the purpose of constructing a canal from Worcester to the Rhode Island border.

At the same time, Rhode Island canal interests, led by merchant Edward Carrington, petitioned their General Assembly for a charter. But unlike legislators in Boston, a number of representatives in Providence fiercely contested the canal measure. Initially, the most vocal foes were Rhode Island farmers, who claimed that out-of-state agricultural goods would crowd them out of Providence's markets. But this was followed by a more powerful group of opponents, namely the leading manufacturers on the lower Blackstone River, between Valley Falls and Pawtucket. These men viewed with alarm the proposal of Wright and Hutchinson to divert Blackstone River water into the southernmost section of the canal, the route of which was to veer from the Blackstone River above Pawtucket and then extend through the Moshassuck Valley directly to the tidewater wharfs in Providence. They feared this diversion of water would reduce the flow to their factories and limit the power of their waterwheels. In June, the manufacturers formed a committee to meet with Carrington and his associates, with the aim of amending the canal charter to "preserve a sufficiency of the waters for the owners of mill privileges." The mill owners of the Lower Blackstone knew that they held a strong legal advantage over the canal petitioners. Numerous precedents in North American courts of law, dating to the eighteenth century, upheld the right of legal claimants to enjoy the "natural run" of the river.[15]

At the request of Carrington, Hutchinson testified that the canal company would maintain the natural flow in the Blackstone River by building a series of reservoirs and feeder canals. Any water diverted from the river would be replaced by surplus water impounded by the company's reservoirs. Although the company received its charter soon after Hutchinson's testimony, it agreed to series of provisions that not only regulated the company's use of Blackstone River water, but also provided redress to the manufacturing interests should the company's operation of the canal impede the natural flow of the river.

After the charters in Massachusetts and Rhode Island had been granted, however, the petitioners made little progress in organizing their companies. As companies remained idle into the fall of 1824, a newspaper editor in Providence asserted that "the scheme for cutting a canal from this town to Worcester seems about to be exploded." While this editor correctly attributed the "numerous restrictions with which the Legislature of Rhode Island has loaded the charter granted to the proprietors of the enterprise" with hampering the petitioners' efforts, Carrington and his associates were, in fact, actively negotiating with the manufacturing interests along the Blackstone River.[16] In the end, the company agreed to build and operate an extremely complex system of reservoirs throughout the watershed to regulate the flow in the river and canal. A year earlier, Rhode Island mill owner Zachariah Allen and his partners had established a similar hydraulic system of reservoirs and feeders on the Woonasquatucket River—at the time, this was the most sophisticated hydraulic system of its kind in the United States—but no construction on the scale proposed by the Blackstone Canal proprietors had ever been attempted before.

With negotiations concluded and their final plans in place, the Massachusetts and Rhode Island committees met in April 1825 to organize the Blackstone Canal Company. They capitalized their concern at $500,000, offering 5,000 shares at $100 per share. Investors quickly stepped forward and the company found itself oversubscribed by more than two times the stated allotment. Having based its original capitalization on the estimated cost of construction, the company turned back the surplus capital. This would prove to be one of a series of missteps, as construction costs ultimately exceeded the initial projections. In addition to raising capital, the company's principal shareholders, who were largely Rhode Islanders, elected officers and commissioners, the latter group being charged with overseeing the canal's construction. Edward Carrington, the most well-known figure associated with the canal, served as one of the three Rhode Island commissioners. He was joined by Moses B. Ives, a partner in the merchant house of Brown and Ives, and Stephen H. Smith, a manufacturer from a prominent Quaker family in Smithfield. Another Rhode Islander, attorney Thomas M. Burgess, who later was a municipal judge and mayor of Providence, served as treasurer. He would remain in this position until the company disbanded. The three commissioners from Massachusetts were John Davis, John W. Lincoln, who was also an attorney and a cousin of Levi Lincoln, Jr., and Sylvanus Holbrook, a manufacturer and landowner from Uxbridge.

As the first construction season approached in late spring of 1825, the commissioners advertised contracts for work primarily on the Rhode Island sections of the canal, most notably the tidal cove area at Providence. The commissioners also retained Holmes Hutchinson as chief engineer; he, in turn, assembled a crew to re-survey the route of the waterway, test soil conditions, and prepare a final design of the canal. Of its 45-mile length, the canal was to use about 5 miles of slackwater navigation on the Blackstone and Moshassuck rivers. Most of the canal, however, would be composed of a trench measuring 34 feet in width at the top and 18 feet at the bottom. Its depth would range between 4 and 6 feet. To overcome the 438-foot drop over the length of the canal, Hutchinson called for 48 lift locks with one timber-constructed tidal lock in Providence. The lift for each lock would average 9.5 feet. Instead of wood, as originally proposed, the lock chambers were to be built of granite masonry mortared together with a high-quality hydraulic cement that was brought from upstate New York and had been used on sections of the Erie Canal.

With Hutchinson and other Erie Canal veterans, predominantly Irish, engaged to build the Blackstone, it is not surprising that New York's massive waterway influenced the Blackstone's design, materials of construction, and even the hydraulic operations of its lock chambers. The Erie Canal also shaped the way in which the Blackstone's canal commissioners managed the construction work. Although the commissioners awarded several contracts to local builders, they also engaged the services of New York masons who had worked on the Erie Canal. In addition, the commissioners hired two Irish-Catholic contractors, Patrick O'Connor and Tobias Boland. O'Connor and Boland brought in several hundred fellow Irishmen to carry out the back-breaking work of clearing, digging, and grading for the canal. Recruited by agents in New York City and Boston, these Irish laborers represented the first major wave of nineteenth-century immigrants in the valley.[17]

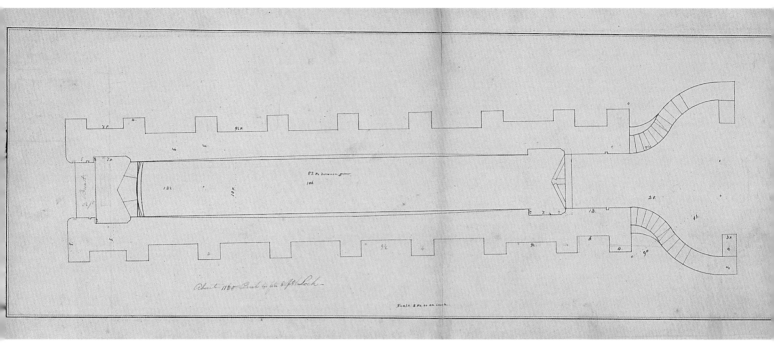

Canal Lock Construction Drawing. This rare construction drawing of a granite lift lock provides insight into canal construction techniques. The lock chamber's length of 82 feet, between the gates, was somewhat shorter than the lock chambers for the Erie Canal, but many of the features, including masonry work, gate valves, and locking mechanisms, were quite similar to those used on the engineering marvel, the Erie Canal. Courtesy American Antiquarian Society

Canal laborers accomplished a great deal of work during the first two years of construction. In Rhode Island, much of the trench was dug and sixteen of the twenty locks were completed by the fall of 1826. Nearly one mile of the canal in Worcester was excavated and workers had finished the earthen embankments for the North and Long (Quinsigamond) ponds, the latter being the largest of the Blackstone company's reservoirs. In 1827, construction continued apace when the season began in early March. Heavy rains in August of that year, however, slowed work and caused an estimated $40,000 in damage. Despite these setbacks, contractors completed the Rhode Island section of the canal in late fall. Finally, in early summer 1828, the entire canal was finished. Its cost had exceeded the original half-million-dollar estimate, possibly by as much $200,000. As a result of this overrun and of stockholders not paying their subscribed amounts, several Providence investors found it necessary to form their own bank, the Blackstone Canal Bank, as a source of additional funds.

The company's financial difficulties did not dampen enthusiasm for opening celebrations of the Blackstone Canal. In July of 1828, the canal boat *Lady Carrington* made the inaugural journey on the waterway, traveling ten miles from Providence to Albion village in Smithfield (now Lincoln) Rhode Island. Among the passengers were the Rhode Island governor, two canal commissioners, and fifty invited guests. When the boat passed Kelly's factory near Albion, passengers "were greeted by the smiling faces of a score of neatly dressed females who thronged the windows of the factory . . . The boat returned to Providence about seven o'clock amid a large concourse of spectators who had assembled to greet her arrival."[18] In October, the completion of the canal to Worcester was greeted by no less pomp and jubilation. Again, the *Lady Carrington* appeared and its crew found the town festooned in colorful bunting. Cannons saluted the boat's arrival and bells tolled throughout Worcester. Before the joyous assembly adjourned to Governor Lincoln's home for obligatory "cups of sparkling wine," town selectman

Millville Lock. One of the best-preserved lift locks along the route of the Blackstone Canal can be found in Millville, Massachusetts. The granite stone walls with recesses built for the large wooden gates when in open position reflect the high degree of craftsmanship of the early nineteenth-century stone masons. Based on cost, wooden locks were preferred; however, maintenance problems associated with wood persuaded Canal Engineer Hutchinson to redesign the locks using granite at a cost of approximately $4,000 per lock. John H. Chafee Blackstone River Valley NHC/National Park Service

Colonel Pliny Merrick proclaimed, "The day then that witnesses the mooring of this boat at the head of this artificial navigation is fitly devoted to our rejoicing. The multitudes that throng these banks and wharfs are yet but few of those who shall hereafter participate in the benefits which may be anticipated from it."[19]

But the heady optimism of the inaugurals in 1828 didn't translate into profits after a first full season of commercial operation in 1829. A short-lived business depression and heavy autumn floods strained company finances. Over the next three years, canal traffic and revenues rose, however, and during the busiest months of the year, Worcester saw as many as a dozen boats each week. Typically, shipping over the waterway commenced with the retreat of ice in March or possibly April, with spring flooding always a strong possibility to curtail canal traffic, and continued often into November. Observing the start of canal op-

Canal and Bridge over Road. Although canal boats on the Blackstone Canal handled far larger volumes of bulk materials, such as stone and grain, than wagons, the amount of goods transported to market by teams of horses or oxen continued to rise throughout the canal era. In this engraving, a horse-drawn wagon crosses the Blackstone Canal and river in a landscape dramatically altered by the need for sound transportation routes. Courtesy of Worcester Historical Museum, Worcester, MA

facing: 1846 Map of the Village of Worcester, Massachusetts. This 1846 map of the Village of Worcester illustrates how central the Blackstone Canal was to the growth of what was barely a village to a full city by 1848. One aspect of Worcester life that has not changed since the days of the canal is the congregation of roads, waterways, and structures that make up today's Kelly Square. With Mill Brook, the Blackstone Canal and Lock #48, bridges over both, a tollkeeper's house, Green Street, and Vernon Street merging together, this area remains a challenge for all pedestrians, horses, wagons, automobiles and trucks. From the collections of Worcester Historical Museum, Worcester, MA

erations in Worcester, one contemporary remarked, "The lading and unlading of boats, the arrival of teams with freight to put on board of them, and the constant passing of trucks with goods brought by the boats to be delivered at different points in town, yesterday and the day before, presented scenes of activity and bustle in the vicinity of the head of the Canal."[20] While some of the horse-drawn boats ran the complete route between Providence and Worcester, many more served local markets along certain stretches of the canal.

Revenues from Tolls on Blackstone Canal

Year	Amount Collected
1829	$8,606
1830	$12,016
1831	$14,944
1832	$18,907
1833	$17,545
1834	$16,464
1835	$14,433
1836	$11,500

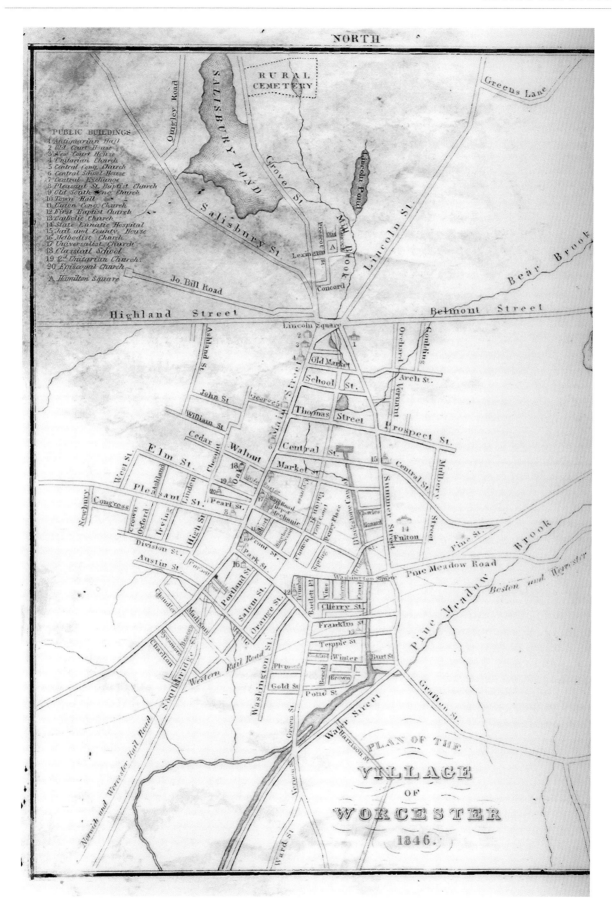

The majority of goods shipped up the canal from Providence included such staples as flour, grains, salt, liquor, and molasses, as well as raw materials, including coal, wool, cotton bales, dyes, and oils. Other consumer goods—tea, dried fish, sugar, china, clayware, and spices—as well as imported manufactured items, namely machinery and hardware, were also conveyed northward from tidewater wharfs. Items shipped down the canal were of two principle categories: farm produce and manufactured goods. Farm produce included fruit and vegetables, grains and flour, dairy products, cider, hay, and firewood. The manufactured goods encompassed everything from hand-crafted, home-spun or sewn textiles and apparel, combs, and baskets, to factory-produced cotton and wool cloth, textile and farm machinery, iron castings, paper, shingles, and chairs. For many farmers, manufacturers, and household producers, the canal offered a substantial savings over shipping via wagon; about $3.80 per ton, roughly one-half the cost between Worcester and Providence, according to one estimate.[21] During its peak years of operations in the 1830s, a dozen boats reached Worcester each week. And activity at the southern end was even brisker, as shippers found that shorter and more frequent runs from Providence's tidewater wharfs to nearby ports were more lucrative than longer hauls to Worcester.

Although some Worcester residents complained that Rhode Island's inland ports received better service, the Blackstone Canal was proving to be a boon to commercial and manufacturing expansion in their city and throughout the region. The upper Blackstone villages of Millbury, Grafton, Northbridge, and Uxbridge experienced unprecedented population growth, as industrial and commercial development reached new heights. Many of the goods produced in these locales were shipped to Worcester for transport to other commercial centers. In fact, tonnage up the canal and into Worcester heavily outstripped, by nearly five to one, the amount shipped to Providence. While the canal accelerated Worcester's status as the premier inland port in Massachusetts, its position was further enhanced in 1835 with the completion of the Boston and Worcester Railroad. Between 1820 and 1850, Worcester's population grew fivefold, to about 17,000 people,

and its value of manufactured products approached the $5 million mark.[22]

The Blackstone Canal helped the region become more mobile and more mercantile, but it also became an integral part of the extensive waterpowered manufacturing development in the valley. One such enterprise that was tied closely to the canal was the Lonsdale Company, formed in 1831 with Rhode Islander Wilbur Kelly serving as its agent. Kelly, a former ship's captain in the Brown Family fleet of ships, was backed by a group of Providence capitalists, including Edward Carrington, Nicholas Brown, and Thomas Ives, and had acquired, in 1825–1826, several large parcels of land, as well as a small textile mill, north of Valley Falls where the canal was projected to run. In exchange for allowing the canal to pass through nearly four and one-half miles of his property, Kelly, operating as the front man for the Lonsdale Water Power Company, obtained the right to tap the canal's waterpower potential. In the years after its establishment, the Lonsdale Company constructed an extensive waterpower system from the canal, operating a series of large textile mills and becoming one of New England's major textile producers. Similarly, mill owners in the upper Blackstone who constructed or expanded their factories after 1825 located their mill ponds, raceways, and waterwheels in relation to the waterway or hydraulic works of the canal company. As a result, they came to depend on the company for supplying and regulating the flow of water to their mills.[23]

In 1832, the company's most prosperous year, Blackstone shareholders received a return of 2 ½ percent on their holdings. Never again would these investors reap even this modest return. Problems of high water in the spring and drought in late summer hindered regular service, especially in the slackwater sections of the Blackstone and Moshassuck rivers. The company also struggled to maintain the waterway and its many associated structures, which were continually subjected to harsh winters, floods, and general wear from regular use. Moreover, sections of the canal reportedly were sabotaged by disgruntled mill owners, angered over the loss of water to their factories. Even more costly were the actions of the lower Blackstone manufacturers who filed numerous claims against the ca-

BLACKSTONE CANAL.

WORCESTER,
MASS.

CANAL
TRANSPORTATION.

The Providence and Worcester Boat Co., grateful for past favors, respectfully give notice, that they will commence running, soon as the Canal is navigable, a daily line of Boats from Providence to Worcester and the intermediate places.

Having engaged the upper Basin and Store-House at Millbury, they feel confident that they can give better satisfaction to Merchants, Manufacturers, and the public generally, whose freight is left at Millbury, than any other company.

Their Boats will be put in good repair, and under command of steady, experienced, and temperate masters; and they pledge themselves that nothing on their part shall be wanting, to accommodate all who may favor them with their custom.

All freights consigned to Oren Nichols or S. R. Jackson & Co., Providence, E. Southwick, Millbury, S. R. Jackson & Co. or Cyrus Aldrich, Worcester, will be forwarded promtly and without delay.

Providence, Feb. 15, 1836.

Canal Transportation Broadside. This broadside of the Providence and Worcester Boat Company, the largest shipping concern on the Blackstone Canal, announces its canal operation business for 1836. Typically, the canal shipping season began in March or April due to flooding and ended in November or whenever the canal iced over. Pictured at the top is the Turning Basin in Worcester, which marked the final terminus for the canal even though the company highlights its storehouse and canal property in Millbury as the preferred port of entrance for merchants and manufactures. From the collections of Worcester Historical Museum, Worcester, MA

KEEP THIS UNTIL CALLED FOR.

CHECK. BOSTON & WORCESTER RAIL ROAD.

GEO. HAVEN, Conductor.

Ticket Stub Boston & Worcester Rail Road. From the collections of Worcester Historical Museum, Worcester, MA

PROVIDENCE & WORCESTER

RAILROAD CORPORATION.

Whitin's Station, Jan 22 1863

C. C. P. Moody, Steam Job Printer, 52 Washington St. Boston.

Received from P. WHITIN & SONS,

ARTICLES.	MARKS.	WEIGHT or MEASURE.

Numbered and marked as above, which the Company promises to forward by its Railroad, and deliver to _____ or order, at its Depot in _____ and will not hold itself responsible beyond the sum of two hundred dollars on any package that may be lost, stolen or damaged, unless otherwise agreed to by special contract; freight therefor to be paid. _____

N. B.   If merchandise be not called for on its arrival, it will be stored at the risk and expense of the owner _____ *For the Corporation.*

Bill of Lading for Whitin Machine Works. These two engravings of steam locomotives—one on the ticket stub of the Boston & Worcester Rail Road, the other on a bill of lading of the Providence & Worcester Railroad—show the extent to which steam railroad technology and design had changed between the 1840s and the 1860s. From the Collection of Laurel Moriarty

nal proprietors for exceeding their allotment of Blackstone River water. This legal action culminated in a new agreement in 1837 that restricted the amount of water available to the Blackstone Canal Company, and in an 1838 Rhode Island Supreme Court decision that awarded the plaintiffs some $8,450. This amount far surpassed the annual revenue of the company for that year and further drained its limited capital.[24]

Competition from the railroad, too, hurt the canal. Seeking to capture the trade lost to Providence, a group of Boston capitalists organized the Boston and Worcester Railroad, and began constructing the line in 1831. The road was completed and service begun in the summer of 1835. From the outset, the railroad secured the vast majority of Worcester's freight traffic. Although the canal continued operations and, even of-

fered lower rates, its traffic and revenues plummeted. The company dispensed with its fleet of boats and even ceased hiring its own lock tenders. (Boat masters who remained in business formed associations, which hired lock tenders to keep the canal operating.) For a few years, the section of the canal between Providence and Woonsocket, Rhode Island, remained relatively busy. Yet even here, declining service led the Lonsdale Company, one of the canal's principal shippers, to employ its own teamsters and rely increasingly on overland transport. In 1841 and again in 1844, Carrington, Burgess, and other canal officials petitioned Rhode Island's General Assembly to dissolve the company's charter and enable them to retire from business. These actions, however, were contested by Lower Blackstone manufacturers who feared their properties

Providence & Worcester Train along the abandoned Blackstone Canal. Following the completion of the Providence & Worcester Railroad in October of 1847, the connections from Worcester to the major cities of New England were just about complete and the story of Worcester as a railroad center would begin. By 1850, twenty-four trains would be arriving and departing from Worcester on a daily basis. Courtesy D. Craig Travers, Hopedale, MA

would suffer if the company abandoned its dams, reservoirs, and canal. The Blackstone Canal Company was forced to struggle on.[25]

The final blow to the canal was dealt by the Providence and Worcester Railroad. Incorporated in 1844, this concern, like the canal a generation earlier, received the backing of Providence's most powerful capitalists. Several, including Moses Brown Ives and Edward Carrington, who retained their investments in the failing canal company, stood to lose even more if the railroad succeeded. Nonetheless, they believed a railroad was necessary to help Providence—as well as their businesses—regain a larger share of the western trade. Charters for the railroad company quickly passed both the Rhode Island and Massachusetts leg-

Canal in Winter. Never as successful as its advocates had hoped, the
Blackstone Canal nonetheless opened the center of Massachusetts
to the port city of Providence and changed Worcester into a central
railroad hub that spurred industrialization. Today, remnants of the
Blackstone Canal still catch the imagination of canal buffs, tourists,
and valley residents alike. Its preservation reflects a broad base of
understanding by the local communities, state and federal agencies,
and local citizenry of the importance of preserving our historic past.
John H. Chafee Blackstone River Valley NHC/National Park Service

islatures and construction soon was underway. By September 1847, a 23-mile section of line from Providence to Millville, Massachusetts, was opened. The following month, workers completed the entire 43-mile route to Worcester, and the line opened to great fanfare. At a gathering in Worcester, railroad officials offered a toast: "The two Unions between Worcester and Providence—the first was as weak as water, the last as strong as iron."[26]

The canal collected its final toll in November 1848. Two months later, the Rhode Island legislature approved the company's application to dissolve. While some of its land had been acquired by the railroad, other parcels acquired in the 1820s by eminent domain reverted to their original owners. Of the various canal properties tied to the manufacturing concerns, the company received permission to sell the land and structures, provided that the sale would not injure the interests of the affected parties. Treasurer Thomas Burgess handled the various transactions involving company property, much of which was sold at public auction in 1849. Another two years would pass before the company's last holdings—several storage ponds—were sold to manufacturers in the valley. In the end, stockholders received $1.25 per share from property sales, while losses totaling more than half a million dollars over the life of the company were absorbed by Carrington, Ives, Brown, and other principal investors.[27]

The financial failings of the Blackstone Canal Company long overshadowed the important role the waterway played in the capitalist transformation of the valley's countryside. Up to the time of the canal's construction, the rural economy that dominated much of the region was a blend of agricultural and artisan production, much of which was oriented toward household consumption. Such long-standing customs as bartering for goods and services, as well as the nonspecialized production of goods for local use, were reinforced by the relative isolation of valley's rural communities. After the canal was completed, more formal economic practices, ranging from the use of legally binding contracts, to cash transactions, to specialization of production for distant markets—in short, the underpinnings of a modern capitalist economy that was becoming ever more powerful in Boston, Providence, and other cities in the young nation—took hold in the valley. Equally as dramatic, the advent of the Blackstone Canal accelerated the growth of factories that were themselves a product of the emerging capitalist order. Residents and newcomers alike moved into the growing industrial and commercial towns. And within a generation, the largest share of the valley's working population found employment as wage laborers in the textile factories.[28]

These changes were nothing short of revolutionary. The railroads that overtook the canal helped propel the social and economic transformation that was already underway. Perhaps Worcester's Pliny Merrick sensed this larger significance when, among the din and uproar at the canal's dedication, he closed his oration, declaring, "Nor can the pealing canon, which is even now to proclaim our rejoicings to a wider circle than is here assembled; send the faintest echo of its thunders to that far distance; which shall feel the grateful and awakening influence of the great work, which we may say to day is done."[29]

NOTES

1. Michael Merrill, "Cash is Good to Eat: Self Sufficiency and Exchange in the Rural Economy of the United States," *Radical History Review* 7 (1977): 43–46, 60–61; James A. Henretta, "Families and Farms: *Mentalité* in Pre-Industrial America," *The William and Mary Quarterly*, 3rd ser., 35 (January 1978), see especially 14–20.

2. Winnifred B. Rothenberg, "The Market and Massachusetts Farmers, 1750–1855," *Journal of Economic History* 41 (June 1981): 288–95.

3. George Rogers Taylor, *The Transportation Revolution, 1815–1860* (New York: Harper Torchbook Edition, 1968 [originally published in 1951]).

4. William Cronon, *Changes in the Land: Indians, Colonists, and the Ecology of New England* (New York: Hill & Wang, 1983), 82–84, 108–12, 127–28.

5. Richard E. Greenwood, "A History of the Blackstone Canal, 1823–1849," unpublished manuscript, copy available at the Rhode Island Historical Commission, 14–16. I would like to thank Dr. Greenwood for making this manuscript available to me. This and his excellent essay "Natural Run and Artificial Falls: Waterpower and the Blackstone Canal," *Rhode Island History* 49 (May 1991): 51–62, were invaluable in the writing of this chapter.

6. Cronon, *Changes in the Land*, 85–90, 103.

7. Quote of Samuel Thurber is from Greenwood, "History of the Blackstone Canal," 18.

8. Ibid.

9. Taylor, *Transportation Revolution*, 15–16; Daniel P. Jones, "Commercial Progress versus Local Rights: Turnpike Building in Northwestern Rhode Island in the 1790s," *Rhode Island History* 48 (February 1990): 22; Jones, "Turnpike Building," 20–23.

10. Taylor, *Transportation Revolution*, 22–28; Jones, "Turnpike Building," 22–24.

11. Jones, "Turnpike Building," 20–23; Greenwood, "History of the Blackstone Canal," 20–21.

12. Short biographical sketches of Benjamin Wright and Holmes Hutchinson may be found in Nobel E. Whitford, *History of the Canal System of the State of New York, together with Brief Histories of the Canals in the United States and Canada*, v. 2 (Albany, N.Y.: Brandow Printing, 1906).

13. A copy of the report by Wright and Hutchinson appeared in "An Account of the Canal from Worcester to Providence, *Providence Gazette*, January 8, 1823. The quotes are from this reprint of the report.

14. Worcester County Committee on [the] Canal Survey, 1822, quoted in Greenwood, "History of the Blackstone Canal," 32.

15. Ibid.

16. Greenwood, "History of the Blackstone Canal," 39.

17. Greenwood, "Waterpower and the Blackstone," 57.

18. *The Microcosm*, July 4, 1828.

19. Pliny Merrick, quoted in the *[Worcester] National Aegis*, October 15, 1828.

20. *[Worcester] Massachusetts Spy*, April 25, 1829.

21. Tom Kelleher, "The Blackstone Canal: Artery to the Heart of the Commonwealth," unpublished research paper, Old Sturbridge Village, Massachusetts, 7–8.

22. For a concise summary of Worcester's nineteenth-century industrial growth, see Roy Rosenzweig, *Eight Hours for What We Will: Workers and Leisure in an Industrial City, 1870–1920* (Cambridge: Cambridge University Press, 1983), 11–16.

23. Greenwood, "Waterpower and the Blackstone," 59.

24. Greenwood, "History of the Blackstone Canal," 84–85.

25. Ibid., 90–92.

26. Quote in ibid., 95.

27. Ibid., 96–97.

28. One of the best studies of the industrial capitalist transformation of the New England countryside is Jonathan Prude, *The Coming of Industrial Order: Town and Factory Life in Rural Massachusetts, 1810–1860* (New York: Cambridge University Press, 1983). See especially chapters 4 and 9.

29. Pliny Merrick, quoted in the *[Worcester] National Aegis*, October 15, 1828.

"At Night, You Could Hear the Looms for Miles"

RANGER CHUCK ARNING

Life in a mill village was an intimate affair. Everyone knew everyone, for at least one person in every family worked in the mill. Whole families could be seen, roused by the mill bell, making their way to their work in the mill. A mill family's entire life revolved around the mill: work, play, church, courting, friendships—all encapsulated by the mill. And, of course, there were stories.

There is a story about a young loom fixer who worked at the Fisherville Mill in South Grafton. It seems that one particular loom kept breaking down, and Fred Small, the young loom fixer, continually had to climb the mill stairs to a young lady's loom to make the repair. This seems to have happened frequently, so much so that Fred finally asked the young lady to attend the Annual Corn Husking Festival at St. James Church with him. Fred ended up marrying Pulcheri St. Onge. We will never know whether it was simply a poorly constructed loom or if Miss St. Onge had a crush on that young loom fixer.[1]

But mill life was not all about courting; there were pressures too. Finding a job in a new country is never easy. Each immigrant group struggled to find a way to fit in. Language was always an issue. There is the story of a young Cape Verdean man, who landed in Providence and found work in a mill in Blackstone. His niece, Yvonne Smart, said that when he got off the boat, "he placed one foot on the land and the other in the mill." It was not that he didn't want to learn English; there just wasn't any time to learn English.[2]

Each mill village reflected the traditions of the immigrant groups that lived and worked there. For the French Canadians, they had no desire to "fit in" to this new country. They were not going to be here long. Make some money, go back to Quebec, and buy some land. It was their faith and their language that made them French. They had no desire to change. The mill villages in Social, Globe, and Bernon in Woonsocket all reflected that aspect of the French-Canadian character. By 1880, 75 percent of Woonsocket was French Canadian.

The Swedes had a totally different strategy. They were going to be the "best" Americans; hard-working, Protestant, temperate and Republican. Whether you lived in the Village of Rumford in East Providence or Quinsigamond in Worcester, the same basic traits could be found. John Agren's grandfather arrived in Rumford in 1901 and made it a point to speak the best English. No accent. He insisted that his children and his children's children learn and speak English perfectly. He joined the Lincoln Historical Society. Later, John would speculate that his grandfather believed that this membership made him a real American.[3]

All these tensions and pressures of everyday life, all these stories played themselves out within the confines of the mill village. Each worker's sunrise and sunset was dictated by the mill and its owners—benevolent, perhaps, but still, the owners governed the rhythms of the mill. While the mill villages had many similarities, each had a unique aspect that made them different and distinct.

NOTES

1. Video oral history of Anita (Small) Hudson, November 1997, National Heritage Corridor Office/NPS.

2. Video oral history of Yvonne Smart, March 1997, National Heritage Corridor Office/NPS.

3. Video oral history of John Agren, September 1998, National Heritage Corridor Office/NPS.

4 Mill Villages and the Diversity of Industry RANGERS CHUCK ARNING, RAY BOSWELL, PETER COFFIN, KEVIN KLYBERG, AND JACK WHITTAKER

Shift Change at the Whitin Machine Works. Whitinsville, Massachusetts, circa 1920. Courtesy of Spaulding Aldrich

The obvious flagship for the evolution of industry in the Blackstone River Valley is the Slater Mill in Pawtucket, Rhode Island; America's first successful waterpowered cotton-spinning mill. This mill was the foundation for the rise of industry across the region and the nation. However, it is possible for the Slater story to overshadow the other elements of this story, which is an understandable, but unfortunate mistake. What made the rise of industry here truly

International Exhibition, 1876.

The Great Corliss Engine.

Advertisement for the Corliss Steam Engine. The impact that the power of the Corliss Steam Engine had on the congregation of manufacturers in Philadelphia for the 1876 Centennial Fair was enormous. As this advertisement illustrates, the ability of this massive engine to power all of Machinery Hall at the fair captured the world's imagination. Courtesy the Rhode Island Historical Society

revolutionary was not the success of a single mill, but the fact that the Slater Mill served as a blueprint that was repeated and imitated across the region, changing the landscape from agricultural to manufacturing, altering the way that people worked and lived.

The core of this transformation was the chain of mill villages that ran along the waterways of the Blackstone Valley. At either end of this chain were two massive anchors, Providence and Worcester, which served not only as the region's key transportation and financial centers, but were also major industrial centers in their own right. At the time of the Cotton Centennial in 1890, Providence was promoting itself as the home to the "Five Great Industrial Wonders of the World." This group of industrial titans included the world's largest machine tool factory (Brown and Sharpe),

the largest producer of steam engines (Corliss Steam Engine Company), the largest file factory (Nicholson File), the largest manufacturer of screws (American Screw Company), and the largest maker of silver hollowware (Gorham Manufacturing Company). Providence's rise to national significance as an industrial center had been highlighted at the Philadelphia Centennial Fair in 1876, where each of these firms had prominent displays.

At the headwaters of the Blackstone River, the City of Worcester also had developed into an industrial center by the post–Civil War period and steel, not cotton, was its medium. Washburn and Moen produced thousands of miles of barbed wire to tame the American West, along with a plethora of other steel goods. Worcester's growth as an industrial center was hin-

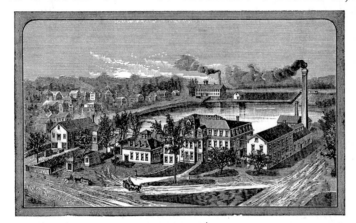

L. COES'

GENUINE IMPROVED PATENT

SCREW WRENCHES,

Manufactured by

L. COES & CO.,

WORCESTER, MASS.

Established in 1839.

Registered March 31, 1874.

CUTS REPRESENT OUR NEW

KNIFE HANDLE PATTERN.

Patented July 6, 1880, and July 8, 1884.

THE BEST MADE AND STRONGEST

WRENCH

IN THE MARKET.

left and facing: Advertisements from the Worcester City Directory of 1886 for Washburn and Moen and L. Coes & Company. The diversity of metal products that streamed out of Worcester was stunning. Between the Washburn and Moen barb wire that settled the American West, the L. Coes & Company wrenches, and the Royal Worcester Corset Company's famous corsets, Worcester manufacturers felt that there was nothing that they could not make. From the collections of Worcester Historical Museum, Worcester, MA

dered at first by the limited power provided by the headwater streams of the Blackstone River. The advent of steam technology allowed it to become a center of production. At the height of its manufacturing prowess in the 1920s, Worcester boasted 527 firms, whose products ranged from envelopes, railway cars, train wheels, ladies corsets, grinding wheels, wallpaper, rugs and carpets, and machine belting to iceskates, monkey wrenches, lunch wagons and diners,

bicycle and car chains, vehicle crankshafts, looms, and other textile machines.

Pawtucket and Woonsocket also developed diverse industrial bases that went beyond textiles. Yet, it was in the mill villages situated along the banks of the Mumford, the Branch, the Clear, and the Blackstone rivers where the real industrial significance of the Blackstone Valley lies. It was here that the social interactions between the mill and its village; the own-

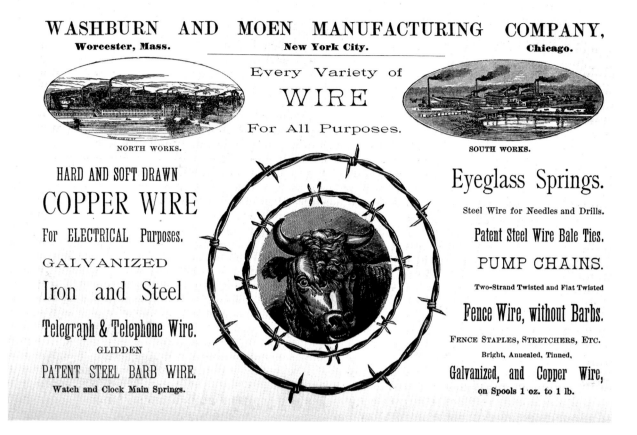

ers, mill managers, and their workers; and the various ethnic groups participated in this dynamic industrial landscape. It was within these close-knit villages that industrial life took on a rhythm and character of its own. The social constructs of company-sponsored athletic teams and bands, of company outings and Field Days, of quadrilles and community events centered on life in the mill village. Sometimes even the conflicts and strikes gave the Blackstone Valley a distinctive feel.

While the villages often differed dramatically in architectural style, from the utilitarian to the elaborate, each village centered around the mill. The mill was the dominant force not only upon the landscape, but in the lives of the workers and their families. It was the mill that brought these people together, and served as the linchpin of their work, their homes, and their identity. And while new advancements in technology in the form of electric street cars and telephone lines would bring the people scattered across the Blackstone Valley closer together, they still would be identi-

fied by their strong individual alliance to their village and their mill.

The following brief narratives and photographic essays highlight but a small sampling of these villages, their identities, and the mills that governed their daily routines. These villages present unique stories and different voices far too diverse to be covered in these pages, but their strength comes through being a part of a greater whole, the industrial landscape of the Blackstone River Valley.

With the growth of the industrial mill village based on an engineered landscape of waterpower, the hilltop villages that were so important to the early development of the valley were fast becoming obsolete. "Mother Mendon," the second-oldest town in Worcester County, originally included all or parts of Blackstone, Millville, Milford, Hopedale, Upton, Uxbridge, and Northbridge. However, due to their proximity to waterpower, the mill villages grew in numbers and wealth along the river, leaving the rural "hilltop village" of Mendon and Northbridge Center distant and

Women's Orchestral Group, 1914, and Rockdale Mill Village Band. The work day was long and hard and everyone needed some form of entertainment. Between the village baseball team, dramatic clubs, musical groups of all types including the village band—generally sponsored by the mill owner, other civic or cultural groups—there was something for everyone. *Top:* From the collections of Worcester Historical Museum, Worcester, MA; *Bottom:* Courtesy of Steve & Renee Leoncini & Family

Electric Street Car stopping at Plummer's Corner, Northbridge, Massachusetts. The electric street cars brought mobility to the people of the Blackstone Valley. A special day trip to Worcester, Woonsocket, or even Lake Nipmuc in Mendon or Hunt's Mill Arcade in Rumford, East Providence was part of the new modern reality for working families. Technology was transforming their lives at unheard-of speeds. Collection of Philip C. Becker

removed from the industrial landscape. With their increased political power, the mill villages split off to create their own towns over a period of time, allowing the rural "hilltop villages" of Mendon and Northbridge to retain their agricultural landscape.

Lime Rock village in Lincoln, Rhode Island, an equally remote village, managed to maintain its significance. Beginning in the 1660s, the mining of lime became a central activity of this rural community. The significance of lime cannot be overstated; it was critical to building. The new colonies required well-constructed homes and the previous material, crushed shells, had proved to be a weak and inefficient substitute for lime. Roger Williams was overjoyed at the discovery of the lime quarries and wrote to all the co-

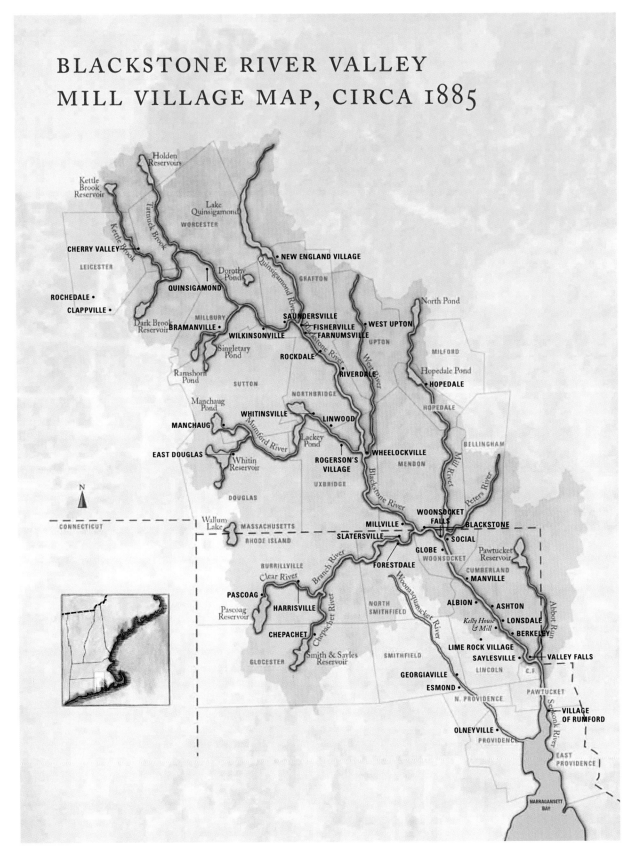

BLACKSTONE RIVER VALLEY
MILL VILLAGE MAP, CIRCA 1885

Illustrated Map of Mill Villages circa 1885. While the space is too small to show and list all of the mill villages in the Blackstone Valley in 1885, the one characteristic of most of the villages is their connection to moving water.

John H. Chafee Blackstone River Valley NHC/National Park Service

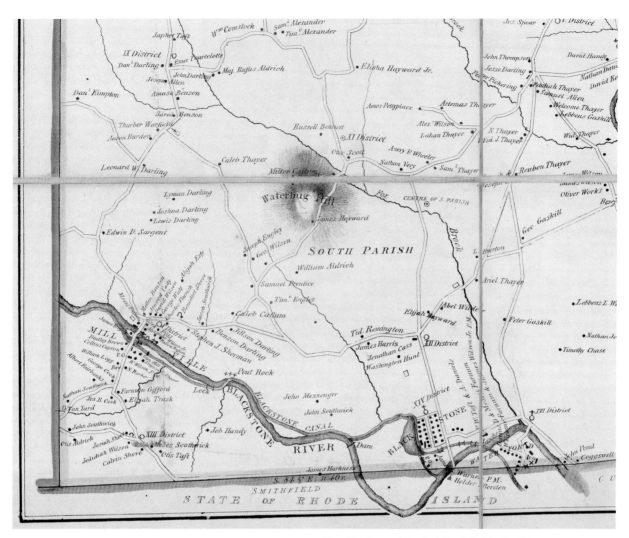

Map of the Town of Mendon's South Parish, 1831. This map of the Town of Mendon's South Parish illustrates the growing economic power of those villages located along the Blackstone River. A river location brought greater access to new technology, power for the mills, and new transportation routes, as seen here as the Blackstone Canal snakes its way north through the villages of Blackstone and Millville. Courtesy American Antiquarian Society

lonial governors alerting them to his find in Rhode Island. Although the Moshassuck River was little more than a brook, lime kept this village vibrant. Later, the Blackstone Canal allowed the lime to be transported efficiently. Lime was a central manufacturing product that could be found stacked in barrels along the sides of the canal boats heading in both directions. While the Louisquisset Pike, opened in 1806, provided an early direct route to Providence for the lime haulers, the canal expanded the lime dealers' market.

While steam would change everything, early in the development of manufacturing in the Blackstone Valley, the amount of water and the consistency of its flow dictated what could or could not be produced. Those communities located on small streams and subject to the whims of nature simply could not produce the power necessary to compete with the massive cot-

Limestone Quarry. Limestone quarries in this village date back to the mid–1600s and the quarrying of lime makes this site one of the oldest industrial sites in the United States. John H. Chafee Blackstone River Valley NHC/National Park Service

ton mills on the Blackstone. Instead, they produced woolen goods, because the greater value of these allowed the mills to make a profit with a smaller production run.

The Village of Chepachet is a good example of this "small is beautiful" concept. From its early beginnings with the opening of the Benefit Mill in 1810, and continuing over the next thirty years, a series of small mills, mostly specializing in woolens, were established in Chepachet, increasing the village's size and cementing its place as the center of Glocester. Today, only one small mill along with artifacts of old raceways and stone ruins remain to tell the story of the work that once went on here.

The Chepachet River. Even small streams like the Chepachet River, with a properly designed water management system, could provide enough power to create at least one ingredient of a successful mill. John H. Chafee Blackstone River Valley NHC/ National Park Service

Sometimes opportunity played a role. In 1825, at the edge of the sprawling village of North Grafton, William Hovey built a dam at the southern tip of Lake Quinsigamond to provide a reservoir for the soon-to-be-completed Blackstone Canal. With the dam in place, new manufacturing opportunities presented themselves along the Quinsigamond River, where the New England Manufacturing Company purchased several mill privileges. At the base of the dam, the owners erected a stone mill for the manufacture of linen cloth. They also built an orderly set of worker housing around a large open common area, creating New England Village.

Open fields to the west and north of the village created a bucolic setting, with horses and cattle grazing within the din of the linen, and later thread and cotton cloth, manufacturing. Factory management created a farm that provided horses for their wagons as well as for pulling the mill's fire apparatus. A large dairy herd, with 72 cows at one time, provided milk for the worker's families. While manufactured products would change, from linen threads to abrasives, the rustic farm landscape still captures the essence of this early mill village.

Smaller sources for power would force early entrepreneurs to be more creative. It was not uncommon that several different industrial processes would occur within the same mill complex over time. Harrisville, in Burrillville, Rhode Island, is another example of such creativity. The emerging textile industry came to town in 1825 and town namesake Andrew Harris opened a shop to make spindles and flyers, followed by a cotton-spinning mill in 1832. The village took a major leap forward in 1856, when William Tinkham and his brother-in-law Job S. Steere bought the Harrisville mill to produce woolens. They expanded operations,

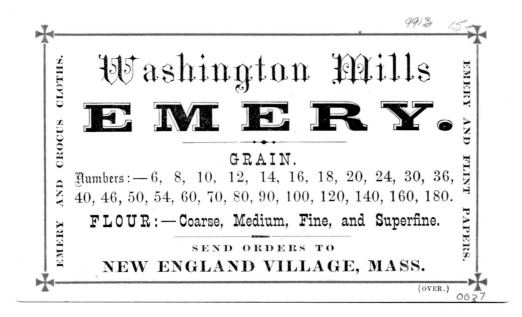

Washington Mills Advertisement. Washington Mills Emery Manufacturing Company, one of the largest manufacturers of abrasive materials in the world, purchased the lower mill in 1878 and has since expanded to owning the entire mill complex, which is still surrounded by the mill houses and common—all a part of the original New England Village. Courtesy American Antiquarian Society

brought rail service to the village, and built numerous worker housing units along Chapel Street.

The face of modern Harrisville was shaped through the efforts of Austin T. Levy, who began operating the mill in 1912. The 1920s and 1930s saw a period of general decline in the textile industry in New England, but Harrisville continued to thrive under Levy's management. He created an efficient and harmonious community where management and workers worked together toward a common goal.

Of all the mill villages that make up the Blackstone Valley, Upton stands out for resembling, not the traditional "Blackstone Valley" family-owned and operated mill village, but the Lowell "corporate" model where boardinghouses for young ladies were the key to developing a stable work force. William Knowlton took advantage of the straw-goods market in Upton and in 1837 began a very serious venture into making straw hats. Hats were, and still are, fashion statements. Keeping abreast of the latest in fashions was a demanding job that required Knowlton to utilize his brothers, Eben and Edwin, as fashion watchdogs in New York City. Knowlton made recruiting forays, much like the Lowell Mill agents, into rural villages in Maine, Nova Scotia, and eastern Canada, looking for young women who could learn to stitch hats.[1] The boardinghouse was an important part of the Upton mill village landscape.

The quiet, peaceful dale of the Hopedale Community of Practical Christians, where nonresistance was taught and practiced, is an unlikely spot to talk about an ideal planned mill community. One of the more successful of the utopian experiments, Hopedale managed to combine progressive land-use practices with a profitable heavy-manufacturing process. The aggressive business practices of the Drapers did not overlook the basic concept of open space promoted by the utopian community. When additional housing was required for a growing work force while protecting upstream water sources for the mill, the Olmstead-trained Arthur Shurcliff placed worker housing facing the waterway, with only the access road between the mill pond and the housing.[2] This allowed all to enjoy the beauty of nature without having to view the normal backyard trash and living "necessities." This picturesque housing arrangement set Hopedale apart from other mill villages.

Considering the great diversity of manufacturing processes that could be found in the Blackstone Valley, the village of Rumford, East Providence, Rhode Island stands out. While the common manufacturing mill village is based on textiles, Rumford was based on calcium acid phosphate and sodium bicarbonate, with a little corn starch thrown in for good measure. Yes, a mill village based on baking powder. The Village of Rumford was known as the "Kitchen Capitol

Hat Stitchers at the Knowlton Hat Company. The journey to becoming a good stitcher took several years of training. Finding the right work characteristics in a young lady took time and effort, requiring agents for the Knowlton Hat Company to recruit from the hinterlands of northern New England and eastern Canada for such talent. Courtesy of the Upton Historical Society

Boardinghouse and Mill. The significance and power of the mill, as it hovers over the young female workers' boardinghouse to its right, cannot be mistaken. The mill dominated the industrial landscape here in West Upton as it did in towns throughout the Blackstone Valley. Courtesy of the Upton Historical Society

Mill Housing, Hopedale, Massachusetts. Not all mill housing was created equal. Whether it was the influence of the Practical Christian Utopian Community or simply the fact that the Draper Manufacturing Corporation required a higher skilled worker, the mill housing in Hopedale is of a significantly higher stylistic quality than any of the other villages in the Blackstone Valley. John H. Chafee Blackstone River Valley NHC/National Park Service

Interior of the Draper Mill Complex. The same mill complex that manufactured the looms that powered the textile industry around the world, and the Boott Mill in Lowell today, also manufactured artillery pieces during the Second World War. Such a retooling effort speaks volumes about the skills of the Draper work force. Courtesy D. Craig Travers, Hopedale, MA

Rumford Baking Powder Ad. The entrepreneurial spirit of the Blackstone Valley is well represented by the partnership of Eben Horsford and George Wilson. The test kitchen for their "leavening agent," Rumford Baking Powder, was in the field kitchens of the Union Army during the American Civil War, where bread could be made almost instantly for the weary and hungry troops using the new baking powder. Courtesy the Rhode Island Historical Society

of the World." The mill village pattern here was much the same as found throughout the valley: mill housing, churches, company store, fire station—all key elements of any mill village, with one very large exception—few mill villages also had their own amusement park. Rumford Chemical Works purchased the Hunt's Mills site and additional land along the Ten Mile River to build their amusement park for entertaining their employees and the general public.

Diversity is thy name, Quinsigamond. From a paper mill operated by Isaiah Thomas, one of America's earliest, as well as one of its wealthiest, visionaries, to the wire mill that settled the American West, Quinsigamond Village, located at the "headwaters of the Blackstone River," has had a history of being an isolated stepchild to the bustling industrial center of Worcester. Although it provided an ideal location for the use of waterpower, even Isaiah Thomas, the noted printer and patriot, couldn't transform the village's isolation through his paper mill in 1793. It wasn't until the construction of the Providence & Worcester Railroad, and the purchase by Henry S. Washburn of the mill privilege for the construction of a steel rod-rolling mill roughly fifty years later, that the village began its journey to economic success. However, what gave the village its unique charm was its Swedish influence. Skilled, hard-working, temperate Swedish iron workers from Varmland and other iron counties in Sweden came to work for Washburn and Moen and brought with them their Swedish culture and their desire to be the "best Americans."

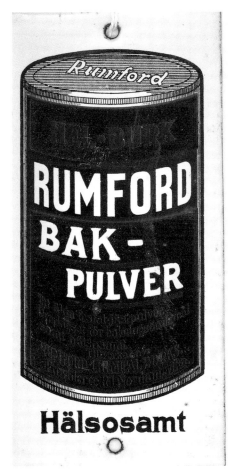

1 Ounce Baking Powder Can in Swedish. Historically, Rumford Chemical always focused on the housewife, making their product easy to use and keep. When a thriving Swedish community developed in the village, Rumford accommodated them by creating a 1 ounce "one use" can of baking powder—just enough for one baking with no waste. Courtesy of the East Providence Historical Society

Crown and Eagle Mill. The mills fell into the Whitin Family Empire when they bought out the creditors in 1849, maintaining the creditors' original charter name, the Uxbridge Cotton Mills. It was the Whitins who added the brick building connecting the two mills in 1851. John H. Chafee Blackstone River Valley NHC/ National Park Service

When one thinks of classic architectural lines and agelessness of design, the brick, almost Monticello-esque look of Rogerson's Village in North Uxbridge, Massachusetts, comes to mind. Robert Rogerson, a one-time Boston merchant and president of the Handel and Hayden Society of Boston, most likely designed the elegant stone Crown Mill (1825) and the Eagle (1829), both cotton textile mills. The village, with its brick two-family homes, its two-story company store with a second floor meeting hall overlooking the Mill and the Mumford River, presents an almost romantic view of the pastoral New England mill village.

Naming the Crown Mill after his former homeland, and the Eagle to represent his home in the New Republic, Rogerson and his partner, Oliver Eldridge, designed a mill and village that seemed so elegant, so indestructible that they would last forever.[3] Unfortunately for Rogerson and Eldridge, while the village

Crown and Eagle Mill Housing. This mill house, with its brick façade, gives this industrial landscape
an almost pastoral feel. John H. Chafee Blackstone River Valley NHC/National Park Service

Mill Workers. Formal portraits of mill workers, taken here at the Wuskanut Mill in Farnumsville, South Grafton, with their supervisor, was not unusual at the turn of the century. However, such an image provides us with real faces to match the concept of "the mill worker." The context is important; surrounded by the machinery of the mill, the men stand a little straighter, and the women sit with a professional air. The pride these mill hands had in their work is evident. Courtesy of Judy Zaleski & Family

they developed had staying power, their ownership of the mill did not. They lost the Crown and Eagle Mills to creditors in the financial Panic of 1837, which took down many early Blackstone Valley mill owners.

Since 1827, when Peter Farnum chose to build his first mill near the confluence of the Quinsigamond and Blackstone Rivers, Farnumsville always has supported an operating mill. Despite fire, financial difficulties, and partners buying out partners, the Farnumsville mill site has captured the imagination of aspiring mill owners.

When the mill at Farnumsville shifted from cotton manufacturing to the more profitable business of spinning and weaving woolens, it needed to attract a

1896 Memorial Day Parade, Whitinsville. This picture of the 1896 Memorial Day parade of schoolchildren down Main Street in Whitinsville illustrates the dominating presence of the mill, in this case the Whitin Machine Works, not only on the industrial landscape it created, but in the hearts and minds of its residents. Courtesy of the Whitinsville Social Library

more skilled work force. The owner hired a manager and weavers from England. Besides exercising their weaving experience, the English workers sought to express their own cultural identity. The village soon boasted a bowling green suitable for cricket matches, and company housing often was surrounded by flower gardens. Cricket has given way to baseball and football and the gardens have been replaced by garages, but some of the privet hedges are still present, silent witnesses to an earlier cultural migration.

The mill villages of Rockdale and Riverdale in Northbridge share a common history from their start in the 1820s, when a man named Holbrook bought the water rights and privilege for both sites. The Upper Holbrook Mill burned down soon after it was built in 1832. In 1856, a year after Holbrook died nearly bankrupt, the Whitin family bought both the Upper and

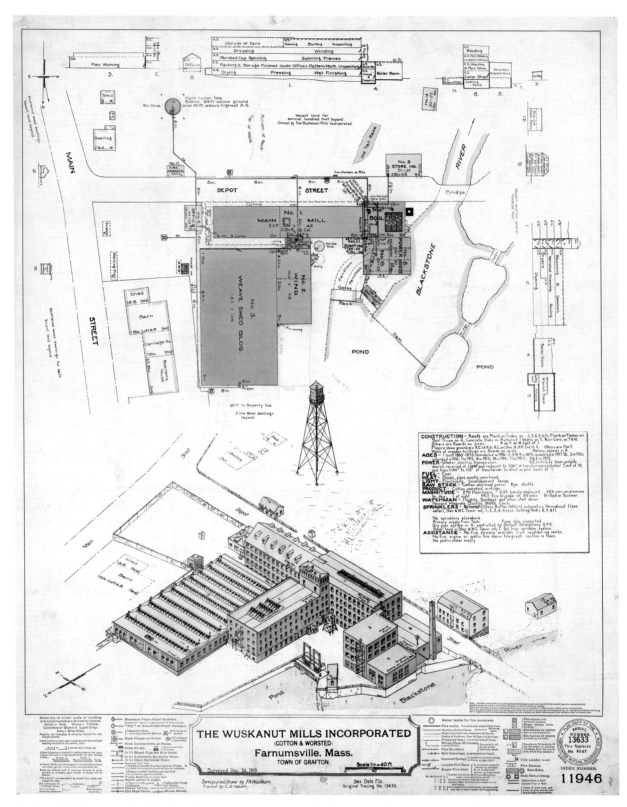

Wuskanut Mill Insurance Map. This December 30, 1919, insurance map of the Wuskanut Mill complex provides a fascinating look at fire safety applications and mechanisms. Types and location of sprinkler systems, availability of fire streams, number of night watchmen (in this case just one), and power source are just some of the details found in this map. In 1919, Grafton did not have a public fire-alarm telegraph system. American Textile History Museum, Lowell, Massachusetts

Douglas Baseball Team. On any given day during the summer months, chances are you would find more people attending the ball game than actually lived in town. Contrast the slow pace of the game, played outdoors in fresh air, with the noisy, humid, dark mill floor filled with rapidly moving machines. It is easy to understand the allure of the game of baseball to mill workers and their communities. Courtesy—Douglas Historical Society

Lower Holbrook mill sites, giving them the more po-etic names of Rockdale and Riverdale. The Whitin family soon operated six cotton mills: Rockdale, Riverdale, Linwood, East Douglas, the Crown and Eagle in North Uxbridge, and their original Cotton Mill in Whitinsville.

The imposing mill of the Whitin Machine Works that dominated the Mumford River and the surrounding mill village landscape sent a clear message of just where the focus of the community resided; along the river where water power ruled.

The Whitin family had enough financial assets to weather the economic depression of 1857, and chose to keep their work force busy by building and equipping a new mill in Rockdale. Steady employment and the close-knit nature of early mill villages helped attract skilled hands to work in the mills.

Tucked away in the far western corner of the Blackstone Valley and better know for its timber resources

ata and
ver, to
strong—
e been
newhat
mental,
ng the
it may
s have
asses—
bonds
their
princi-
to give
dity of
ity and
l solve
st care
e wind
ut will
singu-
ut very
is one
accom-
gimen.
t pre-
ear, is
cle of
l little
I. for
ted by
15th of
person-
e mu-
f War-
e town
by Mr.
ct and
conve-
in New
vill ac-
steam
to Fall
ning of

it will soon disclose itself, and rather advance, than retard the cause.

We have been favored with the returns of the business done on the Blackstone Canal, the past month. It exhibits a gratifying increase over those of the two preceding months. Last year there was a decrease, in the month of June.

Transportation for the last month on the Blackstone Canal to June 30th, 1830.

	To	From.
Worcester,	298 tons.	66
Millbury,	130	31
Wilkinsonville	10	5
Lelands Landing,	76	3
Northbridge,	100	234
Uxbridge,	162	82 1-2
Millville,	110 1-2	19
Blackstone,	204 1-2	53 1-2
Waterford,	6 1-2	
Woonsoket,	167	32 1-2
Mansville,	12 1-2	4 1-2
Albion Mills,	5	5 1-2
Kelly's Mills,	56	3 1-2
Wilkinson's Basin,	—	22
	1338 tons.	562 tons.

The principal articles comprised in the above were as follow.

Up.	Down.
5399 Bush Corn	1015 bales cotton goods
749 do Rye	4463 pieces do do
1626 bales Cotton	73 boxes woollen do
282 sacks Salt	441 ps. hemp Bagging
4349 galls. Molasses	38 boxes Cards
4038 do Foreign and	83 do Cards
domestic Spirits	1205 reams Paper
2044 do oil	199 doz Scythes
630 3-4 M. Shingles	996 Chairs
30 do Clapboards	5000 Bricks
184581 feet Boards and	19 bales Twine
Plank	26 3-4 cords Tanners'
148 casks Lime	Bark
910 bales Cotton	150 1-2 do Wood
133 do Wool	8 bales Cotton
76 1-4 tons Gypsum	137 casks Lime
7 tons Coal	496 Pails
75865 lbs Iron	4000 lbs Soapstone
67 casks Nails	48 tons ship Timber
14 do Wire	
50 boxes Sugar	
34 bbls do	
66 quintals Fish	

The Chancellor Livingston, we learn, arrived at Boston Light, about 7 o'clock, on Saturday

scenue
appear
culprit
wrist,
cord ac
being t
read by
finishe
the dre
special
a minu
man c
He c
slight
drop t
the cro
broke,
quence
ed dow
shawls
doubt,
kind o
and th
tended
mass o
Porter
this ca
wide, c
which
the rus
in the
The
ten o'c
til after
nearly
two or
must h
sufferir
It m
lent dis
pressed
absurd
son.
were id
dent; tl
where
of deatl
The
leaving
steps of
up with
to the c
of pun
prayer
we beli
followe
pronou
devour
descent
er's eye
bold, a
he an

Newspaper column, Inland Navigation for the Blackstone Canal. The success of the canal can be seen in the amount of space the local newspapers gave to its comings and goings. What began as general announcements of arrivals or departures of canal boats, rapidly expanded to exact listings of products and raw materials with quantities and purchaser or customer of the products identified. Courtesy American Antiquarian Society

and its rocky, barren landscape, East Douglas was indeed off the beaten path. Its one advantage was the powerful Mumford River, a major tributary of the Blackstone. Such a major source of power drew early innovators to its banks. In 1835, the Douglas Axe Manufacturing Co. was formed and by 1870 it was operating six large mills stretching one mile down the Mumford, generating 300 jobs.

The year 1904 would bring the greatest change to Douglas and bring unparalleled notoriety in the world of sports. Walter Schuster came to town, and together with the W. E. Hayward, began producing woolen suitings that generated 500 jobs. But of equal importance, Schuster made Douglas into a major center of industrial league baseball. With his flair for sparing no expense to bring quality baseball to the valley, Schuster brought a steady stream of former or soon-to-be major leaguers through his mill. Working with the other mill owners, he formed the Blackstone Valley League, one of the more successful semi-professional baseball leagues prior to the development of today's minor league systems.

The Blackstone and its tributaries constitute a huge drain that empties the Worcester Hills, and surrounding highlands of the Blackstone Valley, into Narragansett Bay. While the fall of the rivers of the Blackstone watershed is significant, the consistency of the water flow is not; it would run from too much to too little without management. The two places where the engineering of the river and its landscape was most effective are in Slatersville in Rhode Island, and Whitinsville in Massachusetts. The series of reservoirs, interconnecting spillways, and step dams allow water to be saved and converted to energy by the hand of the mill owner, not by Mother Nature's will. This engineered system of water power plays itself out throughout the valley, but on a much smaller scale, except when it comes to the mills located on the main stem of the Blackstone River. Here, big water means big mills.

The Lonsdale Company is perhaps the quintessential Blackstone Valley textile firm, combining the investment of Providence merchants, direct connections with the Blackstone Canal, and a chain of mill villages that still dominate the landscape today. Nicholas Brown, Jr., and Thomas Ives made their first foray into the textile industry in 1809 with the establishment of

Ashton Mill with Blackstone Bikeway bridge in foreground. With the end of the Civil War, the Lonsdale Company began its rapid expansion, beginning with the Ashton Mill in 1867. Massive in size, these and other similar mills would signify to the world America's industrial might. John H. Chafee Blackstone River Valley NHC/National Park Service

Ann & Hope Mill. The pinnacle of the Lonsdale Company's growth came in 1886, when they built this 684-foot-long flagship mill, the Ann & Hope, seen here with the "new" mill village in the background. By this time, the ethnic face of the villages were changing as a steady flow of Irish and French-Canadian workers became employees of the Lonsdale Company. Collection of Wells Pile

Bird's-Eye Map of Valley Falls. This bird's-eye view of Valley Falls, with its concentration of industry, highlights the perspective that it was the rivers that drew the innovative entrepreneurs and their workers to its banks. The 1850 census showed that the Chace Mills employed 90 men and 120 women operating 252 looms with 11,000 spindles. John H. Chafee Blackstone River Valley NHC/National Park Service

the Blackstone Manufacturing Company, in what was then the South Parrish of Mendon, Massachusetts.

Their experience with this firm taught them many key lessons that they used to their advantage when they decided to make a second venture into textiles in the 1820s. In 1825, they established the Lonsdale Water Power Company, whose purpose was not to spin thread, but to acquire land and water rights along the Blackstone River, starting at Scott's Pond and eventually stretching upstream to Ashton. Brown and Ives' interest in the land came in part because they were also major investors in the newly chartered Blackstone Canal Company, and they knew that the canal's route through the area would make it more valuable for future mill activity.

It was not until 1831 that construction began on the new factory village of Lonsdale. Constructed by the company, the village included not only workers'

Dam on the Blackstone River, Millville. The dam here in Millville was constructed before the opening of the Blackstone Canal in 1824. The array of mills that once lined the banks of the Blackstone River, giving Millville its name, are gone, leaving behind granite and brick remnants of its industrial past. From the Collection of Laurel Moriarty

houses, but churches, schools, stores, and community buildings. A large dairy farm and company gardens provided nearly all the needs of the hundreds of worker families who thrived on this portion of the river. Utilizing steam was part of the expansion process, beginning when Lonsdale opened the Berkeley Mill in 1871 as their first exclusively steam-powered mill operation.

By 1890, the Brown and Ives holding company ran the four Lonsdale Company mill villages in Lincoln and Cumberland, as well as the Blackstone Manufacturing Company and some other sites outside of the Blackstone Valley. The owners and managers of the mills believed that they had the best interests of their workers at heart, but their employees sometimes disagreed. Long hours and wage reductions led to a series of strikes and retaliatory lockouts throughout the early 1880s. Eventually, the workers began to organize, and by 1885, several hundred Lonsdale employees were also members of the Knights of Labor.

One of the Blackstone Valley's largest textile empires began in 1839, when Oliver Chace, who had begun his career working for Samuel Slater, purchased several small mills located on both sides of the Blackstone River at Valley Falls. Oliver Chace passed management of the mills to his sons Samuel and Harvey, who played a marked role in the development of this community. Almost immediately after purchasing the Valley Falls Mills, the Chaces began improving and

Pay Day. The weekly ritual in every mill where the payroll manager would come through each department handing out small manila envelopes with each worker's pay, in cash, is a relic of the distant past. In today's world of direct deposit, this image, circa 1938, of a Knowlton Hat Company payroll manager personally distributing the weekly payroll is a classic. Courtesy of the Upton Historical Society

expanding operations. The 1850 census reported that the mill was producing 2,400,000 yards of cotton print cloth a year.

Even with their new holdings at Albion and Manville, the mills at Valley Falls continued to expand. As they did so, the population of Valley Falls changed, showing the influence of immigration in the region as new workers were needed to fill these larger mills. What was once an English settlement began to attract Irish workers in the 1840s, and by 1862, the Irish population had grown large enough to warrant the establishment of St. Patrick's Church, the first Catholic parish in Cumberland. Later waves of immigration brought in French-Canadian and later Polish workers throughout the 1800s. In the early 1900s, Valley Falls became home to a solid Portuguese community that is still prevalent today.

Millville, the youngest community in Massachusetts, split off from Blackstone in 1916, fueled by Joseph Banigan's U.S. Rubber Company, the dominant industrial concern in town. Banigan, the most successful Irish and Catholic mill owner of the time, built New Village, also known as Banigan City, in 1885 to house his workers. He built a bridge over the Blackstone River, so the workers could easily walk to work. The path from the bridge to the mill just happened to pass the celebrated Rubber Shop Oval, Millville's home ballfield, where Gabby Hartnett, Hall of Famer for the Chicago Cubs, honed his baseball skills. This connection between the mill, the mill village, and the baseball diamond became the signature landscape artifact of the mill village from the late 1870s right up to the development of minor league baseball.

In summary, these snippets of mill village history with their diverse supporting industries lay the groundwork for better understanding how America became industrialized. It wasn't a revolution, but more of a process, spurred on by risk-taking innovators, the marshalling of resources, and productive workers. The distinctive features of the mill villages that have been highlighted throughout this chapter define the "Rhode Island System of Manufacture." The great concentration of this model of industrialization with these "individually owned and operated mill villages" within a cohesive and highly developed landscape with their prominent water source can be found only here in the Blackstone River Valley.[4] The density of mill villages and the integrity of an industrial landscape that includes an agricultural component make the Blackstone River Valley the place to see and understand the industrialization of America.

NOTES

1. Donald Blake Johnson, *Upton's Heritage: The History of a Massachusetts Town* (New Canaan, N.H.: Phoenix Publishing, 1984), 129–31.

2. John S. Garner, *The Model Company Town: Urban Design through Private Enterprise in Nineteenth-Century New England* (Amherst: University Press of Massachusetts, 1984), 157–58.

3. "The Crown and Eagle Mills: A Remarkable Massachusetts Relic of the Industrial Revolution in Danger," *Boston Sunday Globe Magazine*, August 15, 1971.

4. Larry Lowenthal, "Blackstone River Valley Statement of Significance: Historical Background," Special Resource Study, Northeast Region, National Park Service, March 2008, 2–3.

"Slavery Has Lifted Up Her Voice in Our Streets"

RANGER CHUCK ARNING

The capture and forcible return to his master of runaway slave Anthony Burns may have happened in Boston three months earlier, but it was still hotly contested and discussed throughout the region. Not surprising, then, that the Worcester County Anti-Slavery Society, South Division, chose such troubled times to announce its September Anti-Slavery Bazaar, seeking "all saleable articles."[1] Earlier in the summer, the citizens of Uxbridge held a meeting to consider the recent outrages of the slave power upon the rights of the North. A similar meeting in Upton of citizens of different political parties in late June resolved:

> That the time has come for the formation of a great Northern party, whose purpose shall be to make no truce with the Slave power, until Kansas and Nebraska are rescued from the clutches of slaveholders, and restored to freedom; the infamous fugitive slave law forever repealed, and the National Government cease to be the propagandist of despotism, and become the instrument for the conservation and perpetuation of the principles of universal liberty.[2]

The citizens of Blackstone, Massachusetts, at their annual town meeting in April of 1851, voted not to enforce the fugitive slave law. Up and down the Blackstone Valley, a great unrest was brewing within the populace; their moral indignation over slavery was growing stronger, as was their voice. The above-cited announcement of the Anti-slavery Bazaar contained just such a passionate voice:

> Slavery has lifted up her voice in our streets; has met us at our doors, and they who have persisted in having her confined to the plantation, helpless for evil beyond her own borders, blindly awaiting her own destruction, have been deceived at last—Liberty is struggling as if for life; that here in New England she needs the service of every true head and heart, and hand. No time is to be wasted, no faculty spared; the air grows thick with the shadows of a coming crisis, and they who would work, must hasten while it is yet day.[3]

In Rhode Island, Elizabeth Buffum Chace used her home as a stop on the Underground Railroad, assisting fugitives to find their way to freedom in Canada. She would give each group that passed through her home instructions and a self-addressed envelope that she asked them to mail back to her upon their arrival in Canada, alerting her that they had successfully escaped "beyond the baleful influence of the Stars and Stripes."[4]

Yet it was here in the Blackstone Valley where these great contradictions resided. The economy of the mill villages—from the Draper family's Hopedale in Massachusetts to the several textile mills owned and managed by Samuel Chace, Elizabeth's husband, throughout northern Rhode Island—depended upon the southern plantation economy. The Blackstone Valley and Yankee New England as a whole was connected to the very same slave-dependent plantation system that Northerners railed against so passionately, using the cotton picked by enslaved Africans and the machinery that ran the hundreds of mills up and down the Eastern seaboard.

How could this be? The very industrialists who built and ran the mills considered themselves to be good friends of Abolitionists. Did they not see what their work involved? The Blackstone Valley remains an example of this national conflict between passionate abolitionists and their fight to end slavery versus the interests of the southern plantation economy and the northern textile mills to maintain the system that allowed New Englanders to earn their keep.

NOTES

1. *[Worcester] Massachusetts Spy,* September 6, 1854.

2. *Massachusetts Spy,* July 5, 1854.

3. *Massachusetts Spy,* September 6, 1854.

4. Elizabeth Buffum Chace and Lucy Buffum Lovell, *Two Quaker Sisters* (New York: Liveright Publishing Corporation, 1891), 128.

5 Slavery and Abolition along the Blackstone DR. SETH ROCKMAN

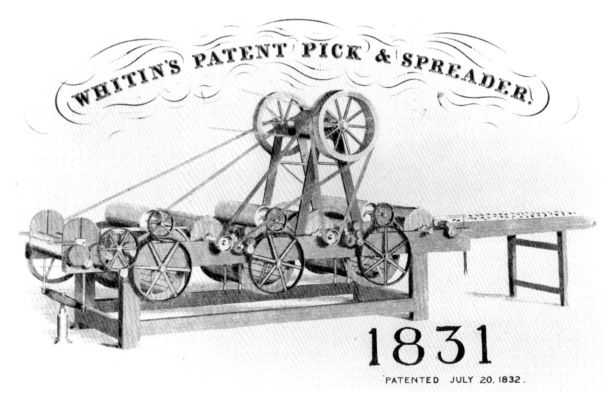

Whitin Machine Works Pick and Spreader Advertisement. Beginning with Eli Whitney and the cotton gin, New England inventors developed the machinery to prepare slave-grown cotton for manufacture in Blackstone Valley textile mills. Courtesy of the Whitinsville Social Library

Resolved, that the people of the North, as citizens and as Christians, have something to do with American slavery. —Rhode Island State Anti-Slavery Society, 1836

Cotton did not grow along the banks of the Blackstone. This unexceptional fact had enormous consequences for the region's history, tying its industrial development to the production of cotton in faraway places under a labor regime that increasing numbers of New Englanders found abhorrent. To be sure, most residents of places like Worcester and Woonsocket gave little thought to the plight of enslaved African Americans, even as their lives and livelihoods were tied together through cotton. At the same time, other Blackstone communities organized to fight against slavery, regardless of their own economic interest in maintaining cordial relations with Southern suppliers of cotton and purchasers of their machinery, tools, and textiles. No one could dispute that Blackstone residents had "something to do with American slavery," but what the delegates to the 1836 Rhode Island antislavery convention left unclear was the nature of that something: as partners in crime? as interested spectators? as agents of its destruction?[1]

Blackstone industry progressed hand-in-hand with plantation slavery in the decades following the American Revolution. How could it have been otherwise, when enslaved Africans and African Americans produced the bulk of the world's cotton supply? As textile manufacturing grew to dominate the New England economy, the plantation regime of American slavery expanded with equal haste. Louisiana, Mississippi, Alabama, Missouri, Arkansas, Florida, and Texas entered the Union just as Rhode Island and Massachusetts textile mills came to epitomize American industrial promise. These histories were inextricably linked.[2]

Ironically, textile manufacturing was intended to free New England from its involvement with slavery. Providence's Moses Brown had hoped that manufacturing would entice Rhode Island investors who might otherwise underwrite African slave-trading voyages. Noting that the Blackstone River and its tributaries offered obvious potential for mechanizing yarn production, Brown touted manufacturing as a more sound investment, both morally and economically. It was his brother John who pointed out the problem: "I can recollect no one place at present from whence the cotton can come, but from the labour of the slaves," he wrote in an acerbic 1789 letter to skewer Moses and the other leaders of the Providence Society for Promoting the Abolition of Slavery. Despite John Brown's loathsome defense of slave trading (especially during his 1800 term in Congress), his hard-nosed analysis cut to the heart of the dilemma for several subsequent generations of Blackstone entrepreneurs and reformers: Even the most altruistic and philanthropic ambitions could mire them further in the world of slavery.[3]

Scholars have long puzzled over the relationship of slavery, abolition, and industrial development. A recent focus on Northern "complicity" conveys the significant stake New Englanders held in the regime of slavery throughout the Americas.[4] Some historians, for example, have traced the capital investment in nineteenth-century manufacturing back to eighteenth-century mercantile fortunes generated in the lucrative business of provisioning Caribbean plantations with New England salt-fish and African slaves. Indeed, some of the most prominent families in Blackstone industry—the Browns, the Allens, the Arnolds—had first found their wealth in the maritime carrying trades. As John Brown had observed, the shift from commerce to manufacturing would reorient the region's relationship to slavery, but by no means end it.[5]

Other historians have suggested that Northern industry needed Southern slavery not merely for raw materials, but also to serve as an ideological foil. With labor radicals like Seth Luther decrying the exploitation of New England mill workers, the viability of the wage system depended upon its favorable comparison to slavery; after all, in a nation with actual slaves, workers who got to keep their wages—no matter how low—were relatively well-off. When striking textile workers declared their refusal to submit to "Wage Slavery," their claims often fell on the deaf ears of employers who increasingly defined wage-earning as freedom itself. Slavery proved indispensable to the rise of what nineteenth-century Northerners called "free labor."[6]

From a different perspective, historians have linked nineteenth-century industry to the rise of organized abolitionism. The values of an entrepreneurial society—efficiency, sobriety, and self-discipline—lent themselves to a critique of slaveholding as economically backward and morally indulgent. Moreover, new bourgeois values cultivated sensitivity to human suffering and fostered confidence that right-minded individuals working collectively could end long-standing social ills such as poverty, capital punishment, and slavery. Leading reformers often hailed from families and communities reaping the benefits of economic development. Elite and middle-class sensibilities, especially when coupled with religious perfectionism, could foster the moral imperative to combat slavery, racism, and all vestiges of social inequality.[7]

Abolitionism may have been a product of industrialization, but it was not the most common form of antislavery advocacy in the Blackstone region—nor anywhere in the North for that matter. Historians have shown how many opponents of slavery were openly hostile toward free people of color and scornful of the abolitionists whose social critique extended to women's oppression, marriage, and organized religion. Many Northerners saw themselves as the primary victims of the "Slave Power," especially as the expansion of plantations into arguably "free" territories like Kansas threatened the future prosperity of Northern farmers and laborers. If slavery was bad, emancipation conjured the specter of millions of freed people moving into Northern cities to rival whites for jobs. The owners of Blackstone factories had no history of hiring black workers, but operatives still resented employers who appeared more sympathetic to slaves thousands of miles away than to the plight of local laboring families. Working-class antislavery was largely hostile to African Americans, a disheartening development for free people of color, few in number but active in fighting against slavery and discrimination in Rhode Island and Massachusetts. The Blackstone region deserved its antislavery reputation, but whatever consensus emerged against the expansion of slavery into the territories fell far short of the racial egalitarianism espoused by black and white abolitionists.[8]

How then to tell the story of slavery and abolition along the Blackstone? Beyond the competing interpretations of historians, the simple facts resist easy categorization. The region purchased enough cotton to make Southern slaveholders rich, while nurturing men and women committed to slavery's abolition. The region became prosperous by producing hats, shoes, tools, and machinery for slave plantations, but also offered unrivaled support to politicians aspiring to keep plantations from spreading into the Western territories. The region witnessed the repression of its own black population, yet when local African Americans voted, they overwhelmingly supported the party of the powerful industrialist over that of the downtrodden worker. The distinct individual experiences of an Uxbridge farmwife, a Grafton shoemaker, a Worcester minister, or a free black laborer in Providence make it nearly impossible to generalize how Blackstone residents engaged slavery. Owning a textile mill did not predispose a person to defend slavery, no more than working in a textile mill promoted a sense of solidarity with slaves. Suffice it to say, the region's dependence upon *and* distance from Southern plantations reverberated in the ways that local families worked

and worshipped, as well as in the ways that they voted and socialized. Precisely because cotton did not grow there, slavery—as an engine of economic development and a spur to social reform—warrants a central place in history of the Blackstone region.

Worlds Apart

No one who toured the United States in the nineteenth century would have confused Oxford, Massachusetts, and Oxford, Mississippi. Both were small villages with adjacent farms and woodlands, but whereas the former was located in the midst of a burgeoning industrial economy, slave plantations surrounded the latter. Working families in one community made woolen textiles, while those in the other produced cotton through compulsory field labor. To all appearances, the two Oxfords were worlds apart—and not only different, but increasingly antagonistic in their customs and cultures. The Civil War confirms this popular version of American history: North and South diverged in the nineteenth century to create two separate and incompatible societies. However, this perspective overlooks the many relationships and dependencies linking the regions. Marriage, migration, and commercial connections did not collapse the differences between the two Oxfords, but they bound Northerners and Southerners, black and white, to one another in the decades between the American Revolution and the Civil War. If slavery was the obvious point of division between the two sections, it was also an institution that connected them.

Consider, for example, the career of Providence's Richard Arnold, an investor in the Blackstone Canal Company, a Brown University trustee, a founding member of the Providence Athenaeum and the Rhode Island Historical Society, and an owner of nearly two hundred Georgia slaves. Arnold spent half of each year managing his investments in Providence, and the other half at White Hall, a plantation outside Savannah. Mum Phebe, one of his slaves, shuttled between Georgia and Rhode Island annually until her death in 1841 (just a year before Rhode Island officially abolished slavery). Arnold was so efficient a rice planter that he earned the admiration of Frederick Law Olmsted in a widely read 1850s Southern travelogue. Arnold's "practical talent for organization and administration," explained Olmsted, had been "gained among the rugged fields, the complicated looms, and the exact and comprehensive counting-houses of New England."[9]

Arnold, as a northerner seeking wealth through slavery, was hardly unique. "A great number of the worthiest sons of Massachusetts, Connecticut, and Vermont have of late years pushed their fortunes to the El Dorado of cotton speculators," commented one observer of the growing Yankee population in New Orleans.[10] Arnold had married into his first parcel of slaves, but he confidently invested his own inheritance into more slaves and plantation lands in the 1820s. Arnold's path would be less noteworthy but for his storied family connections. His father was Welcome Arnold, a powerful merchant in the New England–Caribbean trade, but also a leader in the fight to end Rhode Island's involvement in the African slave trade. His mother was Patience Greene, daughter of one of the colony's wealthiest families and cousin of General Nathanael Greene, the Revolutionary War hero who also split his time between a Georgia plantation and a Rhode Island home.

The 1773 marriage of Welcome Arnold and Patience Greene consolidated landed and mercantile power in colonial Rhode Island, but the couple's four living children played key roles in the industrial transformation of the state's nineteenth-century economy. Elder daughter Mary married Tristam Burges, a zealous manufacturing advocate in Congress. Their elder son Samuel invested in numerous Blackstone enterprises and shifted the family fortune toward industry as did Richard, even as his investment capital came from the rice and cotton his Georgia slaves produced. The youngest daughter (and Richard's twin) Eliza Harriet married Zachariah Allen, an innovative textile manufacturer whose operations included the Allendale and Georgiaville mills. Notably, the wealth that Allen devoted to industry had its origins in eighteenth-century shipping and at least three trans-Atlantic slaving voyages. The remarkable family tree of intermarried Arnolds, Greenes, Burgeses, and Allens tells the story of Rhode Island's decisive shift from a maritime economy to an industrial one. However, that transformation maintained the state's economic reliance upon slavery, a fact made vivid whenever a bale of Rich-ard Arnold's cotton arrived at one of Zachariah Allen's mills.[11]

Family ties assured the intimate connection of North and South, and transplanted relatives like Richard Arnold helped shape the perception of slavery in New England through the letters they sent home. Joseph Goffe, who served as Congregational minister in Sutton (then Millbury) for nearly forty years, received telling letters from his three children in Georgia. Joseph Jr. first arrived in Savannah in 1826 in search of a teaching position, but instead found himself "entirely in the company of northern people" seeking their fortunes in cotton. Struck by Savannah's demography, the recent Amherst College student recalled the near-absence of people of African decent in Massachusetts. "You may consider yourself happy in Millbury with only one family of them," he wrote his parents. In contrast, Savannah seemed like "an Ethiopian city." Despite complaining of slaves "in the house, in my chamber, and under my nose," Joseph Jr. overcame his initial reservations when confronted with the promise of wealth in the plantation economy. By September 1828, Joseph Jr. had married a Southern woman and purchased a plantation in Alabama.[12]

During the 1840s, Maria L. Goddard Davis kept her Worcester family similarly apprised of her new life in Limestone Springs, South Carolina. She and her husband had departed Massachusetts shortly after their marriage, with James pursuing opportunities at an iron works and Maria teaching school. As Maria's letters apologized for not returning home, they also extolled the comforts of Southern living. "I think you must not think I love my Mass[achusetts] friends any less than I did when with them but I have many things here I dislike very much to leave which I cannot carry to the North with me or have if I were there," Maria explained to Ezra Goddard in 1841. "I can have chickens every meal here if I like + all kinds of fine meat killed any time with half the cost at the north now," she added, plus "I [can] have it cooked + brought to me + that is very comfortable you know when any one does not feel in a mood to get it themselves." Anticipating disapproval, Maria predicted that Goddard "will say when you read this she has turned from being an abolitionist." But when she tried to reclaim her moral standing, she dug herself a deeper hole. "I would do as much for [abolition] now as ever and think the system as great an evil," Maria offered, "Yet I think many of them are far better to be slaves than they would be were they free."[13]

Like Maria Goddard Davis, Blackstone natives in the South addressed slavery directly in their letters back to New England. Sixteen-year-old Anna Allen (daughter of Eliza Harriet Arnold and Zachariah Allen) sent her parents a detailed report of her first visit to uncle Richard Arnold's Georgia plantation in 1834. Anna was astounded at the greeting she received from the slaves when her carriage arrived at White Hall: "The negroes came to meet us running and tumbling over the fields as if deranged—shouting and screaming how do massa—Oh my dear Fader + Moder my good misses how glad I is to see dis day." Slavery appeared less objectionable than Anna's New England education had led her to believe. "I only wished that an abolitionist was present that I might see the effect produced," she proclaimed. "He could not, I am sure, wish to change the situation of these poor but happy people."[14]

Uxbridge-born Lucretia Sibley heard a similar message from her cousin Mary Ann Waterman in Virginia. Indeed, Waterman had found a local man for the widowed Sibley to marry, provided she would leave Providence for the South. "I suppose this thing of slavery will rise up a mighty bug bear, to fright you from a comfortable home," Waterman conceded. "But it need not," she continued, as "[y]ou had no hand in bringing them into a state of bondage, and if you consent to place yourself in a situation to make their lives more comfortable and pleasant I cannot see that you will be doing wrong." To the contrary, slavery helped complete God's work by bringing the gospel to people of African descent. Sibley was not convinced and responded by subscribing her cousin to a number of abolitionist periodicals. "I know you thought I needed a lesson on the horrors of slavery," Waterman replied unappreciatively. Letters from Waterman and another cousin in Tennessee made slavery something more than an abstraction for New Englanders like Sibley.[15]

As family ties sustained relations between North and South, so too did institutional and commercial connections. From its founding as the College of Rhode Island in 1764, Brown University trained gener-ations of the nation's Baptist clergy. South Carolinians contributed generously to the school's initial endowment, and prominent planters like Virginia's Robert Carter sent their sons to Rhode Island to be educated. In return, Brown University furnished the South with a parade of ministers and university administrators: president Jonathan Maxcy assumed the helm of the new University of South Carolina in 1804; natural philosopher Jasper Adams departed Brown for the presidency of the College of Charleston in 1824; math professor Alva Woods served as the president of University of Alabama during the 1830s. Brown University's expanding influence on the Southern educational system owed to the popularity of Francis Wayland's *Elements of Moral Science*, a widely assigned textbook of moral philosophy. The president of Brown University from 1827 until 1855, Wayland hoped to see slavery ended, but believed that radical abolitionists jeopardized the prospect of peaceful emancipation and the future of the union.[16]

Business relationships cemented the bond between the Blackstone region and the American South. South Carolina's David Rogerson Williams attended Brown in the 1790s, won the hand of Providence's Sarah Power (daughter of Nicholas) in marriage, and learned enough about manufacturing in Rhode Island to start one of the South's first cotton-yarn manufactories in 1812. As his political career carried him to the South Carolina governorship, Williams convinced his old Brown roommate Abram Blanding to move South and serve as superintendent of the state's public works.[17] Other New Englanders took up residence in the South at the behest of their Northern employers. When he was twenty-two years old, Uxbridge-born Orray Taft set out for Savannah in 1815 to procure cotton for Rhode Island mills. Upon his return to Providence in 1829, Taft became a leading investor in Blackstone mills and ultimately served as president of the Providence & Worcester Railroad. John Waterman had a similar experience as the New Orleans purchasing agent for the Blackstone Manufacturing Company during the 1820s. Already famous in Providence for experimenting with merino wool during the War of 1812, Waterman returned from the South ready to invest his capital in new steam-powered cotton machinery.[18]

The federal government's 1832 survey of American manufacturing revealed the Blackstone region's enormous appetite for Southern cotton. The five textile manufactories in Mendon consumed nearly one million pounds of New Orleans cotton annually. The Crown and Eagle Mills in Uxbridge imported 240,000 pounds of cotton from South Carolina's Sea Islands each year, while the Douglas Manufacturing Company purchased almost as much from suppliers in Georgia. Just to make candlewicks in North Providence, Stephen Randal, Jr.'s mill required six hundred pounds of cotton each week.[19]

In turn, the 1832 survey only began to document the importance of Southern markets to Blackstone manufacturers. "Hoes for plantation cultivation, shoes, coarse cottons and woollens, wool hats, paper, and some other articles, find a market in the slave-holding States," explained Bezaleel Taft, Jr., of Uxbridge.[20] The four "sale boot and shoes" enterprises in Leicester produced footwear for slaves, while Millbury's Amasa Wood manufactured fancy shoes for their owners. Seven thousand palm-leaf hats woven in Worcester reached Southern markets annually. However, the 1832 survey obscured Southern consumption of Blackstone textiles and shoes, insofar as most manufacturers listed commission merchants in Boston, New York, and Philadelphia as their primary customers. Southern purchasers typically provisioned their plantations through these urban commission merchants, rather than dealing with the manufacturers themselves.

Blackstone manufacturers found a particular niche in "negro cloth," a generic category of textiles—sometimes woolen, sometimes cotton, sometimes mixed—intended for slave use. Usually distinguished by its coarse texture, "negro cloth" might also bear a distinctive striped or plaid pattern, as well as a bright hue. Whether slaveholders were hoping to make slaves easily recognizable in the visual landscape of the South, to degrade their laborers with outlandish clothing, or merely to protect their work force from the elements, Blackstone manufacturers were eager to supply this growing market. Simon Darling of Douglas produced woolens for the Peace Dale Manufacturing Company, the southern Rhode Island firm with the most extensive distribution network in the plantation states.

When Frederick Law Olmsted toured the plantation South in the 1850s, he observed slave clothing was "mostly made, especially for this purpose, in Providence, R.I." Slaveholders typically distributed clothing (or cloth to be assembled into clothing) twice a year, and their patriarchal aspirations required them to take the matter seriously; but as shrewd businessmen, they also sought to keep their expenditures to a minimum. Former slaves had few kind words for the uncomfortable fabric their owners purchased from New England. Nor was there any enthusiasm for the inferior leather shoes and boots—usually called brogans—manufactured in Massachusetts. Tyler and Ezra Batcheller operated one of the state's largest slave footwear enterprises in North Brookfield, and their carts conveyed cases of shoes to Providence for shipment to the South.[21]

Plantation provisions comprised a leading export from the Blackstone region. In addition to textiles, brogans, and palm-leaf hats, Massachusetts-made farm implements gained many Southern customers. Ebenezer Goffe advised his brother Joseph to have plantation tools shipped to Alabama from Millbury, where forges owned by the Waters family turned out hoe and axe blades through the 1820s. Not long after, the Worcester firm of Ruggles, Nourse, Mason & Co. established a reputation as a dependable producer of plows and other farm implements for the South. Their 1849 catalog touted "an admirable plow for the rich lands on the Mississippi," a rice-trenching plow that "will be found a great labor-saving implement for the South," and a number of planters, sweeps, and gins designed specifically for cotton and sugar cultivation. After visiting several Northern manufactories producing plows "made of inferior metal and materials," a Charleston editor declared Ruggles, Nourse, Mason & Co. far superior to their competition. We "have every reason to be satisfied that the castings were very superior to those usually sent out to the South," he reported after getting a personal tour from Joel Nourse and Draper Ruggles.[22] It is unclear whether the firearms produced in Millbury by Asa Waters & Sons gained a similar following in the South, where guns played a prominent role in the policing of runaway slaves and suppression of slave insurrections. Business was substantial enough for Asa H. Waters to accuse a South

Ruggles, Nourse & Mason Farm Equipment Advertisement. New England manufacturers marketed plows, shovels, and hoes to slaveholders. Were tools "especially adapted to slaves" of more durable construction than those intended for free workers, or simply more cheaply assembled? From the collections of Worcester Historical Museum, Worcester, MA

Carolina firm in 1853 of "cherishing very unfriendly feelings toward us and [having] done what you could [to] prejudice us in the minds of our partners at the South."[23]

Blackstone manufacturers of spinning machinery helped jump-start the emerging Southern textile industry, beginning with the picker that John Whitin developed for cleaning cotton in South Northbridge—soon to be renamed Whitinsville after his father Paul in 1835. P. Whitin & Sons produced drawing frames, railway-heads, and a distinctive ring-spindle for a number of South Carolina enterprises, including the Batesville Cotton Factory started by Pawtucket-born William Bates. Having first visited New England in 1844, William Gregg, a leading advocate of Southern economic diversification, wrote to Whitinsville to recruit managers for his textile factory at Graniteville. For several months after South Carolina seceded from the Union, Gregg continued to place orders with P. Whitin & Sons. Even as Gregg denounced Abraham Lincoln's "Black republican party," he lobbied the Confederate government to permit the duty-free importation of New England machinery.[24]

In contrast to the large textile firms in Lawrence and Lowell, the manufacturers of the Blackstone region expressed little anxiety over technology transfer to Southern competitors. Local manufacturers shared know-how with David Rogerson Williams and William Gregg, despite the goal of Southern entrepreneurs to free their region from dependence on the North. When Isaac P. Hazard invited a young entrepreneur from Georgia to spend a season in the North in 1845, he proposed a visit to Lonsdale to "become thoroughly acquainted with the business." Even more welcoming was Rhode Island's Charles Tillinghast James, who shortly before becoming a U.S. Senator in 1851, offered "practical hints" to aspiring Southern manufacturers. "The south produces the raw material for the cotton mill in abundance—she has but to say the word, and labor and skill will readily offer themselves to convert it into cloth on the spot," he chided. The South could "become the greatest seat of cotton manufactures in the world."[25]

Boasting of his extensive experience—"I have constructed, either in whole, or in part, between twenty and thirty cotton factories, and put in operation be-

tween two and three hundred thousand spindles"—James declared plantations far less profitable than factories:

> Would the northern climate admit of the culture of cotton, and had a Yankee, in either of the New England states, a cotton plantation, with all the requisites for the prosecution of the business, the moment he found he could make more money by the manufacture of that article than by its production, it would be farewell to cotton growing; and the next thing you would hear on his premises, in the way of business, would be the clatter of the loom and the hum of the spindle.[26]

Presenting this hypothetical choice in 1849, James might have reflected on the economic transformation of the Blackstone region over the several previous decades. For young men in the 1810s and 1820s, greener pastures beckoned to the south, and with good reason. When North Brookfield minister Thomas Snell reflected on the state of his community during the early years of the century, he recalled that "the people in this town, with a very few exceptions, were farmers, and were making next to no progress in anything profitable. . . . There were many poor families—poor houses—and poorly furnished." Yet by 1850, North Brookfield had become a "flourishing village with a busy population," the kind of place that no longer lost its ambitious youth to the cotton frontier.[27]

What accounted for the change? It was not because, given the choice, New Englanders had picked factories over plantations. To the contrary, they intensified their relationship with the American plantation regime in the same years that industrial production propelled small places in Massachusetts and Rhode Island to new levels of affluence. North Brookfield's prosperity, pointed out Snell, owed to the profitable manufacture of slave shoes; its fortunes rose with the expansion of plantation slavery several thousand miles away. Likewise for the Blackstone textile industry that Charles James did so much to develop. Although he posited cotton factories and cotton plantations as opposing enterprises, it was pointless to imagine one without the other. Perhaps New England's cool climate spared Blackstone entrepreneurs from having to grow their own cotton, but the resulting geographical separation of the factory and the plantation in no way negated their intimate connection.

Antislavery

Nothing in Charles T. James's counterfactual scenario suggested a consideration other than monetary profit. His imagined Yankee would abandon the plantation for the factory in pursuit of economic gain, not from revulsion over what James called "the requisites for the prosecution of the business"—namely, a captive population of enslaved workers. James was correct not to overstate the antislavery credentials of Blackstone manufacturers, many of whom organized to restrict abolitionists' legal right to file petitions and deliver public addresses. In 1835, an assemblage of Providence's leading men had denounced abolitionists as "dangerous to the existing relations of friendship and of business between different sections of our country."[28] Still, something remarkable had already happened: A growing number of Blackstone residents began to hear the cracking of the slave driver's whip amidst the whirl of the factory's machinery.

Local opposition to slavery did not wait for the industrialization of the Blackstone region. Long before textile milling, Rhode Island and Massachusetts clergy had questioned the legitimacy of human bondage, Quaker testimony became increasingly antislavery, and enslaved men and women petitioned for general emancipation and stood as plaintiffs in the court cases that abolished slavery in Massachusetts. Following the passage of Rhode Island's gradual emancipation act of 1784, Moses Brown and other Quaker merchants founded the Providence Society for Promoting the Abolition of Slavery, for the Relief of Persons unlawfully held in Bondage, and for Improving the Condition of the African Race. The group aided freedom suits, attempted to prosecute Moses's brother John for illegal slave trading, and watched in pride as James Tallmadge, a graduating senior at Brown University, delivered a scathing antislavery commencement address in 1798. After denouncing the Atlantic slave trade as "repugnant to the laws of God," the future Congressman dismissed the absurd belief that "one who was formed with a dark complexion is inferior to him, who possesses a complexion more light."[29]

Although few in number and scattered across a predominately rural landscape, black men and women struggled to break the shackles of slavery and to carve out a meaningful freedom in Blackstone communities. Outside of Providence, slaveholding had been relatively uncommon. A 1754 census located seven slaves in Uxbridge, six in Leicester, and eighty-eight in all of Worcester County. In 1800, fewer than five hundred free people of color resided among the sixty-one thousand residents of Worcester County. People of African descent were similarly scarce in places like Gloucester, Rhode Island, where a 1774 census found nineteen black people living among three thousand whites.[30] Providence's black population was substantially larger, especially as the newly free migrated from the countryside. Providence's free people of color nearly doubled in number between 1790 and 1810, soon totaling 9 percent of the city's population. Excluded from many jobs, relegated to poor housing, and as of 1822, legally disfranchised from voting, free people of color nonetheless sought to build community institutions and to lay claim to public space in celebrations and parades. They raised $500 in 1819 to construct the African Union Meeting House, and when the structure was finished two years later, an African-American militia company in full regalia escorted civic leaders—both black and white—through the streets of the East Side to the building's dedication.[31]

The politics of race in the Blackstone region were oppressive insofar as people of African ancestry were disfranchised in Rhode Island, denied jobs in new mill communities, and left vulnerable to collective violence at the hands of angry whites. Events like the 1806 beating of Samuel Shoemaker at an Uxbridge election picnic or the demolition of black-owned homes on Providence's Olney Street in 1831 revealed the limits of freedom. Anyone heartened by Senator James Burrill's staunch opposition to the admission of Missouri as slave state in 1819 might soon despair over Rhode Island's choice of his successor: James DeWolfe, a notorious slave-ship captain. To many observers, so long as slaveholding was legal in much of the country, the prospects for free people of color would remain grim. The notion of relocating blacks outside the United States gained traction among philanthropic whites, including members of the Providence Society for Promotion the Abolition of Slavery who donated money to the American Colonization Society. Nicholas Brown, Jr., pledged $1,000 in hopes of sending free people of color to Liberia, and a small contingent of black Rhode Islanders sailed away in 1826. Although Moses Brown decried colonization as "a species of delusion," it remained far more popular than abolitionism among whites opposed to slavery.[32]

The threat of colonization galvanized free blacks throughout the North to organize against forced exile. African-American leaders denounced colonization as a scheme predicated on the presumed incapacity of black people for citizenship. "Did not the same Almighty God make me that made you?" asked Worcester barber Henry Scott of his white neighbors. However, not all black New Englanders denied the prospect of a better future elsewhere. Two Providence men, George C. Willis and Alfred Niger, traveled to Philadelphia in 1830 to attend the first meeting of the American Society of Free Persons of Colour, for Improving their Condition in the United States, for Purchasing Lands, and for the Establishment of a Settlement in Upper Canada. The delegates were eager to live in a society where "no invidious distinction of color is recognized." Insofar as the United States denied them their promises of the Declaration of Independence, men like Willis and Niger stood only to gain by becoming British subjects "entitled to all the rights, privileges, and immunities of other citizens." Niger, a barber with two young daughters, remained active in the organization, co-authoring the group's 1835 annual address. A Canadian settlement never became viable, but Niger continued to press for his rights. When Rhode Island instituted a property tax to fund public schools that barred his children, Niger petitioned for an abatement—or else "permission to exercise suffrage and enjoy advantage of free schools." The state exempted all black people from property taxes in 1841, but it was a pyrrhic victory, further removing people of color from citizenship.[33]

The best-known phase of American abolitionism began in 1831, when William Lloyd Garrison launched his newspaper *The Liberator* and gathered like-minded men and women first into the New England Anti-slavery Society and then into the American Anti-slavery Society. Arthur Buffum, a Quaker from Smithfield, spearheaded efforts in the Blackstone re-gion. Buffum was one of the twelve founding members of the New England Anti-slavery Society, affixing his name to a remarkable declaration of principles in favor of "equal civil and political rights" for people of color. "We believe, that every colored person, who is either born in this country, or forced to make this the place of his residence, is as really an American, as any white-born citizen of New-England," read the group's constitution. Buffum lectured in Providence, Pawtucket, Smithfield, Blackstone, Woonsocket, Slatersville, Uxbridge, and elsewhere in the summer of 1832; Garrison spoke in Worcester and Providence that fall. The Free Will Baptist minister Ray Potter proved the most dynamic speaker in the region and organized a Pawtucket Anti-Slavery Society in 1834.[34]

The next several years witnessed a flurry of abolitionist lecturing throughout the Blackstone region. Potter energized audiences in Sutton, Millbury, and Uxbridge, while famed English abolitionists Charles Stuart and George Thompson lectured to free people of color in Pawtucket and in Providence's African Union Meeting House. George C. Willis and other African-American leaders published a note of thanks to Thompson "for your labour of love in our behalf." As Henry B. Stanton and others crisscrossed Rhode Island in 1835 and 1836, the abolitionist message came to places like Chepachet and Woonsocket. Women filled many audiences, raised funds to distribute antislavery tracts, and founded the Providence Ladies Anti-Slavery Society in 1835. When the nonagenarian Moses Brown died the following year, the profile of Blackstone abolitionists looked quite different than it did in the heyday of his antislavery activism in the 1780s and 1790s. The leading men were not merchants, but now mechanics, artisans, and shopkeepers who were also active in temperance, the peace movement, and health reform. When their organizational efforts flagged, women picked up the slack and kept the cause alive through networks of friendship, family, and religious observance. Free people of color joined white allies in common cause, but also founded organizations of their own such as the General Colored Association of Worcester.[35]

Time and again, abolitionists declared people of African descent—free and enslaved—to be full and equal citizens denied fundamental rights under the Declaration of Independence and the Bible. A foundational belief that "God hath made of one blood all nations of men for to dwell on the face of the earth" conveyed the abolitionists' radical egalitarianism, and perhaps explains why they met such a hostile response throughout New England. Abolitionist views on matters other than slavery exacerbated hostile public perceptions of the movement. Women's involvement in organizational activities confounded prevailing gender norms, so that when someone like Worcester's Abby Kelley Foster took the podium alongside Frederick Douglass or Wendell Phillips, many observers were scandalized by what they called "promiscuous mixing" of the sexes. A commitment to challenging all unequal relations of power propelled many abolitionists to question traditional conventions of marriage and childrearing, not to mention the relationship of clergy and parishioners. Some abolitionists established unorthodox communal living arrangements, such as the Transcendentalist-inspired Holly Home farm in North Providence. Perplexing even to other abolitionists was the communitarian experiment at Hopedale, where Adin Ballou and his followers put "non-resistance" principles into practice. Their reading of scripture required disengagement from electoral politics, even as their community welcomed abolitionist speakers and gained a reputation as a stop on the Underground Railroad.[36]

The anti-clericalism of Garrison and his followers in the 1830s placed sympathetic Massachusetts ministers in a bind. When the state's Congregational ministers convened in North Brookfield in 1837, for example, they denounced women's participation in the abolition movement. Worcester County ministers sought to clarify their position on slavery, and an interdenominational clerical meeting in early 1838 declared slavery "utterly irreconcilable" with Christianity. Some fifty-eight ministers denounced "the reducing of a rational being to the condition of a thing, an article of merchandise, a machine of labor, to be bought, sold, held, and used at the will of and for the benefit of another." Although the gathering conceded that only slaveholders could end slavery, several dissenting ministers feared that the clergy would jeopardize its status by engaging so political an issue. The premise that ministers ought "not touch a great moral

and social evil" so infuriated Leicester's Samuel May that he soon delivered a fiery sermon from Isaiah on the obligation to "set the oppressed free and break every yoke."[37]

Abolitionists' racial egalitarianism also ran into trouble in the heated context of constitutional reform in 1840s Rhode Island. By its still-operative colonial charter, the state was one of the last in the North to enforce substantial property requirements on the franchise. In 1841, a People's Convention nominated Thomas Dorr for the governorship on a platform of "democratizing" political reforms that nonetheless reasserted a ban on African-American suffrage. Dorr, who had spent the 1830s trying to pass abolitionist resolutions in the state legislature, urged his followers to abandon their commitment to white-only voting, but they refused. Dorr ultimately accepted their nomination, and when the normal electoral process broke down in 1842, he became the head of a shadow state government. The traditional state leadership coalesced under the auspices of the Law & Order party and called up the state militia to suppress Dorr's uprising. They also enlisted several hundred black men from Providence to form a company and confront Dorr in Chepachet. At first glance, people of color had little incentive to fight for the established political order; but the Dorrites' exclusion of blacks from their "People's Constitution" made them deserving adversaries. Moreover, the Law & Order party promised modest constitutional reforms, including a new emancipation law (to free the handful of people still enslaved by the gradual emancipation act of 1784) and a revised property requirement that would enfranchise middle-class African Americans but not working-class whites. The alliances formed in the heat of the "Dorr War" estranged logical antislavery constituencies from one another, allying free people of color with the wealthiest and least-democratic elements of the state (including slaveholder Richard Arnold) under the banner of the Whig Party, and at the same time fostering lasting hostility toward black people among the largely working-class constituency of the Democratic Party.[38]

Although radical abolitionists positioned themselves outside electioneering, the 1840s witnessed the arrival of slavery in national politics. Worcester County emerged as the center of political antislavery in Mas-

THE NON-RESISTANT AND PRACTICAL CHRISTIAN.

☞ Absolute Truth, Essential Righteousness, Individual Responsibility, Social Reform, Human Progress, Ultimate Perfection. ☜

VOL. IX.   HOPEDALE COMMUNITY, MILFORD, MASS. SATURDAY, MAY 27, 1848.   NO. 2.

THE NON-RESISTANT AND PRACTICAL CHRISTIAN
Is published every other Saturday, at One Dollar per annum, payable in advance. Persons responsible for six copies receive the seventh gratis.

ADIN BALLOU,
EDITOR AND PROPRIETOR.

☞ All letters, remittances and communications to be addressed (post paid) to the EDITOR, Milford, (Hopedale) Mass.

A. A. BALLOU, PRINTER.

We love all, but can flatter none. Therefore we solicit no person to subscribe who is not willing we should utter all our moral convictions as freely as the winds blow and the waters run. To all such, 'of whatever name or persuasion, we make our respectful salutation, and would say—'' Come and see if any good thing can come out of Nazareth.''

BELIAL'S CORNER.

Quit the principle, or be content with the results.

Sayres, English and Drayton.

These are the three men who helped off the 77 slaves from Washington a short time since. When brought back to the city after their capture, the pro-slavery mob like furies incarnate, were ready to rend them in pieces. Many people are anxious to know something more about them and their treatment in the metropolis of slave-holding republicanism. The following from the Cleve-

are Northern men, report in favor of the payment! And this is but one solitary case out of one hundred and eighty, in which the Marshal asks pay.

IN THEIR ACCOUNT of the capture of Vera Cruz, the Mexicans say:—"Days and dark nights passed, and the enemy did not approach our walls; remaining concealed behind his works, and selecting, as was most agreeable to him, and most in accordance with his character, the barbarous manner of assassinating the unoffending and defenceless citizens by a barbarous bombardment of the city in the most horrible manner, directing his first shots to the powder magazine, to the quarter of hospitals of charity, to the hospitals for wounded, and to the points he set on fire, where it was believed the public authorities would assemble with persons to put it out, to the baker's houses, designated by their chimneys, and during the night raining over the entire city bombs whose height was perfectly graduated with the time of explosion, that they might unite in falling, and thus cause the maximum destruction. Such infamous proceedings indicated from the first day, the cowardice of the enemy. His first victims were women and children, followed by whole families perishing from the effects of the explosion, under the ruins of their dwellings. In a short time the hospitals were crowded with the wounded, the dead being simultaneously buried. The bombs entered the walls of the church of Santo Domingo, killing the unfortunate wounded, frightening away the nurses and doctors, who, after arriving with haste and risk at the church of San Francisco, and the chapel of the third order, encountered the same dismal fate, as well as at the hospitals of Belen and Loretto, where it is well ascertained, one bomb assassinated 19 innocent persons. In all quarters perished unfortu-

testimonials of their religious character, to help the sale in Georgia. I understand he was accustomed to preach to them here, and especially to urge upon them an obedience to their masters.

Some of the colored people outside, as well as in the car, were weeping most bitterly. I learned that many families were separated. Wives were there to take leave of their husbands, and husbands of their wives, children of their parents, brothers and sisters shaking hands, perhaps for the last time, friends parting with friends, and the tenderest ties of humanity sundered at a single bid of the inhuman slave broker before them. A husband in the meridian of life begged to see the partner of his bosom. He protested that she was free—that she had free papers, and was " torn away from the windows of the jail to see his wife, and as she was reaching forward her hand to him the black-hearted villain Slatter, ordered him down; he did not obey. The husband and wife, with tears streaming down their cheeks, besought him to let them converse for a moment. But no! a monster more hideous, hardened, and savage, than the blackest spirit of the pit, knocked him down from the car and ordered him away. The bystanders could hardly restrain themselves from laying violent hands upon the brute. This is but a faint description of that scene, which took place within a few rods of the Capitol and under enactments recognized by Congress. Oh! what a revolting scene to a feeling heart, and what a retribution awaits the actors. Will not these wailings of anguish reach the ears of the Most High? " Vengeance is mine ; I will repay saith the Lord."—*Washington Corespondence of the Boston Whig.*

Downingtown, April, 19, 1848.

free to discuss all questions that pertain to the welfare of human beings. He seems to think the pulpit is for man, and not man for the pulpit. The pulpit has no value except as an instrument to benefit man, and derives its sole importance from its adaptation to this end. This evening, at 5 1-2 o'-clock, I lectured in the Unitarian meeting-house in the centre village of Norton. Several in this meeting have their eyes open to the evils and murder of war. I am most happy to find some 15 or 20 numbers of the Non-Resistant taken in this town and read. Indeed I believe that paper is *read* wherever it is taken. I ask, what can be done to extend the circulation of that paper? We have talked over, also, the importance of raising a *Tract* fund. Lectures, without tracts and papers, lose half their usefulness. If 2000 subscribers could be had to the Non-Resistant, it could be published weekly, could it not?—2000 *paying* subscribers. This is the only paper in the land that takes the strong ground of Non-Resistance, in its application to governments of violence and blood. This is the great question—the Thermopylæ of the anti-war agitation. Cannot subscribers be obtained? Cannot the friends of peace and order, of Christianity and Humanity, sustain it as a weekly paper? Then, during the pending presidential election, tens of thousands of tracts might be *sold* at a cheap rate, if friends in different localities would send in and get them, and sell them to their neighbors. Every Non-Resistant should be a tract distributor.

Broadway Tabernacle, New York, Tuesday,
11 o'clock, A. M. May 9, 1848.

Hopedale's *Non-Resistant and Practical Christian* 1848 Masthead. Newspapers linked abolitionists throughout New England, New York, and the Midwest. Adin Ballou's *Non-Resistant and Practical Christian* represented Hopedale's radical communitarian experiment. Courtesy American Antiquarian Society

sachusetts, characterized by the willingness of its residents to sign petitions against slave auctions in Washington, D.C., or the annexation of Texas. Nowhere did Massachusetts voters offer more support to the Liberty Party than in Worcester County, albeit at a rate of only 14 percent in the 1844 presidential election. Four years later, the Free Soil ticket drew its strongest Massachusetts support from Worcester County, but its platform of protecting Western lands from the expansion of slavery was a far cry from the abolitionist commitment to immediate emancipation and equal citizenship rights for people of color. At the end of the decade, Blackstone voters helped propel an antislavery coalition to power in the state legislature. The Free Democracy convention met in Worcester in September 1849, and standing against the Compromise of 1850, the fusion party gained enough seats to choose Massachusetts's new Senator: Charles Sumner.[39]

If any one event helped shift Blackstone residents to a position against slavery, it was the passage of a

GOVERNOR KING'S EXTRA.

DEDICATED TO HIS EXCELLENCY WITHOUT PERMISSION.

Phantasmagoria
OF THE
RHODE ISLAND WAR!
Drawn from "Nature."

Cum sound de loud strumpet, and blow de sweet bugle,
An tune de soft banjo to glorious war,
Massa Gubner King has got us to fugle,
An gibben de fair sex to our lubbin care—
He took down on us from hit hi king-ly station,
His court friends in peace, an his life guard in war,
An we swear we will g'aard de fair part ob creation,
Til our king he cum back wid full many a scar.
Song of King's Troops.

When drawn up in battle array, and all "eyes right," the King mounted a gin cask, and, by a set speech proceeded to infuse into them some of his own martial spirit and invincible courage, to say nothing of copious doses of patriotism, &c.;

'Fellow-citizen-soldiers—Once more has the iron tocsin of war rung like thunder through our hills and vallies and hemlock swamps—once more have you left your hearth-stones, your corn-fields and tater patches, armed for the fight, to pour out your red gore for "law -and-order," like true and loyal spirits. [talking of spirits puts me in mind that I am almighty dry, so just pass along that mug of punch.] We must toe the scratch and not be afeared. These times is trying—times that will try your soles—(though I perceive that most of you are barefoot)—if you don't stand by me and fight like the d—l for your King and the old Charter. [Cheers and hiccups, and a bomb shell thrown.] Fellow sogers and them 'ar sea-fencibles over there, a-liquoring—remember that the price of vigilence is eternal liberty, whether or no ; and if you'll only lead where I'll follow, I have only to say that "them pistols" of mine shall tell a bloody tale in the field, and make them 'ar rapscallion Dorrites rue the day when they bearded me, and cause their blessed wives and sweet-hearts to weep like gun trees in autumn time—I will. [Tremendous cheering and calls for more liquor.] And, follow-citizen sogers, [pass along that mug, again] don't forget that "law-and-order" is on our side, which will justify us in firing our shooting irons into that hot-bed of rebellion at Chepachet, where, I trust, you will soon be

"King's Troops Assembled."

Immediately, tracks, both thick an' fast, were being made in the direction of the "inimy !" encampment. The drums did rattle, the war-horns blew, and the valient army regaled itself on the long march through swamps and 'severe weather,' with patriotic songs and copious draughts of brandy cocktail, expressly for the occasion. But as the distance shortened, the "fluid" they had inhaled, began to ooze freely—hearts palpitated—'long drawn' and anxious glances were cast behind—and their nether limbs shook like bean-poles in a December blast! Nearer and nearer they approach, when, lo ! and behold ! the bird had flown—the camp was evacuated ! Then, quicker than thought, the thermometer of courage in the breasts of the King's invincibles, arose to boiling heat, and, dead or alive, they would have "Dorr and that sword," if they had to navigate a sea of human blood! Just then one of the 'people' was descried, who immediately blazed away at their ranks and seriously damaged a private's cartridge-box and the rear skirt of his tunic; but the sharp-shooters soon made him

Going to fight the rascals !

But where is Dorr ? alas, he had again vanished ! and his troops were off like a leaf on the north wind, no one knew whither. King's invincibles determined not to be thwarted in this manner, however ; and some immediately started in hot pursuit of the fugitive chieftain. One of the pursuers, it is reported, more fortunate than the rest, descried Dorr making "clean heels" for Connecticut, and came up with him as his valiency was in the act of scaling a garden wall, when, pouncing upon him, like a hawk upon a June bug, he succeeded in detaining him until some of his coadjutors came up ; but, anticipating

SAMUEL WARD KING, Ex-officio, and non-Ex-officio, probably the biggest mountain of dignity, valor, bravery, courage, and gubernatorial authority, that at present looms up against the heaven of recent events, —not even excepting his redoubtable adversary, the "claw" &c.—having been apprised of the "contracting opposition" against his rule, in Chepachet and elsewhere, which would be down upon his Excellency and Council in Providence Plantations sooner or later, if not before, like a shower of brick upon a field of rotten punkins, forthwith ordered his tall boots brushed, his nag equipped, and "them pistols" secured ; then, after scattering a squad of his loyal bravos around on the outer line of his King-dom, to keep foreign foes from meddling with his "law-and-order," a tattoo was thumped upon the kettle-drum, whereat, by scores and fifties

These 'skirmacrages' being performed, the noble bandier called his gallant troops around him—applauded them for their daring deeds of valor—told them how much better it was to make war upon a deserted and defenseless village, than to meet a desperate foe—talked to them of traitors, and of patriots—implored them ever to cherish a due respect for the King-ly government ; and, finally, said he, (having become much excited) you have bravely stormed the citadel of the rebel chief (containing five defenseless women)—killed one man (pointing with an air of triumph to the mangled corpse that lay beside him)—wounded one, and protected your neighbors' "hen-roosts" and punkin patches, from these merciless desperados ; and now, after rendering you my grateful acknowledgments for the respect you have shown me ,in your prompt adherence to my orders during your recent campaign of privation and suffering, you may go home to your anxious mamas, bearing LAURELS fresh from the field of FAME and GLORY.

Reports of the brilliant victory achieved by King's arms were immediately made out and sent post haste to the Head Quarters at Providence by the

Despatch Bearers.

Food for Powder.

What was to be done now ? Return home again ! And accordingly, home they went ;—the invincible army of the King marched up the hill and then marched down again. His Excellency, the commander-in-chief of Providence Plantations, &c., eulogized them with the most flowery epithets for their unswerving loyalty, as well as their conduct and bravery in the fields of Chepachet and vicinity ; said he challenged the world to produce troops their superiors, but he said it could not be done, if it could he wished he might be busted, or teetotally chawed up &c &c.— After having freed himself from his over-load of patriotism and love of his country, and more particularly, his loyal subjects, he told his victory-flushed army that the present soul-stirring occasion had untied his purse-strings, and that a sumptuous banquet, prepared expressly for them, at his own expense, was now patiently waiting their pleasure. And there, forsooth, we find

The Providence City Guards celebrating their Victory over the Dorrites.

His Excellency, the King, then repaired forthwith to Head Quarters, to ascertain the amount of

Damages Received.

The $5,000 Reward
which the King had offered, rather too strongly, Dorr leapt the wall, (positively for the last time,) and once more escaped through the treachery of his coat tail !

A Foraging Expedition,
Chartered by SAMUEL WARD (the) KING.

Three Jolly 'Soap Locks'
—Three Hired Ass-ass-ins, who for their deeds of chivalry would have been renowned, in the marvelous days of knight-errantry, after coursing their lances and breaking those of their enemies, set out for their homes, thus discoursing on their way :

We, the bold spirits of the land,
Return with stars ; and crown'd with glory,
The Fair will give us heart and hand,
'Posterity will tell our story.'

They thus trudged on in safety, till they discovered the smoke from their native city curling in the breeze, above the towering forest, that now shed their homes from view. Elated with success—with thoughts of home and friends, and above all, with their King-ly companion, (Alchohol) who had, during the day, inspired them with new hopes, and more exciting prospects, they pushed on with hurried pace, when, unconscious of their steps, they were suddenly precipitated from the banks of the rolling Providence. Noble Fellows !

Their day of toil is o'er—
Their day of Wondrous Valor, too,
They strangle with the water tide,
And sink to rise no more.

Peace is again within the Kings dominions ; and the sterile desert, and the barren rock, are, by the royal edict proclaimed, again as sacred. But lo ! the CHIEF-TAIN of the People's Band—IS VANQUISHED.

Pursued by hounds, more greedy far,
Then those of foreign climes,
He shoots the Rail-way's rolling car,
And hopes to cross the lines
Of Hampshire's noble State, where,
Floats pure freedom's air.

'But,' says King, 'I'll haunt him, even there,
'Tho' earth and Heaven oppose ;
'And, as my gallant troops shall hunt
'His secret hiding place,
'I'll stand upon this sacred spot,

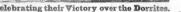

'This halter in my hand.'
And, when he shall have suffered, Haman like, upon the gallows he erected for the destruction of my King-ly authority, I will cast him out, as SPORT for CARRION CROWS and BIRDS OF PREY.

PRICE, TWENTY-FIVE CENTS.

THE
BOSTON SLAVE RIOT,
AND
TRIAL
OF
Anthony Burns,

CONTAINING THE
REPORT OF THE FANEUIL HALL MEETING; THE MURDER OF
BACHELDER; THEODORE PARKER'S LESSON FOR THE DAY;
SPEECHES OF COUNSEL ON BOTH SIDES, CORRECTED
BY THEMSELVES; VERBATIM REPORT OF JUDGE
LORING'S DECISION; AND, A DETAILED AC-
COUNT OF THE EMBARKATION.

BOSTON:
FETRIDGE AND COMPANY.
1854.

Press of J. S. Potter & Co., 2 Spring Lane and 130 Washington Street.

Anthony Burns Book. The 1854 extradition of Anthony Burns alerted many white Northerners to their obligation to defend slavery under the provisions of the Fugitive Slave Act. The case was crucial in the radicalization of Worcester minister Thomas W. Higginson. Brown University Library

facing: Caricature of Dorr's War, 1842. Efforts to lower the property requirement for voting in Rhode Island fanned racial animosity, as free people of color in Providence helped suppress the 1842 uprising of working-class whites. This caricature of the Providence City Guard attests to the hostility of disfranchised white men toward African-American rivals for the franchise. Brown University Library

new Fugitive Slave Act in 1850. "Merciful God! has it come to this?" asked minister Kazlitt Arvine from a Worcester pulpit that December. "Can it be possible in the middle of the nineteenth century, in a land boasting of liberty, in a national assembly which conceives itself unrivaled for intelligence and moral principle, that such iniquity should have been framed into law,—a law trampling on the weak and helpless, and blackening Christian virtues into civil crimes!" When Peter C. Bacon became Worcester's mayor soon af-

ter, he essentially nullified the federal law by prohibiting the city police from assisting in the recapture of a presumed runaway slave. Attempts to seize black men and women in Massachusetts met resistance, and generated sustained outrage, most notably when federal marshals captured Anthony Burns. Thomas Wentworth Higginson left his Worcester pulpit and hastened to Boston to participate in the forceful liberation of Burns. The assault on the prison failed, and Higginson sustained injuries to his face. After Burns

CELEBRATION
— OF —
BRITISH WEST INDIA EMANCIPATION,
AT WORCESTER, AUGUST 1, 1850.

Jubilee Song.
AIR — Away the Bowl.

I.
Our grateful hearts with joy o'erflow,
   Hurrah, hurrah, hurrah!
We hail the Despot's overthrow,
   Hurrah, hurrah, hurrah!
No more he'll raise the gory lash,
And sink it deep in human flesh,
   Hurrah, hurrah, hurrah, hurrah,
   Hurrah, hurrah, hurrah!

II.
We raise our song in Freedom's name,
   Hurrah, hurrah, hurrah!
Her glorious triumph we proclaim,
   Hurrah, hurrah, hurrah!
Beneath her feet lie Slavery's chains,
Their power to curse no more remains,
   Hurrah, hurrah, hurrah, hurrah,
   Hurrah, hurrah, hurrah!

III.
With joy we'll make the air resound,
   Hurrah, hurrah, hurrah!
That all may hear the gladsome sound,
   Hurrah, hurrah, hurrah!
We glory at Oppression's fall,
The Slave has burst his deadly thrall,
   Hurrah, hurrah, hurrah, hurrah,
   Hurrah, hurrah, hurrah !

IV.
In mirthful glee we'll dance and sing,
   Hurrah, hurrah, hurrah!
With shouts we'll make the welkin ring,
   Hurrah, hurrah, hurrah!
Shout! shout aloud! the bondman 's free!
This, this is Freedom's jubilee!
   Hurrah, hurrah, hurrah, hurrah,
   Hurrah, hurrah, hurrah!

British Emancipation.
BY REV. JOHN PIERPONT.

I.
Where Britannia's emerald isles
   Gem the Caribbean sea,
And an endless summer smiles,
   Lo! the Negro thrall is free!
Yet not on Columbia's plains
   Hath the sun of Freedom risen:
Here, in darkness and in chains,
   Toiling millions pine in prison.

II.
Shout! ye islands disenthralled,
   Point the finger as in scorn,
At a country that is called
   Freedom's home, where men are born
Heirs, for life, to chains and whips —
   Bondmen, who have never known
Wife, child, parent, that their lips
   Ever dared to call their own.

III.
Yet a CHRISTIAN land is this;
   Yea, and ministers of Christ
Slavery's foot, in homage, kiss;
   And their brother, who is priced
Higher than their Saviour, even,
   Do they into bondage sell; —
Pleading thus the cause of Heaven,
   Serving thus the cause of Hell.

IV.
Holy Father, let thy word,
   Spoken by thy prophets old,
By the pliant priest be heard;
   And let lips that now are cold,
(Touched by Mammon's golden wand,)
   With our Nation's "burden" glow,
Till the free man and the bond
   Shout for Slavery's overthrow!

Hope for the American Slaves.
BY WILLIAM LLOYD GARRISON.
AIR — America.

I.
Ye who in bondage pine,
Shut out from light divine,
   Bereft of hope;
Whose limbs are worn with chains,
Whose tears bedew our plains,
Whose blood our glory stains,
   In gloom who grope :—

II.
Shout! for the hour draws nigh,
That gives you liberty!
   And from the dust,
So long your vile embrace,
Uprising, take your place
Among earth's equal race —
   'T is right and just.

III.
The night — the long, long night
Of infamy and slight,
   Shame and disgrace —
And slavery worse than e'er
Rome's serfs were doomed to bear,
Bloody beyond compare —
   Recedes apace!

IV.
Speed, speed the hour, O Lord!
Speak, and, at thy dread word,
   Fetters shall fall
From every limb — the strong
No more the weak shall wrong,
But LIBERTY's sweet song
   Be sung by all!

The Nation's Guilt.
BY ELIZABETH M. CHANDLER.
AIR — Missionary Hymn.

I.
Think of our country's glory,
   All dimmed with Afric's tears;
Her broad flag stained and gory
   With th' hoarded guilt of years!

II.
Think of the prayers ascending,
   Yet shrieked, alas! in vain,
When heart from heart is rending,
   Ne'er to be joined again!

III.
Think of the frantic mother,
   Lamenting for her child,
Till falling lashes smother
   Her cries of anguish wild!

IV.
Shall we behold, unheeding,
   Life's holiest feelings crushed?
When woman's heart is bleeding,
   Shall woman's voice be hushed?

V.
O no! by every blessing
   That Heaven to thee may lend,
Remember their oppression!
   Forget not, sister — friend!

Hymn.
BY OLIVER JOHNSON.
AIR — Zion.

I.
Hark! a voice from heaven proclaiming
   Comfort to the mourning slave;
God has heard him long complaining,
   And extends his arm to save;
     Proud Oppression
Soon shall find a shameful grave.

II.
See, the light of Truth is breaking
   Full and clear on every hand!
And the voice of Mercy speaking,
   Now is heard through all the land;
     Firm and fearless,
See the friends of freedom stand.

III.
Lo! the nation is arousing
   From its slumber, long and deep;
And the friends of God are waking,
   Never, never more to sleep,
     While a bondman
In his chains remains to weep.

IV.
Long, too long, have we been dreaming
   O'er our country's sin and shame;
Let us now, the time redeeming,
   Press the helpless captive's claim,
     Till, exulting,
He shall cast aside his chain!

Progress of the Cause.
BY MARIA W. CHAPMAN.
AIR — Old Hundred.

I.
What sound, among the shaken hills,
Rolls awful as the tempest's voice,
And tyranny with terror fills,
And bids the trembling slave rejoice?

II.
It is the thronging of the free
'Round thy high places, Liberty!
By Truth, and Love, and Freedom led,
Till the land trembles to their tread!

III.
What shout, through all the region sent,
So sharply cleaves the startled air,
And shakes the hollow firmament,
As if the judgment trump were there?

IV.
'T is the strong watch-word of the North,
That earthquake voice which thunders forth!
By every stream, and hill, and wave,
It cries, "Deliverance for the Slave!"

Worcester Celebration of British West Indies Emancipation. Blackstone abolitionists found numerous opportunities to bring the plight of the slave before a larger audience. Petition drives, picnics, fundraising sales, and celebrations also helped maintain the solidarity of the activist community. Brown University Library

had been returned to the South, a despairing Higginson declared June 4, 1854, as a day of mourning for the now-dead freedom of Massachusetts. "We talk of the Anti-Slavery sentiment as being stronger; but in spite of your Free Soil votes, your Uncle Tom's Cabin, and your New York Tribunes, here is the simple fact: the South beats us more and more easily every time."[40]

Here was the obvious moment for Worcester abolitionists to gain new adherents to their cause. They had not been inactive in recent years, orchestrating public celebrations of emancipation in the British West Indies and bringing a distinguished array of lecturers to speak in town. They found a public willing to denounce the Fugitive Slave Act (witness the so-called Butman riot in Worcester later in 1854) and to reject efforts to open Kansas to slave settlement, but incapable of embracing immediate emancipation and black equality. Perhaps emblematic were the popular *Uncle Tom's Cabin* plays that ran in Worcester theaters during the mid-1850s, evoking the horrors of slavery and simultaneously offering levity in the form of caricatured black speech and dance. Indeed, a popular culture of minstrelsy went hand-in-hand with the return of the Massachusetts Democrats—now increasingly comprised of Irish immigrants—to a party politics predicated on white supremacy and the right of slaveholding states to control their own institutions.[41]

A majority of Blackstone voters came to identify themselves as slavery's primary victims. "The Slave Power," as they saw it, was not merely content with holding African Americans in slavery, but now sought to strip free white Northerners of political equality. Fifteen hundred Providence citizens convened that March to decry Stephen Douglas's Kansas-Nebraska Act and the proposed repeal of the Missouri Compromise. An emboldened Francis Wayland noted that if new territories were opened to slavery, then a handful of Southern aristocrats would rule the nation through the Senate. "The question ceases to be whether black men are forever to be slaves," warned Wayland, "but whether the sons of the Puritans are to become slaves themselves." Eli Thayer, a Brown graduate and resident of Worcester, diligently raised funds to send New Englanders to settle in Kansas and prevent slaveholders from gaining the upper hand in territorial politics. After the caning of Charles Sumner on the Senate floor

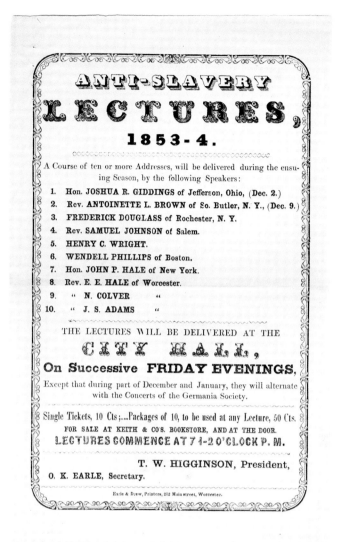

Worcester Anti-Lecture Series, 1853–1854. The abolitionist movement had been organized on the principle of moral suasion, and a cadre of orators spent nearly three decades convincing Blackstone audiences of the fundamental sinfulness of slaveholding. Courtesy American Antiquarian Society

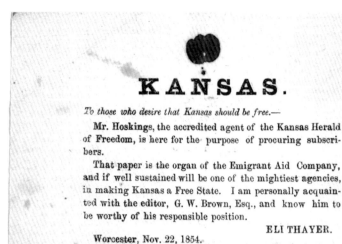

in 1856, politicians and ministers grew angrier. From his Millbury pulpit, Lewis Jessop took solace that "every blow of the assassin's bludgeon that fell upon the defenseless head of Sumner, added thousands of new friends to the anti-slavery cause." At a Providence public meeting, Reverend Frederic Hedge explained that "slavery is one thing, and the policy of the slaveholding power is a very different thing. The former is an institution with which we may not politically interfere; the latter is an armed invader, which, if not repelled, and that speedily, will involve us in a civil war of which no mortal can calculate the cost or predict the result." Hedge's prescient speech nonetheless highlighted the difference between the abolitionist agenda of immediate emancipation and the antislavery appeal of the new Republican Party.[42]

If opposition to the "Slave Power" had become a mainstream position by the end of the 1850s, Black-

stone abolitionists continued to call for radical action. Worcester's City Hall hosted a statewide "Disunion Convention" in 1857. Thomas Earle, S. D. Tourtelotte, Elbridge Boyden, and Thomas W. Higginson represented Worcester as officers, and Leicester's Samuel May declared it "high time" to "cut for ever the bloody bond which unites us to the slaveholders, slave-breeders, and slave-traders of this nation." Stephen S. Foster insisted "that the mass of the people were ripe for revolution." Three years later, when Blackstone voters rallied around Abraham Lincoln (who spoke in Woonsocket in March 1860), abolitionists again met in Worcester, this time to found a new party "with the avowed purpose of abolishing slavery in the States, as well as Territories of the Union." Republican opposition to slavery was too limited in its ambition, insisted abolitionists as they tried to rally "all who desire to see slavery speedily and peacefully abolished, and our beloved country free, united, and happy." Disunion would follow rather quickly at the hands of South Carolina secessionists, but there was nothing speedy nor peaceful about the abolition of slavery.[43]

Connections

One of the striking things about the industrial history of the Blackstone Valley was how infrequently abolitionists connected the region's prosperity to slave-grown cotton and Southern markets for manufactured plantation provisions. Northern merchants who coordinated interregional trade from the financial centers of Boston and New York earned criticism, but rare was the indictment of Blackstone manufacturers on account of the source of their cotton or the destination of their coarse fabrics. In 1836, Theodore Weld issued one of the few condemnations of those who "deputi[zed] the master . . . to plunder the slave," and by paying top price for cotton, "bribe[d] him to plunder again." Weld remarked on Rhode Island's mixed historical legacy as "the land of Roger Williams, and Samuel Hopkins, and Moses Brown; veterans, pioneers, patriarchs, in the cause of human liberty," but also a place "steeped in the guilt and infamy of the African Slave Trade." Referring to Rhode Island as the "the most profitable customer of the South in her great staple of cotton," Weld might have recalled Moses Brown's unrealized aspiration to liberate the state's economy from slavery through textile manufacturing.[44]

Moses's brother John Brown had been more realistic about the interdependency of manufacturing and plantation regimes. An economy powered by cotton was an economy powered by slavery. This observation won John few friends in 1790s Providence, even as his prediction was borne out in subsequent decades. The bane of the Providence Society for Promoting the Abolition of Slavery, John Brown candidly embraced slavery as crucial to New England's economic ambitions (even as he preferred ships to mills). For those old enough in 1859 to remember John Brown, Providence mayor Amos C. Barlow's speech on the failed raid on Harper's Ferry must have come as a surprise. A veteran of the first Rhode Island Anti-Slavery Society meeting in 1836, Barlow paired the martyred freedom fighter with Moses's brother, the cool defender of slavery and a rebel in his own right. "Why should

any man be proud of his relationship to the first John Brown," asked Barlow, "and at the same time frown upon the man who is moved, despite his faults, to express the least sympathy for the second John Brown?" It is hard to imagine that either of the John Browns would have appreciated the company of the other, but both were more candid than their friends and enemies about the national reach of slavery.[45]

Barlow's ability to celebrate Providence's John Brown in the context of a speech opposing slavery was strange, but telling: Even long-time abolitionists like Barlow could lose sight of the relationship of the New England economy to slavery. Several generations of industrial development and general prosperity blunted the thorny problem of whence cotton came. The "complicity" of Blackstone manufacturers might have proven a powerful argument in the abolitionist arsenal, but instead, Southern defenders of slavery seized the point to attack sanctimonious Northern adversaries. In response, Blackstone politicians, ministers, and even abolitionists denied that Northern industrial development had anything to do with slavery; it was as if cotton *actually* did grow on the banks of the Blackstone.

NOTES

Research support for this essay provided by the Gilder Lehrman Center for the Study of Slavery, Resistance, and Abolition at Yale University, the Institute for Southern Studies at University of South Carolina, the National Endowment for the Humanities, and the American Antiquarian Society.

1. *Proceedings of the Rhode-Island Anti-Slavery Convention, held in Providence, on the 2d, 3d, and 4th of February, 1836* (Providence: H.H. Brown, 1836), 13.

2. For the post-Revolutionary growth of American slavery and the history of the cotton supply, see Adam J. Rothman, *Slave Country: American Expansion and the Origins of the Deep South* (Cambridge, Mass.: Harvard University Press, 2005); Sven Beckert, "Emancipation and Empire: Reconstructing the Worldwide Web of Cotton Production in the Age of the American Civil War," *American Historical Review* 109 (December 2004): 1405–38.

3. *Providence Gazette and Country Journal*, February 18, 1789. For the history of Moses Brown's antislavery ideals and rivalry with brother John, see Mack Thomp-

son, *Moses Brown: Reluctant Reformer* (Chapel Hill: University of North Carolina Press, 1962); Charles Rappleye, *Sons of Providence: The Brown Brothers, the Slave Trade, and the American Revolution* (New York: Simon & Schuster, 2006).

4. Anne Farrow, Joel Lang, and Jennifer Frank, *Complicity: How the North Promoted, Prolonged, and Profited from Slavery* (New York: Ballentine Books, 2005).

5. Ronald Bailey, "The Slave(ry) Trade and the Development of Capitalism in the United States: The Textile Industy in New England," *Social Science History* 14 (Fall 1990): 373–414; Martin H. Blatt and David Roediger, eds., *The Meaning of Slavery in the North* (New York: Garland Publishing, 1998); Don E. Fehrenbacher, *The Slaveholding Republic: An Account of the United States Government's Relations to Slavery*, ed. Ward M. McAfee (New York: Oxford University Press, 2001).

6. For the notion that slavery helped give legitimacy to wage labor, see Eric Foner, *Free Soil, Free Labor, Free Men: The Ideology of the Republican Party before the Civil War* (New York: Oxford University Press, 1970); Marcus Cunliffe, *Chattel Slavery and Wage Slavery: The Anglo-American Context 1830–1860* (Athens: University of Georgia Press, 1979); Jonathan A. Glickstein, *Concepts of Free Labor in Antebellum America* (New Haven: Yale University Press, 1991).

7. On the broader relationship of capitalism and antislavery, see Thomas Bender, ed., *The Antislavery Debate: Capitalism and Abolitionism as a Problem in Historical Interpretation* (Berkeley: University of California Press, 1992). For the specific link between abolitionism and middle-class reform, see John S. Gilkeson, *Middle-Class Providence, 1820–1940* (Princeton: Princeton University Press, 1986), 36–52. For the combination of abolitionism and religious perfectionism, see Robert Abzug, *Cosmos Crumbling: American Reform and the Religious Imagination* (New York: Oxford University Press, 1994).

8. David R. Roediger, *The Wages of Whiteness: Race and the Making of the American Working Class* (New York: Verso, 1991); Joanne Pope Melish, *Disowning Slavery: Gradual Emancipation and "Race" in New England, 1780–1860* (Ithaca, N.Y.: Cornell University Press, 1998); Jonathan A. Glickstein, *American Exceptionalism, American Anxiety: Wages, Competition, and Degraded Labor in the Antebellum United States* (Charlottesville: University of Virginia Press, 2002).

9. Charles Hoffmann and Tess Hoffmann, *North by South: The Two Lives of Richard James Arnold* (Athens: University of Georgia Press, 1988). Arnold served as "Mr. X" in Frederick Law Olmsted, *A Journey in the Seaboard Slave States, with Remarks on their Economy* (New York: Dix & Edwards, 1856), 409–51.

10. Louis Fitzgerald Tasistro, *Random Shots and Southern Breezes, containing Critical Remarks on the Southern States and Southern Institutions, with Semi-Serious Observations on Men and Manners* (New York: Harper & Brothers, 1842), I, 173.

11. Hoffmann and Hoffmann, *North by South*, 7. For the rise of Rhode Island's manufacturing economy, see Daniel P. Jones, *The Economic and Social Transformation of Rural Rhode Island, 1780–1850* (Boston: Northeastern University Press, 1992); Peter J. Coleman, *The Transformation of Rhode Island, 1790–1860* (Providence: Brown University Press, 1963).

12. Joseph Goffe, Jr., to Joseph Goffe, October 26, 1826, Joseph Goffe Papers, Box 1, Manuscripts Department, American Antiquarian Society.

13. Maria L. Goddard Davis to Ezra Goddard, February 5, 1843, James S. M. Davis Papers, South Caroliniana Library, University of South Carolina.

14. Anne Crawford Allen to Eliza Harriet Arnold Allen, December 3, 1834, William D. Ely Family Papers, ms. 944, Series I, Box I, Folder 11, Manuscripts and Archives, Sterling Memorial Library, Yale University.

15. Mary Ann Waterman to Lucretia C. Sibley, April 22, 1847, May 5, 1851, Lucretia Carter Sibley Correspondence, Box 1, Manuscripts Department, American Antiquarian Society.

16. *Slavery and Justice: Report of the Brown University Steering Committee on Slavery and Justice* (Providence: Brown University, 2007), 13–31. In 1830, a Southern student named Hazel Crouch delivered a pro-slavery commencement address at Brown. See *The Brunonian, edited by the Students of Brown University* (October 1830). For Wayland's success as an anti-slavery interlocutor, see *Speech of Rev. Wm. H. Brisbane, Lately a Slaveholder in South Carolina; Containing an Account of the Change in his Views on the Subject of Slavery* (Hartford: S.S. Cowles, 1840); *Domestic Slavery Considered as a Scriptural Institution: in a Correspondence between the Rev. Richard Fuller of Beaufort, S.C. and the Rev. Francis Wayland of Providence, R.I.* (Boston: Gould, Kendall, and Lincoln, 1845). Many aboli-

tionists read Wayland's *Limitations of Human Responsibility* (1838) as excusing the sin of slaveholding. See Jeremy Chase, "Francis Wayland: A Uniting Force in an Era of Disunion," A.B. Honors Thesis, Brown University, 2006.

17. Harvey Toliver Cook, *The Life and Legacy of David Rogerson Williams* (New York: Country Life Press, 1916), 47–64, 140–43, 162.

18. J. Leander Bishop, *History of American Manufactures from 1608 to 1860*, 3rd ed., (Philadelphia: Edward Young & Co, 1868), II, 531–33; Rhode Island Historical Preservation Commission, *Providence Industrial Sites*, Statewide Historical Preservation Report P-P-6, July 1981.

19. Generally known as the McLane Report (after Andrew Jackson's secretary of the treasury, Louis McLane), the survey is officially titled *Documents Relative to the Manufactures in the United States, collected and transmitted to the House of Representatives, in compliance with a resolution of Jan. 19, 1832, by the Secretary of the Treasury* (1833; reprint, New York: Burt Franklin, 1969), 474–577 (Worcester County), 927–77 (Rhode Island). For additional data for Worcester County, see John G. Palfrey, *Statistics of the Condition and Products of Certain Branches of Industry in Massachusetts, for the Year ending April 1, 1845* (Boston: Dutton and Wentworth, 1846).

20. *Documents Relative to the Manufacturers*, 83.

21. Depending on who was to wear them, cassinets, ozneburgs, satinetts, kerseys, and linsey-woolseys could be classified as "negro cloth." On basic production, see Robert B. Gordon and Patrick M. Malone, *The Texture of Industry: An Archaeological View of the Industrialization of North America* (New York: Oxford University Press, 1994), 248–49. Simon Darling to Isaac P. Hazard, May 8, 1831, Peace Dale Manufacturing Company Papers, Case 4, Baker Library, Harvard Business School; Frederick Law Olmsted, *The Cotton Kingdom: A Traveller's Observations on Cotton and Slavery in the American Slave States*, 2nd ed. (New York: Mason Brothers, 1862), I, 105; Helen Bradley Foster, *"New Raiments of Self": African American Clothing in the Antebellum South* (Oxford: Berg, 1997), 145–47; Susan Oba, "'Mostly Made, Especially for this Purpose, in Providence, R.I.': The Rhode Island Negro Cloth Industry," A.B. honors thesis, Brown University, 2006.

22. Ebenezer Goffe to Joseph, Jr., and Eliza Goffe, July 28, 1828, Joseph Goffe Papers, Box 1; *Descriptive Catalogue of Agricultural and Horticultural Implements, Machines, and Seeds, by Ruggles, Nourse, Mason & Co.* (Worcester:

Henry J. Howland, 1849); *The Southern Cabinet, of Agriculture, Rural and Domestic Economy, the Arts and Sciences, Literature, Sporting Intelligence, &c.* I (September 1840).

23. A. H. Waters & Co. to Joseph G. Ives, March 25, 1853, Waters Family Papers, Octavo Vol. 8, Manuscripts Department, American Antiquarian Society.

24. Thomas R. Navin, *The Whitin Machine Works since 1831: A Textile Machinery Company in an Industrial Village* (New York: Russell & Russell, 1969); Archie Vernon Huff, Jr., *Greenville: The History of the City and County in the South Carolina Piedmont* (Columbia: University of South Carolina Press, 1995), 83–84; Tom Downey, *Planting a Capitalist South: Masters, Merchants, and Manufacturers in the Southern Interior, 1790–1860* (Baton Rouge: Louisiana State University Press, 2006). William Gregg to P. Whitin, July 2, 1846, July 11, 1849, September 26, 1857, March 13, 1858, March 11, 1861, April 18, 1861; James G. Gibbs to P. Whitin, October 19, 1857, Records, P. Whitin & Sons, South Caroliniana Library, University of South Carolina.

25. Catharine B. Turner to Isaac P. Hazard, January 17, 1845; Isaac P. Hazard to Richard M. Habersham, March 4, 1845, Case 12, Peace Dale Manufacturing Company Papers; Charles T. James, *Practical Hints on the Comparative Cost and Productiveness of the Culture of Cotton, and the Cost and Productiveness of its Manufacture. Addressed to the Cotton Planters and Capitalists of the South* (Providence: Joseph Knowles, 1849), 48; James, *Letters on the Culture and Manufacture of Cotton: Addressed to Freeman Hunt, Esq., Editor of Hunt's Merchants' Magazine, and Published in the Numbers of that Journal for February and March, 1850, in Reply to the Communication of A.A. Lawrence, Esq., Originally published in the Merchants' Magazine for Dec. 1849 and January, 1850* (New York: Geo. W. Wood, 1850).

26. James, *Practical Hints*, 29.

27. Thomas Snell, *A Discourse, containing an Historical Sketch of the Town of North Brookfield* (West Brookfield, Mass.: O.S. Cooke and Co., 1854), 15–16.

28. "Anti-Abolition Meeting," *Providence Daily Journal*, November 4, 1835; Rhode Island General Assembly, House of Representatives, *Reports of the Select Committee to whom were referred the resolutions of Mr. Wells . . . touching certain resolutions of the House of Representatives of the U. States relating to Petitions for the Abolition of Slavery, &c., &c. . . .* (Providence: s.n., 1839); ibid., *Mr. Whipple's Report, and Mr. Otis's Letter* (Boston: Cassady and March, 1839); Gilkeson, *Middle-Class Providence*, 39–42.

29. For Massachusetts's abolition of slavery, see Roy E. Finkcnbine, "Belinda's Petition: Reparations for Slavery in Revolutionary Massachusetts," *William and Mary Quarterly* 64 (January 2007): 95–104; Emily Blanck, "Seventeen Eighty-Three: The Turning Point in the Law of Slavery and Freedom in Massachusetts," *New England Quarterly* 75 (March 2002): 24–51. For Rhode Island, see Arline Ruth Kiven, *Then Why the Negroes: The Nature and Course of the Anti-Slavery Movement in Rhode Island: 1637-1861* (Providence: Urban League of Rhode Island, 1973); *Address of the Yearly Meeting of Friends for New England: held on Rhode Island, in the sixth month, 1837 . . .* (New Bedford: The Meeting, 1837), 3; *Slavery and Justice Report*, 30.

30. For population statistics, see J. H. Benton Jr., *Early Census Making in Massachusetts, 1643-1765* (Boston: Charles E. Goodspeed, 1905), 14; John R. Bartlett, compiler, *Census of the Inhabitants of the Colony of Rhode Island and Providence Plantations . . . 1774* (Providence: Knowles, Anthony, & Co., 1858), 239. On the isolation of black families, see John L. Brooke, *The Heart of the Commonwealth: Society and Political Culture in Worcester County, Massachusetts, 1713-1861* (New York: Cambridge University Press, 1989), 45. For the broader struggles of people of color, see John Wood Sweet, *Bodies Politic: Negotiating Race in the American North, 1730-1830* (Baltimore: Johns Hopkins University Press, 2003).

31. Henry Jackson, *Short History of the African Union Meeting and School-House, erected in Providence (R.I.) in the Years 1819, '20, '21 . . .* (Providence: Brown and Danforth, 1821); *The Life of William J. Brown of Providence, R.I., with Personal Recollections of Incidents in Rhode Island* (1883; reprint, Durham, N.H.: University of New Hampshire Press, 2006), 47; Shane White, "'It Was a Proud Day': African Americans, Festivals, and Parades in the North, 1741-1834," *Journal of American History* 81 (June 1994): 13–50; Lydia Pecker, "A View of Power': People of Color in Antebellum Providence, Rhode Island," A.B. honors thesis, Brown University, 2003.

32. Sweet, *Bodies Politic*, 312–13, 353–98; James T. Campbell, *Middle Passages: African American Journeys to Africa, 1787-2005* (New York: Viking, 2006), 39–56; Kiven, *Then Why*, 44–45. The seemingly moribund Providence Society for Promoting the Abolition of Slavery met in September 1825 to appoint a delegate to a national antislavery convention. See *Minutes of the Nineteenth Session of the American Convention for Promoting the Abolition of Slavery, and Improving the Condition of the African Race, Convened at Philadelphia, on the Fourth day of October, 1825* (Philadelphia: Atkinson & Alexander, 1825), 5.

33. B. Eugene McCarthy and Thomas L. Doughton, eds., *From Bondage to Belonging: The Worcester Slave Narratives* (Amherst: University of Massachusetts Press, 2007), xl; *Constitution of the American Society of Free Persons of Colour . . . with Their Address to the Free Persons of Colour in the United States* (Philadelphia: J.W. Allen, 1831), 10; Pecker, "View of Power," 81.

34. *Constitution of the New-England Anti-Slavery Society: With an Address to the Public* (Boston: Garrison and Knapp, 1832), 3, 9; John L. Myers, "Antislavery Agencies in Rhode Island, 1832–1835," *Rhode Island History* 29 (Summer–Fall 1970): 82–93. For the best history of Rhode Island abolitionism, see Deborah Bingham Van Broekhoven, *The Devotion of these Women: Rhode Island in the Antislavery Network* (Amherst: University of Massachusetts Press, 2002).

35. *Report and Proceedings of the First Annual Meeting of the Providence Anti-Slavery Society, With a Brief Exposition of the Principles and Purposes of the Abolitionists* (Providence: H.H. Brown, 1833), 5–6; *Liberator*, November 22, 1834; *Annual Report of the Board of Managers of the New-England Anti-Slavery Society* (Boston: Knapp and Garrison, 1835), 6; John L. Myers, "Antislavery Agents in Rhode Island, 1835–1837," *Rhode Island History* 30 (February 1971): 21–31; Gilkeson, *Middle-Class Providence*, 36–52; Van Broekhoven, *Devotion of these Women*, passim; McCarthy and Doughton, *Bondage to Belonging*, xliii.

36. *Proceedings of the Rhode-Island Anti-Slavery Convention, held in Providence . . . 1836*; *Declaration and Expose of the Principles of the Worcester Anti-Slavery Society* (Worcester: s.n., 1836); Dorothy Sterling, *Ahead of her Time: Abby Kelley and the Politics of Antislavery* (New York: W.W. Norton, 1991); Aileen S. Kraditor, *Means and Ends in American Abolitionism: Garrison and His Critics on Strategy and Tactics, 1834-1850* (New York: Pantheon Books, 1969); Lewis Perry, *Radical Abolitionism: Anarchy and the Government of God in Antislavery Thought* (Ithaca, N.Y.: Cornell University Press, 1973), 131.

37. For the challenge that Garrison abolitionism posed to antislavery clergy, see Snell, *Discourse*, 39–40. For ministerial meetings, see *Liberator*, August 11, 1837; *Proceed-*

ings of the Convention of Ministers of Worcester County, on the Subject of Slavery; Held at Worcester, December 5 & 6, 1837, and January 16, 1838 (Worcester: Massachusetts Spy Office, 1838), 16, 18. The Worcester ministers initially considered a far more radical declaration of opposition to slavery, penned by George Allen of Shrewsbury and affirming a "belie[f] in the duty and safety of its *immediate abolition.*" See *Mr. Allen's Report of a Declaration of Sentiments on Slavery, December 5, 1837,* 2nd ed., (Worcester: Henry J. Howland, 1838), 10. Samuel May, Jr., "Slavery: Isaiah 58:6–7," April 15, 1838, Leicester, Mass., Samuel May Jr. Collection, P-470, Massachusetts Historical Society.

38. Marvin E. Gettleman, *The Dorr Rebellion: A Study in American Radicalism, 1833–1849* (New York: Random House, 1973); *Life of William J. Brown of Providence, R.I.,* 92–103.

39. Bruce Laurie, *Beyond Garrison: Antislavery and Social Reform* (New York: Cambridge University Press, 2005); Jonathan H. Earle, *Jacksonian Antislavery and the Politics of Free Soil, 1824–1854* (Chapel Hill: University of North Carolina Press, 2004), 184–87; Brooke, *Heart of the Commonwealth,* 357–81; *Emancipator & Republican* [Boston], September 20, 1849.

40. Kazlitt Arvine, *Our Duty to the Fugitive Slave: A Discourse delivered on Sunday, October 6, in West Boylston, Mass., and in Worcester, December 15* (Boston: J.P. Jewett & Co., 1850), 28; *Inaugural Address of Hon. Peter C. Bacon, mayor of the City of Worcester, April 7, 1851 . . .* (Worcester: Henry J. Howland, 1851), 29–33; Thomas Wentworth Higginson, *Massachusetts in Mourning: A Sermon, preached in Worcester, on Sunday, June 4, 1854* (Boston: James Monroe & Co., 1854), 10.

41. *Worcester Dramatic Museum. Mrs. Harriet Beecher Stowe's Moral and Religious Work of Uncle Tom's Cabin . . .* (Worcester: n.p., 1854); *Brinley Hall! The Great Moral and Scenic Representation of the Free Slave! In Five Acts . . .* (Worcester: Fiske and Reynolds, 1855).

42. *Proceedings of a Public Meeting of the Citizens of Providence, Held in the Beneficent Congregational Church, March 7, 1854, to Protest against Slavery in Nebraska, with the Addresses of the Speakers* (Providence: Knowles, Anthony, & Co., 1854), 16; *The Outrage in the Senate. Proceedings of a Public Meeting of the Citizens of Providence, Held in Howard Hall, on the Evening of June 7th, 1856* (Providence: Knowles, Anthony, & Co., 1854), 10; Lewis Jessop, *God's Honor; or the Christian Statesman. A Sermon preached in Millbury, Sunday, June 15th, 1856* (Worcester: Chas. Hamilton, 1856), 11–12.

43. *Proceedings of the State Disunion Convention, held at Worcester, Massachusetts, January 15, 1857* (Boston: s.n, 1857), 13, 58; *Political Anti-Slavery Convention, in the City of Worcester, Mass.* (Worcester: s.n., 1860).

44. *Proceedings of the Rhode-Island Anti-Slavery Convention, held in Providence . . . 1836,* 85–87.

45. *Speeches of Hon. A.C. Barstow, Rev. Geo. T. Day, Rev. A. Woodbury, Hon. Thomas Davis, and Resolutions adopted at a Meeting of Citizens Held in Providence, R.I., December 2d, 1859, on the Occasion of the Execution of John Brown* (Providence: Amsbury & Co., 1860), 3–6.

"Cannot and Will Not Grant Eight-Hour Day!"

RANGER CHUCK ARNING

"It is evident many Worcester mechanics have caught the strike fever. It is equally evident that, like in any other fever, it has to run its course. The medicine will have to be taken before conditions improve," explained Donald Tulloch, secretary of the Worcester Branch of the National Metal Trades Association to a reporter for the Worcester Telegram on September 24, 1915.[1]

And so it seemed, for 1915 brought a wave of industrial worker unrest throughout the Blackstone Valley. Even Worcester, not known for organized labor activity, was seeing disruptions throughout its diverse industries. In March, the Bottlers, Drivers and Brewery workers went on strike, seeking an eight-hour day, a $2-per-week wage increase and a three-year, twelve-month contract that virtually shut down the two local breweries.[2]

The ladies were not to be denied, either. On October 12, 1915, the corsetmakers of the Royal Worcester Corset Co. formed a union affiliated with the American Federation of Labor. An eight-hour work day was their chief demand, but the workers also wanted the company to eliminate a requirement that the workers pay for the thread they used while on the job.

This heightened industrial unrest could be traced to the growing conflict in Europe. War-related orders meant increased production, high employment, and strong profits; in fact, the industries of the Blackstone Valley were doing so well that company heads had to deny open accusations of wartime profiteering. It seemed only fair that the workers would want their share of the benefits in such a profitable economy. By the fall of 1915, tensions between workers demanding an eight-hour day with an increase in pay and the well-organized National Metal Trade Association, hostile to any union activity and adamantly holding to the "open shop" concept, placed the City of Worcester on edge.

An unsigned "Letter to the Editor," published in the *Worcester Telegram*, captured the feelings of the day:

> The low pay and long hours have been brought about by the Metal Trades Association. They have black listed any and all who have agitated the loudest for more pay and shorter hours ... and should this country ever be drawn into the war on account of having furnished so much war material, it won't be J. P. Morgan, Charles M. Schwab or the rich manufacturers who will do the fighting, but the poor devils who have to work for a day's pay.[3]

The machinists must have taken note. In September, they struck the Reed-Prentice Mfg. Company, followed by walk-outs at Whitcomb-Blaisdell, then Leland-Gifford, all with the "Eight-Hour Day" as the lead demand. But nothing compared to the strike at the Crompton & Knowles Loom Works. The *Worcester Telegram* headline sounded the alarm, "More Than 1000 Go Out," as machinists "with almost military precision, the men formed into marching lines ... led by an improvised drum corps with an American flag and an 'Eight-hour Day' banner ... proceeded to Eagles Hall."[4] It was significant that the ethnicity of the strikers was noted in the newspaper accounts. Loom workers from Poland, Armenia, Greece, Italy, Russia, France, and Great Britain took part in the walk-out. In America, in 1915, where you were from meant a great deal, for it often determined how much was in your pay envelope: being American-born was a clear advantage.[5]

But in such a conflict, there are winners and losers. In the end, the words of James N. Heald, the Treasurer and General Manager of the Heald Machine Company, spoke volumes:

[T]he company made a careful canvass of the men in the factory, with the result that there were but a few men out of the entire force of 275 employees who had any sympathy with the eight-hour movement. Mr. Heald said these men were neglecting their work however to such an extent that it was found necessary to let 21 men out to relieve the atmospheric tension."[6]

NOTES

1. *Worcester (Mass.) Telegram*, "Cannot and Will Not Grant Eight-Hour Day," September 25, 1915.

2. *Worcester (Mass.) Gazette*, "Brewery Workers Strike," March 22, 1915.

3. *Worcester Telegram*, "Machinists Underpaid," March 22, 1915.

4. *Worcester Telegram*, "More Than a 1000 Go Out," October 29, 1915.

5. Bruce Cohen, "The Worcester Machinists' Strike of 1915," *Historical Journal of Massachusetts* (Summer 1988): 158.

6. *Worcester (Mass.) Gazette*, "Heald Machine Company Lets 21 Machinists Go," September 28, 1915.

6 "We Walk!" The Struggle for Worker Rights in the Industrial Blackstone Valley DR. ALBERT T. KLYBERG

Draper Workers. Draper workers listening to labor organizers outside the mill. From the Collection of Laurel Moriarty

"Tumultuous," "unprincipled," and "disorderly" were among the adjectives peppering the newspaper accounts of the "turn-out" of mill workers in the Pawtucket Strike of 1824. Led by 102 women weavers, nearly 500 mill operatives took part in the week-long work stoppage that closed the eight textile mills of Pawtucket and sent seismic waves to other industrial centers around New England.[1] The cause of the May 25 turn-out was the concerted action of the mill owners to lengthen the work day by an hour, shorten the time allowed on the job for meals, and cut the piece-work rate of pay for weavers by 25 percent. Since the pay cut for weavers affected women almost exclusively, it was they who led the walkout. Although the changes were scheduled to take effect June 1, the reaction was immediate. Women weavers gathered at the gates of the mills and encouraged others to join their protest. Sympathy for their position spread beyond their fellow workers, and the mills closed. Boisterous and angry marches to the homes of the mill owners ensued, and there were turbulent days in Pawtucket. Later in the week, a small fire in some cotton bales broke out in the Walcott Yellow Mill, and the mill owners met at a hotel the next day. A compromise was struck, the weavers returned to work, and the owners printed an after-the-fact justification for their actions.[2] Life went on.

The initial small-scale nature of the cotton manufacturing operation often cast the owner or manager on the shop floor alongside the machine operators and tenders; it was common for the boss to work amid the help. For the most part, this familiarity bred contentment, not contempt. There was daily dialogue, discussion, accessibility, and some collegiality, but it was also largely, a "man to man," fraternal relationship. Reflecting the cultural norms of the day, particularly that the home was the "appropriate" place for women's activity, the same collegial bonds did not extend to women. The balance of power and respect for the value of a worker's role in the enterprise was skewed even further when children comprised as much as two-thirds of the work force, as they did in the early decades of the textile mills.

Between 1814 and 1825, the roles assigned to women and children—namely, picking apart the cotton bales and operating hand looms at home—changed as these processes became more mechanized and moved from home to factory. This was particularly true after the introduction of power looms. Women followed the looms into the mills. They were eagerly sought; cash pay was employed as an incentive. By the 1820s, children were no longer used as production workers and were given tasks involving moving stock from one part of the process to the next or refilling spent bobbins. The percentage of children in the work force shrank from nearly 70 percent in 1820 to 40 percent by 1831.[3] Conversely, the percentage of women increased from

NOTICE.

THE members of the Pawtucket Mechanic Society, are hereby notified that their annual meeting will be held at their room, on Thursday next, the 24th instant, at 2 o'clock, P. M. A general and punctual attendance is particularly requested.
By Order,
C. S. TOMPKINS, Sec'ry.

Pawtucket Mechanic Society. Skilled workers organized the Pawtucket Mechanic Society. These operatives were several status rungs above the women weavers who struck in 1824. Courtesy the Rhode Island Historical Society

16 percent to 30 percent and men from 15 percent to 25 percent during the same period.

The contention between worker and owner had many origins in the Blackstone River Valley, this "cradle" of the Industrial Revolution in America. Mills were suspect from the beginning, and there were many disagreements over rights and control as might well be expected when there was a "new order of things." For example, squabbles emerged about whether a company could appropriate the sole use of the public waterway to the disadvantage of other property owners or the public at large. Part of the sympathy for the weavers stemmed from a vestigial grudge over the mill owners' decision to build dams on the river, flooding out the fields of upstream farmers and denying the age-old access to anadromous fish.[4] Then there was the discomfort surrounding the novelty of selling one's time instead of bartering a good or product. The uprooting from farm family life to live as a tenant in a house owned by the boss in the artificially new industrial village was another source of conflict, as was the surren-

COMMONWEALTH OF MASSACHUSETTS.

RESOLVE

IN RELATION TO CHILDREN EMPLOYED IN FACTORIES.

RESOLVED, That the Selectmen of every Town in this Commonwealth, and the Mayor and Aldermen of the City of Boston, be instructed to send to the office of the Secretary of the Commonwealth, before the first session of the next General Court, a statement of the number of persons of each sex, under sixteen years of age, employed by any Incorporated Manufacturing Company within their Town or City, setting forth the length of time during which they are usually kept at work, and the opportunities allowed, and means provided for their education.

Resolved, That the Secretary of the Commonwealth cause a copy of the above Resolve to be sent to the said Selectmen, and to the said Mayor and Aldermen of the City of Boston.

In Senate, February 25, 1825.

Read and passed.   Sent down for concurrence.

NATHANIEL SILSBEE, *President.*

House of Representatives, February 25, 1825.—Read and concurred.

WM. C. JARVIS, *Speaker.*

February 26, 1825.—Approved.

MARCUS MORTON.

A true copy—Attest,   EDWARD D. BANGS, *Secretary.*

Massachusetts Legislation: Resolved in Relation to Children Employed in Factories. Any effort to obtain reasonable working conditions began with the assembling of facts relative to work life in the mills. Massachusetts began collection of data pertaining to child labor in factories in 1825. Courtesy American Antiquarian Society

der of the right to participate in Rhode Island town meetings when workers assumed tenant status as a result of their employment in the mills. Life was regimented by the summoning of bells, so rose the fear, or the resentment, of not having time of one's own, and of losing the ownership of time. When the management possessed the only time piece, time was whatever the boss said it was, hence the fabled effort on the part of the Pawtucket community to install—through the financial support of subscribers—a huge, readable public clock in the tower of the Congregational Church as a reliable, independent arbiter of the rhythms of the work day.[5]

The ink on the Declaration of Independence was not even fifty years dry, and yet the Hamiltonian view of the new order of things—factories, industrial villages, and wage labor tied to hours and regulations—had spun out a new world in the New World of America. This transformation included a new system of social classes. There were owners and industrial entrepreneurs; there was a middle class of artisans, mechanics, shopkeepers, and farmers; and, finally there were the factory operatives selling their time and tending machines.

Balancing these competing interests, which often were at odds with each other, became a tug of war throughout the valley for the better part of the eleven decades from 1824 to 1934. To use a more local metaphor for the struggle: What successful leaders needed in managing these struggles was the political and economic equivalent of the "fly-ball governor," an ingenious mechanical device that automatically lifted gates regulating the flow of water to waterwheels or the flow of water into steam boilers when power decreased. And even the most seasoned mill operators, the most politic politicians, the most impassioned labor rights advocates, were subject to the same laws of popularity and circumstance that made their personal stakes ascendant one day and subordinate the next.

Despite their lower economic status, workers weren't entirely powerless in the mill towns; they could always vote with their feet, even if that vote would cost them. The refusal of workers to bow to the authority of foremen, managers, agents, and owners took many forms: sometimes individual, sometimes parental, and sometimes by group consensus. There were instances where women and children simply refused to handle dirty cotton or to climb out on planks at head races to clear ice from waterwheels and guard-gate flumes.[6] In other instances, parents removed children from mill work when they thought they were in danger.[7] Sometimes, workers just decided to take time off to go berry picking or to watch their fellow mill hand, daredevil Sam Patch, jump from a five-story window ledge into a foaming, boiling, rock-rimmed pool at Pawtucket Falls.[8]

There were serious issues and concerns, as well, such as the specific complaints about wages, hours, and safety in the mill. At a Providence convention in

FACTORY PUNISHMENTS.

Mr. Walter Paine, Jr. of Providence, has pledged himself, as we have been informed, to prove that, if an instance of corporeal punishment has occurred in a Cotton Mill, the person that inflicted it was promptly discharged. If Mr. P. has given such a pledge, we consider him rather unfortunate, as we do *know* it to be out of his power to redeem it. In addition to the solitary instance Mr. Doyle has named, we can, if he demand it, or if Mr. Paine require it, name at least, we think, one hundred instances, that have occurred within two miles of the Artisan Office, some of them recently; in which corporeal punishment has been inflicted in no very gentle manner neither, and in which, the persons that performed the *duty*, so far from being dismissed, have been justified by their employers, and retained in the mills.

No names shall be called unless demanded. But two or three cases shall be given, for the information of Mr. P. and should he ask for further proof of the facts, they are at hand, and at his service. If he will refer to William Aplin, Esq. of Providence, he may probably learn from his records, that an action was commenced and tried before him, against a certain overseer in a cotton Mill in this vicinity, for unmercifully whipping a *Deaf* and *Dumb* boy under his control. The facts were fairly proved; the boy carried the marks of the rod for a week; the overseer was convicted and fined, and yet retained his situation in the mill. The boy was beaten by his *humane* master, until he was unable to stand!

In a certain mill in this place, a certain lad had the thumb and fingers on one of his hands badly lacerated by the cards. The overseer, instead of commiserating the sufferings of the poor lad, and manifesting the least sympathy for him, scolded him severely for the damage done the *cards* and shook him till he fainted and fell to the floor! The same overseer was for some time in the habit of inflicting punishments on *females* as well as boys, some of them arrived at the years of womanhood, that common decency forbids us to name, and yet he was not dismissed.

In a certain cotton mill, not five miles from this ...nt seized on a *young woman of* ...

Factory Punishment. Reports of corporal punishment of mill workers by overseers appeared first in labor newspapers, like the *New England Artisan*, and then were picked up by the general press. Ironically, and sadly, many of the abuses were inflicted upon children and female workers, who were largely disdained and neglected by the early trade union movement that catered to the injustices experienced by male operatives. Courtesy American Antiquarian Society

To the Working-men of New-England.

The FARMERS, MECHANICS and other WORKING-MEN, are reminded that the *sixth day of September next* is appointed for the meeting of Delegates from all parts of New-England, to consult upon measures for the general welfare and improvement of the producing classes of our country.

The meeting will be held at the State House in Boston, by permission of the Legislature of Massachusetts.

A full representation from the manufacturing districts is ex-

— of wisdom, of benevolence, of disinterested love, and god-like charity, were showered with open hand upon all who would receive them. Learned ingenuity might refine upon its plain teaching, and profess to make more clear that simple but divine lesson which God had prepared for the humblest of his children — yet the one true religion required not to be expounded, but proclaimed. — It was published only — and understood by all whom it was intended to bless or to save. So, thanks be to Providence, has it proved with the civil regulations necessary for the best government of freemen. Our pilgrim fathers, with nothing of experience to instruct them but its warnings, and in the true spirit of the founder of christianity instituted a government that should be understood by all, and give equal protection to all. No important difficulties attended its administration, — and our

Broadside: Workingmen's Movement. The workingmen's movement of the 1830s comprised a broad class of mechanics and laborers not yet divided into respective trades, had many general goals of equal protection under law that were primarily designed to give them the same playing field as that enjoyed by merchants and manufactures. Courtesy American Antiquarian Society

1831, one of the first attempts at industrial unionism occurred. The Providence effort led to the founding of the New England Association of Farmers, Mechanics, and other Working Men in Boston the following year.[9] Lasting only until 1834, the association was a political organization, a sounding board, and a breeding-ground for journeymen labor strikes. It was also an advocate for the interests of artisans, farmers, and factory operatives. Its weekly paper published in Pawtucket, *The New England Artisan*, was one of the first labor papers in the country.[10]

The Workingmen's Movement of the 1830s, however, was less about the plight of the textile workers in the area mills than the concerns of tradesmen such as carpenters, shipwrights, shoemakers, and house painters. Despite all the rhetoric about the importance of public education as a key to unlock all the barriers preventing workingmen from enjoying their rights as won by the American Revolution, most of the energies of the Workingmen's Party were directed at obtaining the ten-hour day.[11] In 1828, in Providence, the local mechanic's association actually had persuaded the General Assembly to enact a statewide public school act, making public education a matter of state governmental responsibility, rather than the job of the local town meeting.[12]

Curiously, the basic empowerment of the workingmen, getting the right to vote itself, had a checkered career. As previously noted, the property ownership

qualification for voting was done away with in Massachusetts in the 1820 revision of the state constitution. In Rhode Island, it remained locked in the turmoil surrounding the prevailing document of government, the old 1663 charter granted by King Charles II. While the qualification to vote was established by legislative statute, the power to set the standards for voting was granted as a prerogative to the General Assembly by the charter. Efforts to cure this feature and other annoying conditions were the subject of many calls for constitutional reform in Rhode Island in the decades prior to 1840, because the charter itself had no provision for amendment. The mounting frustration led to the People's Constitution effort, led by Thomas Wilson Dorr and workingmen allies like Seth Luther.

According to John Brooke and Ronald Formisano, political historians of Massachusetts, new access to the ballot box enjoyed by the mill workers was possibly a shell game.[13] The returns from the Worcester County towns, where there was a large mill population, were significantly lower than those from abutting municipalities. Furthermore, it was alleged that when the factory workers did vote, they reflected the interests of the mill owners, either by coercion or by being persuaded that protecting American manufacturing was also in their own self-interest. Also, in many situations, the peripatetic, transient quality of mill workers' lives, moving from job to job, meant they frequently failed the residency time-test required to qualify as voters.

Portrait of Thomas Dorr. Thomas Wilson Dorr (1805–1854), an idealistic, patrician reformer, called repeatedly for a state referendum to draft a modern constitution that would recognize the reality of unrepresented voters and the injustice requiring civic duties of them without voting rights. Courtesy the Rhode Island Historical Society

Two exceptions to this docile deference to the political opinions of the "better sort" were Rhode Island workingman Seth Luther, and the patrician reformer, Thomas Wilson Dorr.[14] While the constitutional crisis in Rhode Island of 1842 was essentially about repealing the real estate requirement for voting, it was also about the extension of suffrage, giving a political voice to the thousands of male mill operatives who had no way to voice their opposition to laws compelling them to serve in the militia, or facing, without recourse, impossible and unfair prison consequences for indebtedness. To a lesser degree, Dorr's Rebellion also sought to redress the lopsided distribution of representatives in the respected towns. The old town of Smithfield, for instance, had a population of 9,534 by 1840.[15] Many of its inhabitants were industrial workers clustered in the several villages along the Blackstone, Woonasquatucket, and Branch rivers. Old Smithfield had only two representatives in the lower house of the General Assembly, the same number as Barrington and James-

town with populations of 549 and 365, respectively. Yet when Barrington and Jamestown delegates voted on issues, their combined population of 914 could trump the interests of Smithfield every time. So, even if all the mill operatives had been enfranchised, under the prevailing apportionment of representatives, their interests pertaining to factory issues stood little chance of fair consideration.

Luther and Dorr shared a common belief that the American Revolution had transferred decisionmaking rights to all of America's citizens (as a doctrine called Popular Constituent Sovereignty), but they shared little else. Luther (1795–1863) was a carpenter and son of a tanner and currier; Dorr (1805–1854) was a lawyer and son of a China Trade merchant.[16] Luther became a professional rabble-rouser, an outspoken enemy of injustice and inequality. He frequently was beaten and jailed for his outbursts and he spent his final years in Providence's Butler Hospital for the Insane before being transferred to the Vermont Asylum

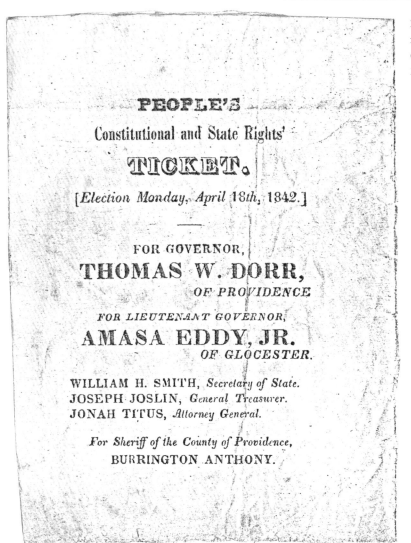

Handbill of People's Constitution. Handbill for the slate of officers under the People's Constitution Party. Courtesy the Rhode Island Historical Society

in Brattleboro. Dorr tried for a dozen years to obtain referenda to overhaul Rhode Island's outdated colonial charter, and, in final desperation, staged a statewide plebiscite for a People's Constitution.

Although it was overwhelmingly approved by a margin of 13,892 to 52 in December 1841, it was rejected by the governor, General Assembly, and state supreme court as being obtained illegally because no property restrictions were placed on those who could vote on its adoption. Citing the example of the American Revolution, and claiming that the power of the king was conveyed to the American people without limits, Dorr attempted to use force to implement the People's Constitution.[17] His military efforts thwarted twice, he fled the state with a price on his head. At last, voluntarily returning from exile, he was arrested, tried for trea-

son, and sent to prison, where he became ill. Agitation growing out of mass political rallies staged by Luther and countless others eventually freed Dorr in 1845, but he died within a decade at the age of 49. Both Luther and Dorr proved more powerful in death than in life, each providing an inspiring martyrdom that energized Rhode Island equal rights reformers for more than a century after their deaths.

At the time of the Dorr War of 1842, however, the Equal Rights Movement won mixed results. In the matter of suffrage for African Americans, Dorr and his supporters left out that provision in the People's Constitution and deferred it to a later, separate referendum for fear it would create opposition to passage of the constitution in its entirety. Ironically, Dorr's opponents, the Law and Order Party, supported enfranchising black property owners and thereby peeled off one layer of the equal rights constituency. One African-American military unit, the Providence Guards, actually marched in the Law and Order Army to put down Dorr's rebellion.[18]

Most of the women's suffrage advocates, like Catherine Williams and Frances Whipple, supported Dorr, expecting to receive fair treatment down the road if he won his case.[19] Elizabeth Buffum Chace was part of this group; Abby Kelley was not. Some women in the anti-slavery movement dropped their support of the People's Constitution when the convention vacillated on enfranchising blacks.

The role of blacks in the region of the Blackstone Valley in the post–Civil War period is a curious one, both from the standpoint of equal rights and as a component of the labor force.[20] For all of the interest and effort in operating a successful Underground Railroad before the Civil War to ensure runaway slaves a safe passage to Canada, the treatment of the resident black population in the Blackstone Valley seemed to function on a separate standard. While Quaker and abolitionist Moses Brown had a few blacks performing tasks for Slater, there was never a large black workforce for Almy and Brown. Similarly, the hiring practices, or lack of, for reformers Samuel and Harvey Chace or Edward Harris, made few places for African Americans in their mills.

During the era of industrialization throughout the Valley—with the exceptions of the urban areas of Providence, Pawtucket, and Worcester, and later still in Woonsocket—there was never a sizeable population of African Americans. In fact, blacks were probably exceeded in numbers by descendents of the Nipmuc nation. The Blacks in the region were never encouraged to work in the mills; prejudice was always present; and discrimination in hiring and in housing persisted to modern times. Census returns and anecdotal stories for the valley towns identify a half-dozen blacks as self-employed in marginal agriculture or as shoemakers and day laborers.

In nineteenth-century Worcester, blacks were numerous enough to form church congregations.[21] The first was the African Methodist Zion Church, gathered around 1846. Three others followed: the African Methodist Episcopal Bethel (1867), the Mount Olivet

Baptist (1885), and the Second Baptist Church (1958), which acquired the Mission Chapel built by Ichabod Washburn in 1854. Repeatedly in the census records of the later nineteenth century, the blacks of Worcester listed their occupations as barbers, laundresses, and laborers. Black populations in Pawtucket and Woonsocket eventually grew large enough to have churches, too: One example was the Union Baptist Church in Pawtucket in 1893, but none of their members played anywhere near the role in the industrialization of the Blackstone Valley that Primus Jenckes did in assisting Slater to make the bobbins on a lathe for his first machines, or that Prince Hopkins achieved in his work for Moses Brown.

Trade union organizations were slow to appear in the textile industry. The mule spinners were first in 1858, but the textile workers didn't organize until 1893. However, turn-outs and strikes, organized by wildcat leaders, were by then a common phenomenon. One of the earliest strikes, again led by young women, occurred in Woonsocket in 1834, just ten years after the Pawtucket turn-out.[22] Strikes came with increasing frequency in the 1870s. As noted, the increased war demands for goods, the improvement of the rail systems, and the demand for cloth across the Great Plains to California and thence around the world, led American producers to expand their mills. The great fleet of red brick factories anchored along the Blackstone, from Pawtucket to Millbury's Bramanville on the Singletary Brook, all with dates in their bell towers, attests to this expansion from the 1860s to the first decade of the twentieth century.

As the mills got larger and the path from the shop floor to the superintendent's office got longer, the grievances of the operatives also grew. With or without unions, there were strikes. Mule spinners went out in Blackstone in 1874, followed in the next year by the cotton workers in Lonsdale.[23] In 1877, it was workers in Uxbridge who struck and, then in 1880, there were work stoppages in Woonsocket, Valley Falls, and Manville.[24] The principal causes were wage cuts, the addition of more machines for a single worker to tend, and the stretching out of the day for the same or less pay.

The issue of the ten-hour day had simmered since the agitation of Seth Luther and the Workingmen's Movement of the mid–1830s. The Knights of Labor revived the issue in the mid–1880s, and making the workday shorter was the Knights' main objective.[25] Federal government employees enjoyed an eight-hour day, and Massachusetts had passed a ten-hour day for women and children in 1874. In 1873, a series of walk-outs in Rhode Island, begun in the Olneyville district of Providence, spread to Pawtucket but achieved little result.[26] Finally, petitions and meetings of the Knights of Labor and its local ally, the Central Labor Union, managed to get a Rhode Island ten-hour law passed in 1885 that exempted some workers such as the horse-drawn trolley drivers.[27] An 1883 law that would have regulated the hours for child labor was already on the books, but it contained no provision for enforcement.

Labor unrest in this period was particularly acute in the villages of the Lonsdale Company. Despite the arrival of some French-Canadian families during the Civil War to fill gaps in the work force and the presence of Irish workers, the real leaders of the Lonsdale dissatisfaction were the workers with an English background. Harkening to their trade union experience in mills of Lancashire, before coming to Lonsdale and Ashton, these workers discovered that they had less economic freedom in their work here than they had been accustomed to in England. They resented the arrogance of the American superintendents who, according to one Lonsdale worker, were the "Policeman, Judge, Jury and Almost King." Said one of the disgruntled English immigrants, the superintendents controlled every aspect of life, making the workman hesitate to "blow his nose" without looking over his shoulder.[28] These British imports even hesitated to continue the workingman's custom of singing at night for fear of losing their lodgings. In 1880, when a congressional investigation reported that the mill owners of the area had disenfranchised some 10,000 to 15,000 naturalized citizens—all mill operatives—the loss of their voting rights and the importance of the ballot was driven home to the proud Englishmen.

It was the Irish-centered leadership of Rhode Island state representative, Charles E. Gorman, however, who helped focus congressional scrutiny on Rhode Island. A brilliant attorney and committed equal rights advocate, Gorman had tried to get ethnicity included in the language of the Fifteenth Amendment to the U.S. Constitution along with blacks. Rhode Island U.S. Senator, Henry Bowen Anthony succeeded in blocking this effort as long as he could. He won the battle in the U.S. Constitution struggle, but Gorman's advocacy prevailed in the Bourn Amendment to the Rhode Island constitution in 1888. By that time, Anthony had died. Equal rights at the ballot box became as important as the issues of hours and wages.

In 1888, the Bourn amendment to the Rhode Island state constitution recognized voting rights for naturalized citizens without property holdings, except in the local election of city councils.[29] Similarly the non-taxpaying citizen could not participate in financial town meetings. The assemblies, or chapters, of the Knights of Labor, which previously had focused on cooperatives, nurseries, and neighborhood clubs, turned to politics and won legislative approval for the ten-hour day for women and children.

Almost as quickly as the Knights became the political muscle of the workingman, however, the muscle atrophied. Unfairly associated with the extremism of the Haymarket Riot and explosion in Chicago in 1886 and with other labor radicalism, and eclipsed by the emerging American Federation of Labor, the Knights had passed from the scene by 1893.[30] In Rhode Island, they left the legacy of the Rhode Island Bureau of Industrial Statistics. This was a seemingly minor accomplishment, but, like the public commotion in Pawtucket to put a clock in the church tower, the bureau crunched the numbers related to industrialization and let the chits fall where they may.

One person who paid attention to this political and economic agitation in Lonsdale was Dr. Lucius F. C. Garvin.[31] Although Garvin was born in Tennessee in 1841, he served in the 51st Massachusetts Volunteer Infantry in the Civil War. After graduating from Harvard Medical School, Garvin became the village doctor of Lonsdale in 1867. Practicing preventive medicine from his home office overlooking the Ann & Hope Mill, he attempted to improve public sanitation in the village, wrote a report about the hazards of exposed gears and pulleys on the shoproom floor, and spoke out on such issues as tuberculosis and the rate of infant mortality.

In 1883, during the ten-hour law agitation, Dr. Garvin won a seat in the Rhode Island General Assembly, beginning a career of public service that in-

14   REPORT OF FACTORY INSPECTION.

the age certificate which would enable them to get employment. I recommend that the law be amended so that in cases where the impossibility of obtaining such proof of age is evident, such evidence, other than the affidavit of parent or guardian, as shall be approved by the Commissioner of Public Schools shall be accepted by him, and he be authorized to issue a special certificate which shall entitle the child to receive employment.

I renew for the tenth time my recommendation that all children under sixteen years of age, who are unable to read and write simple sentences in the English language, be prohibited from employment.

I also renew the recommendation made last year, that provision be made for some physical test for children seeking employment.

PROSECUTIONS.

There have been four cases of prosecution for violation of the child labor law during the year, all of which are still pending.

ACCIDENTS.

During the past year eighty accidents have been reported, seven of which were fatal. Of these fatalities, but three were caused by machinery. The particulars are given as follows:

February 10, 1909. Vaseleos Teuskes, aged 21 years, employed by Forestdale Mfg. Co., Forestdale, to operate an elevator. The elevator was at the bottom floor. A girl on an upper floor signalled for him to come up. He started the elevator and was seen by the girl to immediately fall upon the gate. The girl was so frightened that she did not think to stop the elevator, but shouted for help; but before help arrived his body was caught between the elevator and the floor above, and he was taken out dead. What caused him to fall over is not known.

February 18, 1909. James Abraham, aged 20 years, employed at the Sayles Bleacheries, Saylesville. He was at work guiding a rope of cloth into a white chemic bin. As sometimes happens, the cloth

REPORT OF FACTORY INSPECTION.   15

was caught up by the rollers through which it runs. Instead of throwing off the belt, he followed a common custom of grasping the cloth and setting back his weight upon it to throw off the belt; but in this instance the belt did not slip, and he, becoming entangled in the cloth, was drawn up over the shaft and killed.

April 19, 1909. Charles Rossi, aged 23 years, employed at the Esmond Mills, Esmond, went into the "lint pit," under the napping room, to clean out the dust pipes, which had become clogged with waste, and, in some manner unknown, the lint was ignited and set fire to his clothing and burned him severely all over his body, and particularly about his head and the upper part of his body. Dr. A. W. Hughes, of Greenville, who was passing, was called in, and rendered such aid as was possible, after which the man was removed to the Rhode Island Hospital, for treatment, where he died the next morning. There was no lantern, electric light, or any artificial light in the "lint pit," at the time of the accident.

Sunday evening, October 10, 1909. George B. Carey, employed by the Narragansett Electric Lighting company, was directing the work of some men hoisting a motor to the ceiling in the mill of the Nornay Worsted Co., Providence, when the chain fall broke and Mr. Carey was pitched headlong to the floor, and it is thought, the motor fell on top of him. He died half an hour later at the Rhode Island Hospital.

November 4, 1909. John Brophy, aged 30, a machinist's helper, at the Phillipsdale Paper Mills, Phillipsdale, grasped a belt on a moving shaft, and the belt pulled him in and wound him around the shaft. He received injuries which proved fatal.

November 18, 1909. Gilbert Allen, aged 53 years, employed at the Esmond Mills, Esmond, as a teamster. He was dumping a tip-cart load, and the body of the cart came back, striking him in the stomach, inflicting injuries from which he died a few days later.

December 5, 1909. Antonio Tocci, aged 42 years, employed at the Phillipsdale Paper Mills, Phillipsdale, was working in the boiler

Rhode Island Factory Inspection Report. One of the few reforms to emerge from the efforts of progressive statesman like Garvin in the last part of the nineteen century was the annual inspection of working conditions in the mills that appeared in the reports of the Rhode Island Bureau of Labor Statistics beginning in 1894. Courtesy of Slater Mill, Pawtucket, RI

cluded thirteen years as a state representative, five as a state senator, and two one-year terms as governor of Rhode Island. It was Garvin who introduced the bill for the Bureau of Industrial Statistics and another to curb the mill owners' proclivity to fine children for minor infractions, leading to deductions of more than half of their pay envelopes, and promoted acceptance of the ten-hour law.[32]

Gilded Age America was filled with "rags to riches" stories told by popular writers like Horatio Alger. Certainly, Benjamin and Robert Knight's rise from "bobbin" boys in a Warwick mill to cotton kings with 39 mills under the Fruit of the Loom label seemed to prove the mythology. Rubber entrepreneur Joseph Banigan, a refugee of the Irish Famine, full of luck and pluck, also seemed to qualify, but luck didn't extend to his social skills in personnel management.[33] Banigan's Woonsocket Rubber Company grew out of the need to make quality rubber rollers for Bailey's American Wringer Company, but it was in the boot-and-

The foregoing table comprises the reports from establishments engaged in manufacture or finishing of cotton and woolen cloths and yarns, silk goods, thread, tapes, braids, and twines. The number of employees in these industries was divided as follows:

Males of sixteen years and over...................... 36,277
Females of sixteen years and over...................... 28,064

Total adults................................... 64,341

Males under sixteen years of age...................... 1,942
Females under sixteen years of age.................... 2,000

Whole number of children........................ 3,942

Total number employed in textile industries.......... 68,283

Compared with those of last year's report, the foregoing figures show an increase of four thousand seven hundred and ninety-three (4,793) in the number of adults employed; an increase of two hundred and seventy-eight (278) in the number of children employed; and a total increase of five thousand and seventy-one (5,071) in the whole number employed in the textile industries. The percentage of child labor in these industries remains the same as last year—5.8.

The following table gives a summary of the statistics of the reports of this department for the years that the factory inspection law has been in force:

Year.	Number of places visited.	Number of adults employed.	Number of children employed.	Total number employed.	Percentage of children.
1894	294	55,109	5,217	60,326	8.5
1895	293	53,523	4,473	57,966	7.7
1896	379	50,068	4,065	54,133	7.5
1897	355	56,072	4,786	60,858	7.9
1898	433	63,259	4,539	67,798	6.5
1899	549	72,296	4,666	76,692	6.0
1900	595	76,552	5,253	81,805	6.4
1901	617	81,496	5,068	86,564	5.8
1902	628	86,043	5,477	91,520	6.0
1903	644	90,165	6,451	96,616	6.7
1904	653	88,545	5,895	94,444	6.2
1905	1,508	112,377	6,917	119,249	5.8
1906	1,742	123,112	6,932	130,044	5.3
1907	1,899	131,059	6,150	137,209	4.5
1908	1,913	122,060	4,924	126,984	3.9
1909	1,973	135,947	5,531	141,478	3.9

RECOMMENDATIONS.

Section 22 of Chapter 168 of the General Laws prohibits the employment of women, and minors under sixteen years of age, more than fifty-six hours in a week. I recommend that this section be made a part of the factory inspection law, thereby applying to all classes of employment now covered by that law. I also call your attention to the inconsistency of enacting, in the interest of the physical welfare of women, a provision that prohibits their employment for more than fifty-six hours in a week, and still permits them to work that fifty-six hours on a night schedule—an employment that is manifestly more injurious to the health than a sixty-hour schedule of daytime work would be.

Several cases have been called to my attention in which it has been impossible for children to furnish the necessary birth certificate, baptismal certificate, or passport, and have consequently been denied

Rhode Island Factory Inspection Report. Although the ten-hour day, a major labor victory, had been in place for some time, this 1909 report points out that conditions still permitted women to work a night schedule of 56 hours that was, according to the report, more injurious to health than a 60-hour regimen for day work. Courtesy of Slater Mill, Pawtucket, RI

shoe business that Banigan really hit his stride. He really put his foot in it, however, by seeming to show disrespect for his fellow Irishmen when he cut back on wages in the Millville mill in 1885.[34]

Built in 1882, a model of efficient production, the Millville branch of the Woonsocket Rubber Company hit a difficult patch of business, and Banigan did what any other owner would do: He cut back. The way he went about it, however, rankled the workers, who then approached the Knights of Labor, organized a "local assembly," and promptly went on strike. They were back on the job within three weeks, but Banigan's intransigent attitude drove them out again. In fact, during the year 1885, there were actually three strikes at the Millville mill. The strikers appealed to their Catholic priest to provide moral support for their position, but the Church actually took Banigan's side of the issue, although, in the end, Father McCabe mediated the strike, helping to end the walkout.[35]

Banigan was an enormously generous benefactor

to Catholic charities. The previous year, he financed a home for the aged in Pawtucket, funded numerous projects for nurseries, and built a dormitory for working girls in Providence—so nice they stayed there forever, and it became an old ladies' home. Much to the chagrin of the American Catholic hierarchy, his philanthropy extended to the Mormon Church, perhaps dimming his halo in some eyes. He provided scholarships to Brown University to support its first Catholic students. He built hospitals and an infant asylum. He endowed a chair in political science at the Catholic University of America in Washington, D.C. For his philanthropy, he was made a Knight of St. Gregory by Pope Leo XIII, only the second such honor bestowed on an American.[36]

It was the Knights of Labor, however, that took him to task and made his life miserable in 1885. In mid-July, there was violence over scabs taking the place of strikers; shots were fired, a house attacked. Finally, he gave in, after about ten months, restoring half the pay cut, but not until he embarrassed the Church and had many of his good deeds besmirched by endless wrangles and heated criticisms in the columns of the Woonsocket and Providence newspapers.

The events of Millville in 1885, however, paled in comparison with the Motormen's trolley car strike in 1902.[37] Most of the militancy associated with the rise of labor unions in the Blackstone Valley logically related to worker/management disputes on the shop floor in the hundreds of textile factories in the region. One that did not, however, was the trolley strike of 1902. It sharply silhouetted the base issue of management's low esteem for its employees.

The issue behind the strike was that the Union Railroad—the trolley car company—believed it had enough power through its political connections to ignore the new ten-hour law.[38] The law protected the motormen and conductors from being bullied into working longer days and also sought to protect the public from dangerous accidents that could occur when tired employees lost control of their vehicles. At issue, moreover, was the assumption by the company that it had a right and entitlement to an unequal playing field, tilted in its favor, because the workers' cause was secondary to management's unlimited right to make money.

In the company's view, the workers were not deserving of the same opportunities due to their own mental, moral, ethnic, or congenital defects. Lacking fortune or fortitude, the workers' lot in life was intended to be lowly. According to the popular idea of the time, known as the "survival of the fittest," or Social Darwinism, if the workers had any gumption, they would make something of themselves and not be content to be wage laborers. Pure and simple, it was the Gilded Age's philosophical creed: Some people were just "predestined" to be menials.

One strand of the rope in this classic tug of war reached back a half-century to the equal rights issue framed by the Dorr Rebellion of 1842. Another strand emerged from the coil of nativism and "Know Nothing" prejudices of the 1850s, revived in the American Protective Association of the early 1890s. "True Americans" looked askance at Irish newcomers arriving in rags from their famine-torn homeland, with their superstitious, non-American Catholic religion, their separate schools, and their unquestioning obedience to priests in thrall to a foreign, infallible, dictator: the Pope. A third thread in the rope was the suspicion that workers combining in trade unions unfairly used labor power to hamper, circumscribe, and thwart the business decisions of entrepreneurs risking their fortunes. A fourth strand was that recently arrived workers brought with them the taint of radical syndicalism or socialism, both virulent anti-capitalist nostrums plaguing manufacturing in Europe at the time.

By the 1880s and the 1890s, the owners of companies had banded themselves together to form trade associations such as the Slater Club in the Blackstone Valley. National lobbying organizations, once deployed mostly to obtain tariff laws in Congress to keep out foreign competition, were now used to block the power of the Knights of Labor and its competing organization, the American Federation of Labor. High-handed and illegal worker actions, like Chicago's Haymarket Riot and the abuses of the murderous "Molly Maguires" in Pennsylvania coal fields, were used as excuses for blaming all trade union activities as criminal. The chambers of federal and state courts were open to owners to block "illegal" restraints to trade (strikes). State militia, local police, and sometimes national troops were called in to break strikes. Strike breakers (scabs), politicians, newspapers, and sympathetic clergy were also employed on the side of management.

But the Union Railroad's position in 1902 seemed to go too far. Public opinion turned on the management. Instead of riding the trolleys during the strike, the public sympathized with the carmen—and walked.[39]

A widespread disgust over back-room politics and ham-handed manipulation of the system led to this development. At the center was a trio of manipulators, the first of whom was United States Senator Nelson W. Aldrich, who, by 1900, had gained so much power in Washington that he was known as "The General Manager of the United States." His tariff favors on behalf of the U.S. sugar industry made it possible for him to get an interest-free loan to buy the Union Railroad when the Sprague textile and trolley empire went into bankruptcy.[40]

Using his political alliance with a former Civil War general—Charles Brayton, the second member of the triumvirate, who controlled all political patronage in Rhode Island and issued orders to a pliant General Assembly—Aldrich managed to convince local cities to turn over the use of the public streets to the trolley car company for a few dollars a year. The third member of this team was banker Marsden J. Perry, who cornered all the local utilities that supplied the power to run the trolleys. Because they had the situation literally "wired," and had no worries of being taken to task for high-handed treatment of the trolley car operators from the courts, the mayors, the governor, or the legislature, the Union Railroad Company simply decided to disregard the ten-hour law and force the motormen to run the trolleys as long as necessary. Their pay would be by the day, not by the hour.[41]

This outrageous abuse of power would have gone unchallenged but for the courage, cunning, and celtic insubordination of Pawtucket Mayor John J. Fitzgerald.[42] Where Providence Mayor Daniel Granger— a captive puppet of the trio of Aldrich, Brayton, and Perry—caved in on all their demands to protect the strike-breakers in running the trolleys, Fitzgerald used his police powers to protect the strikers and to keep the sheriffs and marshals provided by Brayton off the trolleys and out of his city.

There were massive marches in support of the strikes in both Providence and Pawtucket. The un-armed trolleys on the Pawtucket routes were the object of verbal abuse, brick-bats, and obstructions on the tracks that caused delays. After about ten days, at the behest of Marsden Perry, Governor Charles Kimball sent the state militia into Pawtucket to secure the streets on June 11. The sentiment of the militia, however, was clearly with the strikers. After two weeks' duty, they were withdrawn. The state supreme court weighed in with an opinion to the governor saying that the ten-hour law was legal and the company was in the wrong. Nonetheless, the state attorney general announced that he would not take legal action against the company until the fall. To underscore his arrogance, Marsden Perry requested an injunction against the attorney general to prevent him from doing his duty, even at a later date.[43] Despite the outpouring of broad public moral support, the strikers couldn't keep the job action going without strike pay from the Amalgamated Association of Street and Electric Railway Employees of America. The national union didn't forward the cash. The strike officially ended on July 5; the Pawtucket hold-outs returned to work on July 8.

Although the workers lost, the furor accompanying the strike swelled the ranks of registered voters. Lucius Garvin, the physician reformer, was swept into office as governor. Like the carmen's strike, however, Garvin's two one-year terms as governor were full of sound-bites, but not much else. Brayton had defanged the governor's office in his 1901 Brayton Act, taking away all its appointive powers, making it toothless. While the governor still could offer names to all the positions in state government, the nominations required senate approval. Once declined by the senate, the governor never had a second nomination; the senate was empowered to fill the positions as it saw fit. As Brayton bragged to Aldrich, "the governor can't do anything but sign notaries' commissions."[44] As if to underscore the lack of gubernatorial powers, when Governor Garvin addressed the legislature on pressing issues, the members rose from their seats and turned their backs on him. The calendar marked the beginning of the "progressive" twentieth century, but the pettiness of the nineteenth prevailed a bit longer.

One of the new ideas in unionism in the twentieth century was the concept of having all workers in one big union. This concept was exemplified by the pat-

Outside labor meeting. Denied space inside their place of work for purposes of assembly, and sometimes in village meeting halls, churches and reading rooms as well, groups of workers, like these employed by the Draper Manufacturing Company in Hopedale, Massachusetts, workers often met under maples to hear politicians or labor organizers—like the IWW—who outlined their labor reform programs often to various forms of company harassment. From the Collection of Laurel Moriarty

tern promoted by the Congress of Industrial Organizations, the CIO; it organized workers on a factory-by-factory basis, mixing both skilled and unskilled workers into one union, rather than using the model of the craft unions offered by the American Federation of Labor, with separate units for the plumbers, the carpenters, the machinists, and so forth.

Another approach to the "one union fits all" approach was the International Workers of the World, the I.W.W., popularly known as the "Wobblies."[45] The brainchild of "Big Bill" Haywood, the Wobblies embraced socialist ideals and confrontational tactics. Many of their strikes took place in Western mining towns. One of their Blackstone Valley forays was in Hopedale, however, where they tried unsuccessfully for six months in 1913 to help the machinists make gains with the Draper Company.[46] An equally bitter strike of machinists against Brown and Sharpe Manufacturing Company absorbed most of 1916. The company stood firm, however, and kept unions out until the Second World War when they had to recognize the Machinists' Union in order to do war work.

In 1922, textile strikes swept across Rhode Island, as the United Textile Union tried to hold on to gains it had made in World War I.[47] The union fought against cutbacks in wages and increases in hours that mills sought in order to stave off losses. This retrenchment occurred as the country tried to adjust and convert production from a war-time to a peace-time economy. Cotton mills were hit particularly hard. Strike actions took more violent turns as strike-breakers were threatened and attacked when they attempted to cross picket lines. When local police were overwhelmed, the Republican governor, a Franco-American by the name of Emery J. San Souci, called out the National Guard to quell disorder. In this confrontation, industrial neighborhoods were treated to the sight of machine guns mounted on the roofs of mill buildings and armed soldiers in the streets.

Something was clearly changing, particularly in the large French-Canadian communities in Pawtucket, Central Falls, Albion, Manville, and Woonsocket in the 1920s. The French, who previously had been a bulwark of the Rhode Island Republican Party, developed a new appreciation of the fraternal and economic interests they shared with other workers of different ethnicities. This new solidarity, coupled with other issues of the day, began to loosen the strong political ties the French-Canadians had with the Republican Party and the management class it represented. Gradually, by the mid–1930s, the French-Canadian and Italian workers had shifted their allegiance to the Democratic Party.

The other issue that provoked the previously "docile" French was the quarrel with Roman Catholic Bishop William Hickey, known as the Sentinellist Controversy.[48] As discussed earlier, it centered on the bishop's goal to build a regional high school, one where English, rather than French, would be the language of instruction. In doing this, Hickey was not only trying to Americanize to a greater degree the French stalwarts, but he was also trying to bring Catholic edu-

cation more in line with the prevailing standard of public school educators. In 1924, the State of Rhode Island had passed the Peck Act, legislation authored by a leader of the Republican Party that required "English only" instruction in the public schools. Hickey's attempt to honor the Peck Act in a Catholic context was costly, but ultimately prevailed: After much public discord, the Sentinellist leaders eventually were punished for their defiance of the bishop. But as a concession to French sensibilities in the matter, Mount St. Charles, one of Rhode Island's premier Catholic high schools, was built in Woonsocket with a French order in charge. Despite this severe, but temporary, rupture between the French community and the Irish church hierarchy, this breach did not have long-term effects for French comity and cooperation within the other major institution dominated by the Irish: the Democratic Party.[49]

In the turbulent decade of the 1920s, immigrant and ethnic groups emerged, threatening and being threatened by the existing labor structures, and eventually fomenting their own changes in the valley. After World War I, the nation experienced a cloud of suspicion unleashed by the Bolshevik Revolution in Russia and the apparent will of the new Communist regime to overthrow the capitalist West that led to a national "Red Scare." Aliens, socialist sympathizers, and radical labor advocates were rounded up. A culture of suspicion that challenged the loyalties of recent immigrants and hyphenated Americans was spawned. In 1921 and 1924, national origins quota immigration restrictions cut off the flow of newcomers to the "Golden Door," especially those from southern and eastern Europe. Programs increased to "Americanize" recent immigrants in order to preserve the American ideals and traditions. Activities that celebrated other "old country" traditions were discouraged, skimmed like fat off the surface of the melting pot. New citizens were molded and minted in the drive for "100 percent Americanism."[50]

Out of this atmosphere erupted another national abscess: the revived Ku Klux Klan with its message of hate against Blacks, Catholics, and Jews, its opposition to international policies like the League of Nations, and its attacks on trade unionism. Klan activity in Rhode Island centered in the country towns west

PUBLIC SCHOOL DEPARTMENT
Division of Immigrant Education

———

Learn English

A free Public Day School for Immigrants is held Monday, Tuesday, Wednesday, Thursday and Friday from 9 a.m. to 4 p.m. at the Lamartine Street School.

For men and women who work nights.

For men and women who can go to school mornings only.

For men and women who can go to school afternoons only.

For all **new** immigrants who wish to learn to speak English before going to work in their new country.

———

Tell your friends about it
Come when you can
Stay as long as you can

PRINTED AT WORCESTER CONTINUATION SCHOOL

left and below: Poster—Learn English; Educational Class for Immigrants. Although immigrants from Ireland, French Canada, Italy, and Eastern Europe had flocked to the Blackstone Valley mills, it wasn't until the early decades of the twentieth century that Americanization classes were offered. Largely the result of the apprehensions of groups like the American Protective Association (APA) that American virtues and traditions would be diluted by waves of illiterate immigrants, classes in evening schools were designed to make sure that the "melting of European nations" would produce those loyal to America. From the collections of Worcester Historical Museum, Worcester, MA

of Providence, but the objects of its hatred lived in the cities and towns of the Blackstone Valley.[51] In Worcester, the Klan's messages seemed to resonate mostly within the Swedish community.

At first glance, the parallels between the cities of Worcester and Woonsocket with respect to industrialization and ethnic labor force appear congruent. However, as far as their history of trade-union organizing, the two towns are a study in contrasts. Two major urban manufacturing centers, with a majority of their populations comprising a blue-collar work force, both on the same river, and using the same transportation services, but their union-building stories could not have been more different. Why were the machinists in Worcester twenty years behind their fellow metal artisans in Massachusetts and a world away from labor activists just 20 miles to the south?

For one thing, Worcester's industrial scene consisted of a variety of industries: wire making, machine-tool building, the manufacturing of everything from railroad cars, paper envelopes, and emery wheels, to railroad cars, carpets, ice skates, lunch wagons, and ladies' corsets. This manufacturing diversity created divides in the work force.[52] Woonsocket's industrialism was more limited: cotton textiles, machine building (mostly tied to textiles), rubber boots, and woolen and worsted fabric. The predominant jobs in Worcester required skilled craftsmen. In Woonsocket, tending the machines of manufacturing needed only semi-skilled or unskilled workers. Unlike in Worcester, a large portion of the Woonsocket work force consisted of women. Well into the 1920s and 1930s, with the major exception of Washburn and Moen, which had been sold to American Steel and Wire, most of Worcester's businesses were still owned by their original local families. Even the Wire Company's management was still largely as local as it been for decades.

With local management came all the networks of family, friends, church, and social groups that formed a barricade against the onslaught of labor militancy. In addition, beyond the owners' group, a broad community opposition to unions comprised of clergy, banks, newspapers, and a city government with police powers supported private enterprise. In Woonsocket, by contrast, the ownership of the mills was spread from the local scene to Providence industrialists and banks,

and as far away as board rooms in Roubaix and Tourcoing, France.[53] In Worcester, besides having a work force spread throughout different kinds of manufacturing, there were major divides and fissures within the laboring population itself, stemming from ethnic antagonisms between the Irish and the Swedes stemming from Catholic versus Protestant points of view (so deep that they fueled the Swedes' affection for the Klan), but also including different attitudes towards Prohibition. In addition, the Irish foothold in the hierarchy of the Catholic Church gave an aura of a different kind of "clannishness" to newcomers like French Canadians and Italian Catholics. There was clearly a hierarchy among the ethnic groups dictated by their order of arrival. It made working-class and ethnic solidarity more difficult in Worcester. These fissures between the Irish and the French Canadians were less prominent within Woonsocket, but they also had manifested themselves outside of Woonsocket in the Sentinellist controversy with the Irish bishop Hickey.

The Worcester business leadership used two other ploys, moreover, to discourage union agitation.[54] The socialist ideas of the Wobblies and other militants never got into the public forum as they did elsewhere. In addition to a full range of economic sanctions, including blacklists and union-busting trade association tactics, there was, on the other hand, a strong community tradition of corporate philanthropy and benefits to workers such as good pay, company housing in progressive neighborhoods for the Norton workers, and support for playgrounds, parks, and company outings at Lake Quinsigamond. Both methods—overt discouragement for unions and a kind of corporate paternalism that served as "positive reinforcement" against unionizing—kept Worcester relatively agitation-free.

Once the labor movement gained a foothold in Woonsocket, however, the entire town was transformed into a labor stronghold. At first, this was an unlikely scenario. Labor success hinged on arousing the ire of the French-Canadian mill hand who had a reputation in labor circles for being too docile, too devoted to his or her church, and too demure for acts of public outrage. The idea of unions was looked upon as being "too American" for an ethnic group that prided itself on maintaining its French culture and tended

American Wire & Steel Workers. The hardened faces of the wire workers was a clear indication of their difficult working conditions. From the collections of Worcester Historical Museum, Worcester, MA

ITU Picket Arm-Band and ITU Union Pin. During World War II, the ITU, which began as the Independent Textile Union in Woonsocket, kept its monogram, but transformed itself into the Industrial Trades Union—a CIO-style conglomeration of several unions. Its influence spread throughout the Blackstone Valley, welcoming workers in machine tools, rubber products and textiles. Courtesy of Museum of Work & Culture Collection

to be corporatist, with its group loyalty to family and church. The spark that illuminated a new view on things came from a recently arrived group of Franco-Belgian workers, imbued with European-style attitudes for controlling the shop room floor, who had appeared in Woonsocket with the new French and Belgian mills, starting around 1905.[55]

Gathering momentum with strikes at the French Worsted Mill in 1913, the General Textile Strike of 1922, and the Manville Jenckes Strike that eventually closed the Social and Nourse mills in Woonsocket, throwing 1,000 people out of work, these "France French" seceded from the United Textile Workers in 1931 to form their own Independent Textile Union.[56] By 1939, this unlikely entity had not only organized all the city textile mills, but represented bakers, barbers, electricians, retail clerks, and public employees; once known for textiles only, ITU came to stand for the Industrial Trades Union.

The transformation of this innovative workers' voice from radical cadre to city-wide union began when these European arrivals shed their European socialist roots, and adopted a conservative fiduciary regimen. They also drew from American patriotic models for marketing and image making. The European-style unionism

appeared on the scene at just the right mood moment to capture the loyalty of the French-Canadian community as it drifted away from its traditional moorings.

The main catalysts for the transformation, however, were the twin historical developments of the Textile Strike of 1934 and the Norris-LaGuardia and Wagner Labor Acts, New Deal legislation that protected union organizing.[57] In September 1934, some 400,000 textile workers walked out on strike throughout the United States, protesting industry speed-ups and stretch-outs and seeking higher wages. The 1934 strikes in Rhode Island particularly affected the village of Saylesville in Lincoln and the textile mills of Woonsocket. Mass demonstrations, attacks on mill property, several deaths, and a tear gas–laden battle between workers and national guardsmen among the gravestones of the Moshassuck Cemetery took place on the boundary line between Lincoln and Central Falls.

This mayhem led Governor Theodore Francis Green to call Washington, D.C., for federal troops under the command of General Douglas McArthur.[58] There was four days of fighting in Woonsocket, too. An innocent bystander was shot to death, and the confrontation made all the newsreels. The ranks of the ITU doubled after this event, from 1,500 to 3,000. By 1936, its

Moshassuck Cemetery Gravestone. A view of the tense days of the textile workers strike in Saylesville, Rhode Island, in 1934 with National Guard troops chasing strikers through the Moshassuck Cemetery can be clearly seen through these prominent bullet holes through a gravestone in the cemetery. John H. Chafee Blackstone River Valley NHC/National Park Service

membership doubled again, and it was 10,000 strong by 1939. The total population of Woonsocket during the period, including women and children, was only 50,000 people.[59]

Despite his stance in quelling the riots and blaming the origins on the communists, Governor Green still managed to hang on to most of his labor support in the fall election of 1934. He had called out the Guard only after the outbreak of violence, and he was careful not to take the side of the mill owners. He was re-elected. His Democratic coalition of labor, ethnic groups, and patrician Yankees of a progressive bent carried the house of representatives and came within two seats of capturing the state senate.

Using some parliamentary sleight-of-hand only available on the first legislative day of the new session, Green and Democratic leaders, including Pawtucket's Harry Curvin and Thomas P. McCoy and the Pawtuxet Valley's Robert E. Quinn, forced a re-count of two senate seats whose outcome were in doubt.[60] By failing to swear in the contested seat-holders, Lieutenant Governor Quinn created a constitutional moment that gave him the deciding vote in the case of deadlocked runs for office. By invoking this rule, the two disputed seats were recounted and the Democrats were declared winners. With a majority now in both houses, Green's floor managers proposed a series of sweeping changes. All the seats on the state supreme court were declared vacant and the state finance officer, the commandant of the state police, and the high sheriff were fired. More than 80 state boards and commissions were dissolved and state administrative departments of government put in their place. All this took place on January 1, 1935, in fourteen furious minutes of legislative legerdemain, later known as the "Bloodless Revolution." Breathless, his pen almost out of ink from signing all the bills, Governor Green announced that, finally, the spirit of Thomas Wilson Dorr had triumphed in Rhode Island.[61] This time, however, unlike the shaming experience accorded his predecessor, Lucius Garvin, no one in the Grand Committee of the General Assembly turned his back.

NOTES

1. Gary Kulik, "Pawtucket Village and the Strike of 1824: The Origins of Class Conflict in Rhode Island," *Radical History Review* 17 (Spring 1978): 21–26.

2. Ibid., 26.

3. Gary Kulik, "Textile Mill Labor in the Blackstone Valley: Work and Protest in the Nineteenth Century," in *Working in the Blackstone Valley: Exploring the Heritage of Industrialization*, ed. Douglas M. Reynolds and Marjory Myers, 112 (Woonsocket, R.I.: Rhode Island Labor Historical Society, 1991).

4. Gary Kulik, "Dams, Fish, and Farmers: The Defense of Public Rights in Eighteenth Century Rhode Island," in *The New England Working Class and the New Labor History*, ed. Herbert H. Gutman and Donald H. Bell, 187–213 (Urbana: University of Illinois Press, 1987).

5. Gary B. Kulik, "The Beginnings of the Industrial Revolution in America: Pawtucket, Rhode Island, 1672–1829," Ph.D. dissertation, Brown University, 1980, 370.

6. James Conrad, "The Evolution of Industrial Capitalism in Rhode Island, 1790–1830: Almy, the Browns, and Slater," Ph.D. dissertation, University of Connecticut, 1973, 108.

7. Ibid., 106.

8. Ibid., 105; Paul E. Johnson, *Sam Patch: The Famous Jumper* (New York: Hill and Wang, 2003), 3–40.

9. Paul Buhle, Scott Molloy, and Gail Sansbury, eds., *A History of Rhode Island Working People* (Providence: Rhode Island Labor History Group, 1983), 1. See also Ronald P. Formisano, *The Transformation of Political Culture: Massachusetts Parties, 1790s–1840s* (New York: Oxford University Press, 1983), 227–38.

10. Formisano, *Transformation of Political Culture*, 227–32. See also Robert Grieve, *An Illustrated History of Pawtucket, Central Falls, and Vicinity* (Pawtucket: Pawtucket Gazette and Chronicle, 1897), 98–99.

11. Formisano, *Transformation of Political Culture*, 227–32.

12. Edward Field, ed., *State of Rhode Island and Providence Plantations at the End of the Century, A History* (Boston: Mason Publishing Company, 1902), 226–32.

13. John Brooke, *The Heart of the Commonwealth: Society and Political Culture in Worcester County, Massachusetts, 1713–1861* (Amherst: The University of Massachusetts Press, 1989), 314–16; Formisano, *Transformation of Political Culture*, 282–84.

14. Scott Molloy, Carl Gersuny, and Robert Macieski, eds., *Peaceably if We Can: Forcibly if We Must: Writings by and about Seth Luther* (Kingston: Rhode Island Labor History Society, 1998).

15. Peter J. Coleman, *The Transformation of Rhode Island, 1790–1860* (Providence: Brown University Press, 1963), 220, 254–62; Patrick T. Conley, *Democracy in Decline: Rhode Island's Constitutional Development, 1776–1841* (Providence: The Rhode Island Historical Society, 1977); Marvin E. Gettleman, *The Dorr Rebellion: A Study in American Radicalism, 1833–1849* (New York: Random House, 1973); George Dennison, *The Dorr War: Republicanism on Trial, 1831–1861* (Lexington: University Press of Kentucky, 1976); Joyce M. Botelho, *Right and Might: The Dorr Rebellion and the Struggle for Equal Rights* (Providence: The Rhode Island Historical Society, 1992); Patrick T. Conley, "No Tempest in a Teapot," *Rhode Island History* 50, no. 3 (August 1992): 67–100; Ronald P. Formisano, "The Role of Women in the Dorr Rebellion," *Rhode Island History* 51, no. 3 (August 1993): 89–104.

16. Carl Gersuny, "Seth Luther—the Road from Chepachet," *Rhode Island History* 33, no. 2 (May 1974): 47–55; Conley, *The Dorr Rebellion*, 3–4.

17. Conley, *The Dorr Rebellion*, 12. See also Patrick T. Conley, *Rhode Island in Rhetoric and Reflection* (East Providence: The Rhode Island Publications Society, 2002), 129–58.

18. Botelho, *Right and Might*, book three, 56.

19. Formisano, "The Role of Women," 89–104.

20. Jan Armstrong, "People of Color in the Blackstone Valley," research report conducted for the Blackstone River

Valley National Heritage Corridor, 1999/2000: Pawtucket, 66–76; Providence, 77–82; Woonsocket, 83–89.

21. Ibid., 37–59.

22. Kulik, "Textile Mill Labor," 116.

23. Ibid.

24. Ibid.

25. Paul Buhle, "The Knights of Labor in Rhode Island," *Radical History Review* 17 (Spring 1978): 39ff.

26. Ibid., 46.

27. Ibid., 49.

28. Ibid., 47.

29. Charles Carroll, *Rhode Island: Three Centuries of Democracy* (New York: Lewis Historical Publishing Company, 1932), vol. II, 655–56.

30. Buhle, "Knights of Labor," 63–67.

31. Buhle, Molloy, and Sansbury, *History of Rhode Island Working People*, 34–35.

32. Ibid., 34. See also Carl Gersuny, "Uphill Battle, Lucius F. Garvin's Crusade for Political Reform," *Rhode Island History* 39, no. 2 (May 1980): 57–75.

33. Scott Molloy, *No Philanthropy at the Point of Production: A Knight of St. Gregory against the Knights of Labor, the 1885 Strike at the Woonsocket Rubber Company* (Kingston: The Rhode Island Labor History Society, 2003). See also Alton P. Thomas, *Woonsocket Highlights of History* (Woonsocket: Woonsocket Opera House Historical Society, 1976), 73–82.

34. Molloy, *No Philanthropy*, 9ff.

35. Ibid., 22–23.

36. Ibid., 5. See also Robert Hayman, *Catholicism in Rhode Island* (Providence: Diocese of Providence, 1995), vol. II, 475–78, 478–91, 502, 504, 505.

37. Scott Molloy, *Trolley Wars: Street Car Workers on the Line* (Washington, D.C.: Smithsonian Institution Press, 1996).

38. Ibid., 131–32.

39. Ibid., 147–50.

40. Ibid., 71.

41. Ibid., 132.

42. Ibid., 140–46.

43. Ibid., 153.

44. Ibid., 169.

45. Buhle, Molloy, and Sansbury, *History of Rhode Island Working People*, 41–42.

46. John S. Garner, *The Model Company Town* (Amherst: University of Massachusetts Press, 1984), 183.

47. Buhle, Molloy, and Sansbury, *History of Rhode Island Working People*, 45–47.

48. Gary Gerstle, *Working-Class Americanism: The Politics of Labor in a Textile City, 1914–1960* (New York: Cambridge University Press, 1989), 58–60. See also Marcel Fortin, ed., *Woonsocket, Rhode Island: A Centennial History, 1888–1998* (Woonsocket: Woonsocket Centennial Committee, 1998), 86–90; Richard S. Sorrell, "The Sentinelle Affair (1924–1929) and Militant Survivance: The Franco-American Experience in Woonsocket, Rhode Island," Ph.D. dissertation, State University of New York, Buffalo, 1975; Richard Sorrell, "Sentinelle Affair: Religion and Militant Survivance in Woonsocket, R.I.," *Rhode Island History* 36, no. 3 (August 1977).

49. Patrick T. Conley, class lecture notes on Rhode Island in the 1920s from course on Rhode Island history at Providence College, 1970s.

50. Ibid. See also Anita Rafael, *La Survivance* (Providence: Rhode Island Historical Society, 1997), 27–28.

51. Norman Smith, "The Ku Klux Klan in Rhode Island," *Rhode Island History* 37, no. 2 (May 1978): 35–45; Charles W. Estus and John McClymer, *ga till Amerika* (Worcester: Worcester Historical Museum, 1994), 124–34; Timothy J. Meagher, *Inventing Irish America: Generation, Class, and Ethnic Identity in a New England City, 1880–1928* (Notre Dame: University of Notre Dame Press, 2001), 306–13, 330, 343, 353–54.

52. Charles G. Washburn, *Industrial Worcester* (Worcester: The Davis Press, 1917).

53. Gerstle, *Working-Class Americanism*, 75–77.

54. Roy Rosenzweig, *Eight Hours for What We Will: Workers and Leisure in an Industrial City, 1870–1920* (New York: Cambridge University Press, 1983), 12–16.

55. Gerstle, *Working-Class Americanism*, 61–91.

56. Ibid., 95–105; Rafael, *La Survivance*, 29–32.

57. Buhle, Molloy, and Sansbury, *History of Rhode Island Working People*, 50–58; Gerstle, *Working-Class Americanism*, 127–40.

58. Erwin L. Levine, *Theodore Francis Green: The Rhode Island Years* (Providence: Brown University Press, 1963), 169–71.

59. Gerstle, *Working-Class Americanism*, 138–39.

60. Levine, *Theodore Francis Green*, 176–83.

61. Ibid., 182.

The Demise of a Mill Village

RANGER CHUCK ARNING

Manchaug Mill Housing. A six-room flat with bath, electric lights, and running water could be rented for a bargain rate of $2 a week back in 1927. Courtesy of Pat Nedoroscik & Family

The village of Manchaug in Sutton, Massachusetts, had managed to survive fires and floods, depressions and wars, but it couldn't survive a lack of orders.

The stone mill, No. 1, built in 1826 from granite quarried from neighboring farms, dominated the village landscape. Cut into the hillside, its unique design allowed the mill five different levels of loading docks to accommodate the B. B. & R. Knights growing textile operation. With 96 years of continuous operation and a close-knit village of French-Canadian and Polish workers residing within walking distance of the mills,

villagers expected the boom of supplying textiles for the Great War (World War I) to usher in an era of full employment and good times.

Instead, what rolled in was a precipitous drop in orders from which the company never rebounded. The mills, the village, and all its properties went on the auction block in March of 1922. The mills closed and left the area. They headed south. Viewed from an economic standpoint as cash cows, mill ownership stopped reinvestment. Old mills used old technology; dirty and gritty, they were a dying breed. While labor costs were far lower in the South, the real issue was the ability to build a new mill with new technology for far less in the South, than it would cost to retrofit the existing mills throughout the Blackstone Valley.

It wasn't an overnight transition, but happened over time, with the textile mills the first to begin the migration south. The machine-tool and wire mills were able to hang on longer and, with the influx of business based on the war orders during World War II, they persevered to the 1950s, while some, like the Draper

Manchaug Mill No. 1. In just the right light and properly cropped, this twenty-first-century picture of the 1826 Manchaug Mill No. 1 could have been taken over 180 years ago. The resurgence of the renovated mill, acting as an incubator for small businesses and industry, continues to dominate the landscape and provide a sense of identity and pride for those who still call the village home. John H. Chafee Blackstone River Valley NHC/National Park Service

Manufacturing Company, maintained their integrity to the 1970s. But the economic downward spiral that pushed the Blackstone Valley, once the leader in the industrialization of the young Republic, seemed inevitable. The broken mill windows and empty industrial buildings made the region look like a backwater of industrial development. The world had changed and left the Blackstone Valley behind.

One thing that did not change was the character of the mill village and the people who lived there. They survived. They adapted. They persevered. Their lives changed, but they found ways to soldier on. They had to commute. The people in Manchaug found work in the Shuster Mills in East Douglas; others found work at the Whitin Machine Works. And thus, it was so throughout the valley. The people adapted.

An example of this ability to adapt can be found with our loom fixer, Fred Small, who managed to fix

Empty Fisherville Mill. This eerie image of the harsh light of reality hitting the barren mill floor where hundreds once worked was duplicated throughout the Blackstone Valley. Courtesy of Skip Michniewicz

that cranky loom at the Fisherville Mill and court its weaver. Small, seen below as a textile worker in a circa 1915 photo inside the Fisherville Mill, then as the loom fixer working in the circa 1930 Machine Shop at the mill, continued to find a way to provide for his family. It was a struggle, but more than merely an individual feat of endurance and tenacity, Small's experience is the standard for the mill villages throughout the valley. People simply found ways to survive.

Small became the night watchman for the Fisherville Mill and, to this day, his youngest daughter Anita remembers how her father had to venture out into every storm, making his way to the mill to ensure all was right inside the hulking relic of an industrial past. He eventually served the community as a police officer for twenty-three years.

1915 Fisherville Mill Textile Workers. A circa 1915 photo of the interior of the Fisherville Mill showing textile workers, among them the young teenager, Fred Small, pictured to the right with dark hair. Courtesy of Anita (Small) & Richard Hudson & Family

1930 Fisherville Machine Shop. A circa 1930 photo of the interior of the machine shop at the Fisherville Mill. Notice the shop supervisor in the straw hat to the right with a more mature-looking Fred Small standing just back of him. Courtesy of Anita (Small) & Richard Hudson & Family

Memorial Day Parade. At a late 1940 or early 1950 Memorial Day parade through the Village of Fisherville
in South Grafton, Massachusetts, a contingent of police officers leads the way with a senior-looking Fred Small
right in the center. Courtesy of Anita (Small) & Richard Hudson & Family

In every corner of the Blackstone Valley, from the village of Rumford to the Globe Village in Woonsocket, to Leicester, families who loved the region worked hard to preserve the lives they lived there, even if they could not preserve their former livelihoods. The mill villages of the Blackstone Valley endure as unique historic sites because of their landscape, their architectural integrity, and the sheer number and close proximity of the villages. They endure in our hearts because of their ability to tell a story of industrialization—and of the families who helped make it happen—that can be found only in the Blackstone Valley.

7 The Past as Prologue The National Park Service and the Reintegration of the Blackstone Valley's Past

DR. JOSEPH F. CULLON

Kayakers and Horse-Drawn Wagon. John H. Chafee Blackstone River Valley NHC/National Park Service

The past that has been recounted in these pages is now prologue to something new in the Blackstone River Valley. Where once the spread of mills along the river as well as the movement of goods upon the canal and railroad gave shape to the valley as a distinct cultural and economic subregion of New England, a new entity has emerged to connect and give meaning to the valley. Nearly a century of mill closings, de-industrialization, and suburbanization had obscured the novelty and vitality of the valley's history. But the John H. Chafee Blackstone National Heritage Corridor has resurrected this past to spur the preservation, restoration, and conservation of the valley's natural, industrial, and urban resources. Just as human endeavors to channel the river's power for manufacturing created the Blackstone as a meaningful unit of social and economic organization at the end of the eighteenth century, now, two centuries later, efforts to exploit not the river's power but its human history remind us just how much the communities of the valley are still bound together—if not by a shared economic base, then by a common past.

In the process, the corridor not only has championed a new sense of place and purpose among the now-disparate communities of the valley, it also has reshaped the presentation of New England's past. Pilgrims, Puritans, minutemen, and goodwives have long been the stock characters of the region's grade-school textbooks. Recreations of their sensible farmsteads, white meetinghouses, and tidy commons have been the standard destinations of countless field trips.[1] Now alongside these mythic characters in New England's public memory stand the enterprising manufacturers, Irish canal diggers, and immigrant mill hands whose labors created the Blackstone.[2] Schoolchildren can visit the Slater Mill Historic Site in Pawtucket to see the humble origins of American manufacturing or they can learn about the work and leisure of French Canadians at the Museum of Work and Culture in Woonsocket. At both sites—and many more throughout the valley—National Park Service rangers working with the John H. Chafee Blackstone River Valley National Heritage Corridor Commission help visitors understand the past and its implications for the region's future. Thus, Irish immigrants, French Canadians, Swedes, and other hyphenated Americans have found their rightful place in New England's drama.

Interpreting the past is only part of Corridor Commission's work to develop and implement "integrated cultural, historical, and land management programs to retain, enhance and interpret" the valley's natural, industrial, and cultural resources.[3] The heritage corridor seeks to preserve the past as a renewable asset that can help support the region's economic development as a foundation for the future. The Corridor

Commission and the National Park Service have undertaken this challenge by collaborating with a host of local institutions in Massachusetts and Rhode Island. Together, the commission and its partners have come to appreciate that, as one institutional partner says, "the river's heritage can be a cornerstone for future prosperity."[4]

These recent efforts to energize the valley rely upon the sound stewardship of historic structures, local traditions, and natural spaces. Local institutions conceive of the past as a resource and platform for improving the valley residents' quality of life, stimulating economic development, and instilling a dynamic sense of place. The Corridor Commission relies upon partnerships with the many keepers of the Blackstone Valley's past: the prestigious institutions, the local historical societies, the private industries, and the diligent preservers of changing ethnic traditions. It also brings to the table those concerned with the region's present and future: state highway planners, local conservation organizations, and local development advocates. By bringing the valley's traditional guardians of the past together with the proponents of economic development for the future, the corridor emphasizes that a more prosperous future in the valley need not disown the region's industrial past; in fact, it should embrace it.[5] The past offers models of innovation and entrepreneurialism to emulate in the new century, as well as a sense of common heritage to draw upon to rebuild the bonds that once held the region's communities together. Thus, the forces that historically have animated the valley in the nineteenth century—invention and entrepreneurialism, work and technology, environment and energy, immigration and identity—might again revitalize the Blackstone that has suffered for too long from the deindustrialization associated with mill closings and the atomization brought about by the placelessness of modern car culture. The past becomes prologue for a new way of living in the Blackstone River Valley.

The National Park Service began their work in the Blackstone Valley more than twenty years ago, when Congress established the Blackstone River Valley National Heritage Corridor Commission to "preserve and interpret the unique and significant contribution of the valley's resources and history to the nation's heritage." The commission's charge was to work with

Turnpike Locator Sign Celebration. To accomplish its objectives in the valley, the Corridor Commission collaborated with a host of partners spanning the nonprofit and for-profit worlds, local, state and other federal agencies, and a wide variety of civic groups and historical societies. John H. Chafee Blackstone River Valley NHC/National Park Service

state, municipal, and private agencies within the corridor to better integrate various cultural, historical, and environmental programs that spanned the river. One measure of the success of the commission is its longevity. It was initially slated to expire in 1996, but Congress extended its charter for another ten years in 1996 and another five years starting in 2006. Between 1987 and 2004, nearly twenty-four million dollars in federal funding has flowed into the valley through the National Park Service, whose rangers do much of the work to further the mission of the Corridor Commission.[6]

A second measure is the corridor's visibility. Although the John H. Chafee Blackstone National Heritage Corridor covers nearly 400,000 acres spread across 13 towns and cities as well as two states, the National Park Service has left its mark on the area. The Blackstone Heritage Corridor logo appears through-

Quinsigamond School and Wayside Sign. Road signs like this one orient traffic to the place of specific sites within the larger history of the valley. John H. Chafee Blackstone River Valley NHC/National Park Service

out the region on highways, museums, and roadside signs. Numerous interpretative panels describe the history of particularly noteworthy sites and do so in a consistent and visually arresting manner.

While the National Park Service does not own many of the historic sites in the valley, its rangers do coordinate programs, sponsor special events, and facilitate cooperation among participating institutions. As a result, NPS rangers orient visitors and its partners to the larger history of the valley and other sites along the Blackstone. Connecting the many sites and communities that comprise the corridor through academic conferences, public festivals, and river tours ties the region together. Appealing to a diverse and large audience, the Corridor Commission has made visibility and consistency the hallmarks of their effort to revitalize the valley's past as a bridge to the future.

Efforts to preserve the river's resources predate the

commission. For example, before the existence of the corridor, both local and academic historians converged on the Blackstone to explore the history of its industrialization. From diverse and nontraditional sources, these authors wrote histories that challenged the popular imagination. Farmers who broke up the dams of mill owners to preserve traditional rights to the river's resources have made their way into countless history books. The tensions created by the earliest mills between workers and mangers, as well as between mill owners and communities, have been documented to demonstrate the conflict that came with the industrialization of the Blackstone's countryside. The cultural politics of constructing urban parks and the struggles between middle-class reformers and industrial laborers over the uses of those spaces in Worcester, Massachusetts, have been exposed and have altered the ways that historians write about the social dynamics of the

Blackstone Canal Wayside Sign in Downtown Worcester.
Although the portion of the Blackstone Canal in Worcester,
Massachusetts, has long been paved over, visitors are reminded
of what history has been buried with signs like this one. John H.
Chafee Blackstone River Valley NHC/National Park Service

period. The struggles of Woonsocket's French Canadians and the Swedes from Quinsigamond Village in
Worcester have also been examined to reveal how various immigrant groups laid claim to an Americanizing
identity. Collectively these histories about the Blackstone have reshaped the way professional historians
write and talk about America's industrialization.

National Park Service rangers working with the
Corridor Commission have brought the existing work
of local historical societies and academic historians
into sustained dialogue. In the process, the commission has drawn upon both the local knowledge of the
valley's stewards and the expertise of historians to develop innovative public history programs. At Woon-

Storm Drain Stenciling. River recovery has been a grassroots activity from the start involving many different groups, including this group of young adults. John H. Chafee Blackstone River Valley NHC/National Park Service

socket's Museum of Work and Culture, interpreters bring to life the immigrant experience in a series of exhibits that include replicas of a French-Canadian farmhouse, the Precious Blood Catholic Church, a mill shop floor, a typical triple-decker interior, and a union hall. As the culmination of the efforts of many partners that include the Corridor Commission, the Museum of Work and Culture exemplifies the rewards of bringing many disparate voices together to interpret history and embodies the spirit of productive collaboration that defines the commission's work.[7]

Just as an old mill in Woonsocket has found new life as a museum and gateway to the valley's past, so too has the river taken on a new life—and again, the Corridor Commission has been central in achieving this task by forging or facilitating productive partnerships that have helped restore the once-polluted Blackstone River. Here too, local efforts laid the groundwork for the more ambitious regional effort that took shape after the arrival of the commission. Long before Congress signed enabling legislation that created the commission, local groups in Rhode Island and Massachusetts already had started to spearhead efforts to clean up the water and salvage crumbling industrial structures along the river's banks. In Lincoln, Rhode Island, ordinary citizens like Henry and Ruth Tetreault and their friends set out to save a section of the

canal. In their effort to rescue a canal that few knew still existed in the 1960s, they also took up the struggle to clean up the river. The Committee for the Advancement of Natural Areas in Lincoln attracted many volunteers who took on the job of pulling industrial debris, tires, abandoned cars, and appliances out of the river.[8]

From such isolated local efforts grew a regional plan for the recovery and restoration of the Blackstone River. The Blackstone's designation as an American Heritage River in 1998 evidenced the success of the first steps taken to restore the river and signaled the beginning of enhanced efforts to protect and restore it. Now, professionals and volunteers work together to monitor water quality. Efforts are underway to bring anadromous fish back to Lonsdale Marsh. A goal of a Fishable/Swimmable Blackstone has been set for 2015.[9]

While water quality improves, other recreational activities beckon. Trails and river access points bring residents closer to the Blackstone's water. These access points can accommodate the launching of boats and canoes, allowing people to experience the river first-hand. In addition to paddles and oars, bikes can propel people along the Blackstone's course, and a planned 48-mile bikeway will connect Providence and Worcester, bringing visitors close to the towpath that

Riverfest. A celebration featuring a canoe and kayak race in Woonsocket, Rhode Island. John H. Chafee Blackstone River Valley NHC/ National Park Service

The Blackstone Canal in Uxbridge, Massachusetts. Bicyclists will soon enjoy a 48-mile bikeway along the old canal, just as these paddlers are getting out on the river. John H. Chafee Blackstone River Valley NHC/National Park Service

paralleled the Blackstone Canal in the 1830s. Such recreational uses would have been unthinkable in the nineteenth century, when the valley's waters powered mills, and would have been a distant dream of those who first undertook the task of cleaning up the river after years of use and abuse.

By revealing the myriad connections that once joined the villages, towns, and cities of the valley, the Corridor Commission has gone a long way toward enhancing a spirited sense of place among the valley's inhabitants. One partner described the valley of twenty years ago as a "repressed, depressed area," where "not so many people claimed with pride the fact that they lived in the Blackstone Valley." This partner and several others see this as having changed. The Corridor Commission did not single-handedly create this burgeoning sense of pride in the valley, but local partners appreciate the positive force the commission has unleashed. One partner describes the Corridor Commission as "a coalescing force" that has helped local partners join together to reclaim the valley's historic past and reinterpret it for the future.[10]

Again, the past has been the key to this transformation. While abandoned mills once represented the valley's declining fortunes, they now convey a host of stories that are increasingly familiar to the valley's residents. One local partner describes the transfor-

Volunteers in Parks. Excitement about the valley's past and numerous volunteers now share their enthusiasm through the Volunteers in Parks program. Here, volunteers gather at the Jencks Store in East Douglas, Massachusetts. John H. Chafee Blackstone River Valley NHC/National Park Service

mation among residents as they engage their shared past: "You actually see people's faces light up when they hear some of the specific stories of the valley, and they tell those to their kids, and then that leads again to this pride of place."[11]

Although the valley covers an enormous geographic area and numerous interpretive sites, the John H. Chafee Blackstone National Heritage Corridor is able to channel visitors through the area by connecting the restoration projects at various sites, such as mill sites in Lincoln and Woonsocket, the Fire Station in Farnumsville in South Grafton, and the mill in the Village of Manchaug in Sutton, Massachusetts. At the heart of the commission's work to promote the historitcal, cultural, and natural attractions of the valley has been the creation of a narrative map that spans time and bridges places. This cartographic interpretative strategy allows for straight paths and winding journeys in historical explanation. It also reveals the connections

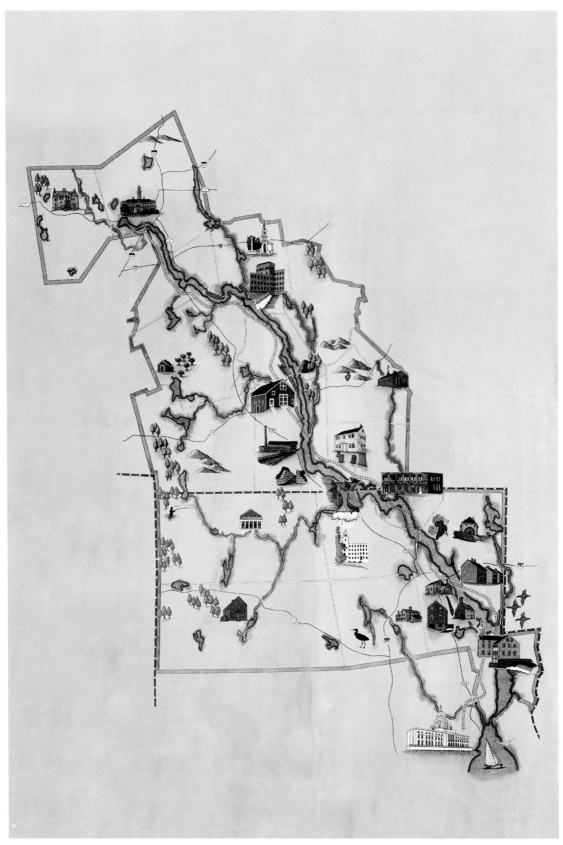

Illustrated Blackstone River Valley National Heritage Corridor Map. John H. Chafee Blackstone River Valley
NHC/National Park Service

that have worked together historically to create a distinct economic and cultural region out of the Blackstone River Valley.

The spatial metaphor of a map for the John H. Chaffee Blackstone Valley National Heritage Corridor is an apt one for the way in which the National Park Service is working to reintegrate New England's many histories. The corridor purposely has been conceived as a journey through time as well as space. The interpretive strategy of the National Park Service and its many partners works because it sets visitors in motion—both literally in their cars to the several sites and also figuratively in their minds—as they reconcile and integrate the many histories that they encounter. New England's old master narrative of Pilgrims, Puritans, and patriots is augmented and enriched by the many other stories that make the valley's history. Since the history of the valley unfolds as a journey through the corridor's many sites, the result is not simply a fragmentation of competing histories, but the accretion of a complicated and contingent past that has room for Puritans and patriots, inventors and entrepreneurs, mill girls and immigrant laborers, reformers and activists. The John H. Chaffee Blackstone Valley National Heritage Corridor sets us in motion and pushes us to ask new questions of New England's past.

As the several essays in this volume suggest, the many histories to be told about the Blackstone River Valley do not coalesce into a linear history. There is no simple unfolding of events. Rather, conceive of the Blackstone Valley as a set of connective histories—each worth telling, each adding a facet previously missing—until a larger image emerges and connects the flow of capital, the movement of people, the formation of ethnic neighborhoods, and the coalescence of working-class culture. These connective stories reveal the forces that created the Blackstone Valley. And while such historic forces may have changed with the waning of nineteenth-century industry, the legacy of the region's vibrant past and the stories of the people who have been part of it remain as vital as ever.

NOTES

1. Useful studies of New England's public memory that make this point include Stephen Nissenbaum's essay, "New England as Region and Nation," in *All Over the Map: Rethinking American Regions*, ed. Edward L. Ayers and Peter S. Onuf (Baltimore: Johns Hopkins University Press, 1996), 38–61; and Joseph A. Conforti, *Imagining New England: Explorations of Regional Identity from the Pilgrims to the Mid-Twentieth Century* (Chapel Hill: University of North Carolina Press, 2001).

2. To explore the rise of public history, see Cathy Stanton, "Serving Up Culture: Heritage and its Discontents at an Industrial History Site," *International Journal of Heritage Studies* 11 (December 2005); and Cathy Stanton, The *Lowell Experiment: Public History in a Post Industrial City* (Amherst: University of Massachusetts Press, 2006).

3. *Cultural Heritage and Land Management Plan for the Blackstone River Valley National Heritage Corridor* (Woonsocket, R.I.: Blackstone River Valley National Heritage Corridor Commission, 1989); *The Next Ten Years: An Amendment to the Cultural Heritage and Land Management Plan* (Woonsocket, R.I.: Blackstone River Valley National Heritage Corridor Commission, 1998); and *Reflecting on the Past, Looking to the Future: Sustainability Study Report* (Woodstock, Vt.: Conservation Study Institute, 2005).

4. Quotation from *Reflecting on the Past, Looking to the Future*, 45.

5. Before 2005, the Corridor Commission has entered into 284 agreements with 87 partners in pursuing its mandate; see *Reflecting on the Past, Looking to the Future*, 6 and 77–80.

6. The statutes creating and extending the life of the Corridor in 1986 and 1996 are Public Law 99-647 (November 10, 1986) and Public Law 104-333 (November 12, 1996). The Corridor was reauthorized most recently by Public Law 109-338 (October 12, 2006).

7. Anita Rafael, "Artifacts and Theme," *Rhode Island History* 55 (1997), 4–41. See also Marie Louise Bonier, *Beginnings of the Franco-American Colony in Woonsocket, Rhode Island*, Claire Quintal, translator (Worcester, Mass.: Assumption College, 1997).

8. On river recovery, see *Reflecting on the Past, Looking to the Future*, 29.

9. Ibid.

10. Ibid., 46, 47.

11. Ibid., 46.

Contributors

Dr. Joseph F. Cullon

Assistant Professor, Department of History, Dartmouth College

Dr. Richard E. Greenwood

Deputy Director, Rhode Island Historical Preservation & Heritage Commission

Gray Fitzsimons

Public Historian

Dr. Seth Rockman

Assistant Professor, Department of History, Brown University

Dr. Albert T. Klyberg

Director Emeritus, The Rhode Island Historical Society

Ranger Chuck Arning

Interpretive National Park Service Ranger, John H. Chafee Blackstone River Valley National Heritage Corridor

Ranger Ray Boswell

Interpretive National Park Service Ranger, John H. Chafee Blackstone River Valley National Heritage Corridor

Ranger Peter Coffin

Interpretive National Park Service Ranger, John H. Chafee Blackstone River Valley National Heritage Corridor

Ranger Kevin Klyberg

Interpretive National Park Service Ranger, John H. Chafee Blackstone River Valley National Heritage Corridor

Ranger Jack Whittaker

Retired Interpretive National Park Service Ranger, John H. Chafee Blackstone River Valley National Heritage Corridor

Jennifer Desai

Editor, Freelance writer, and Assistant Director, Calderwood Writing Initiative at the Boston Athenaeum

Index